CW01083243

To Speak is Never .

To Speak is Never Neutral

LUCE IRIGARAY

Translated by Gail Schwab

continuum
LONDON • NEW YORK

Continuum

Tower Building, 11 York Road, London SE1 7NX
370 Lexington Avenue, New York, NY 10017-6503
www.continuumbooks.com

This edition first published 2002

This English translation © Continuum 2002
Originally published as *Parler n'est jamais neutre* © Les Editions de Minuit 1985

Luce Irigaray has asserted her right under the Copyright, Designs and Patents Act, 1998, to be identified as the author of this work.

The publishers wish to record their thanks to the French Ministry of Culture for a grant towards the cost of translation.
    This book is supported by the French Ministry for Foreign Affairs, as part of the Burgess programme headed for the French Embassy in London by the Institut Français du Royaume-Uni.

Liberté • Égalité • Fraternité
RÉPUBLIQUE FRANÇAISE

All rights reserved. No part of this publication may be reproduced or transmitted in any form or by any means, electronic or mechanical, including photocopying, recording or any information storage or retrieval system, without prior permission in writing from the publishers.

British Library Cataloguing-in-Publication Data
A catalogue record for this book is available from the British Library.

ISBN 0 8264 5904 8 (HB)
      0 8264 5905 6 (PB)

Typeset by Acorn Bookwork, Salisbury, Wiltshire
Printed and bound in Great Britain by Biddles Ltd
www.biddles.co.uk

Contents

I
Introduction

Rereading these texts affected me, and several comments, or ideas, came to mind. In particular, I felt irritated and amused by the language of science. I have for several years been confronting the reality of scientific requirements, those norms or criteria of a so-called rigorous process. I stand before them as if I had to answer to them, to submit to being judged. A kind of tribunal of discourse, deciding what good thinking, good exposition, and valid truth and research are. Supposedly, they are impossible outside of already existing scientific and epistemological frameworks. Off the beaten path, there is only poetry, politics, and demagogic fantasy.

These value judgments – 'positive' indicates the framework of true theory; 'negative' indicates language that does not live up to it – are always stuck in norms of platonic truth. In other words, they remain embedded in an ideology that has never been thought through. This idealism, and its ideological consequences, require the ascendancy, or the authority, of a sentence or formula of the type: *one says that x is equal to, greater than, or less than y.* That is nothing more than an encoding of the world from which subjectivity is removed, and which is subordinated, under cover of the universal, to one single subject, or to several subjects. No feelings apparently … A language divested of all *pathos*, absolutely neutral and detached, is transmitted by someone to someone else, who has no acknowledged origin or source either. This language is supposedly a translator, or a perfect translation, an adequate copy of the universe, and today, of the subject as well. The formula, its mechanics, and its machinery are supposedly enough. No more creation of life. Everything has already been realized in sterile duplications. The subject has become a machine, with no becoming – finished.

Hence my anger and my laughter! Such is the danger we face today. This is also what makes certain discourses successful – or unsuccessful – some complicit with the general mechanics, but somehow beyond time – without past, present or future – and some with an anarchy, or a demagoguery, lacking rigor and logic, flip sides of the others. The most rigorous discourses supposedly correspond to the defensive destiny of humanity: mimicking nature as closely as possible? The most exact science is supposed to be simultaneously atemporal and chameleonesque, versatile enough to change color in order to blend into the background. At the end

of an era, the most highly elaborated aspect of culture seems to turn back
into the most elementary. What we lack is the creation, the affirmation,
that says: *I live*.

This affirmation is sought – perhaps – in the esthetically variable graphisms of science and of art. They meet up in fabrications that claim to be
detached, closer to the world than to their producers. They're supposedly
faithful to reality, and can only be interpreted obliquely, in surfeit. As
always? All that can be told about the subject would be its itinerary, its
directions, its profiles, and its colors? Numbers are supposedly better
vehicles than language, which is either too subjectively invested, or not
enough. Formulas, figures, painting … and religion. Non-numeric scientific discourse claims to be neutral, a duplicate of reality, untainted by
emotion.

This science is not without naivety, especially when it claims to be a
science of the subject, as in psychology, sociology, psychoanalysis, or linguistics. However, it is difficult to comprehend its imperatives, except as preten-
sions to a childish type of objectivity: a moral code of 'good conduct,'
political economy of the truth. Neutral language supposedly could and
should be spoken by everyone. Which is obviously impossible …

But science does not say 'I,' or 'you,' or 'we.' Science stays out of that
polemic, forbids it. Science's subject is 'one.' Who is this *one*? Are its verbs
already substantives, already officially recognized and consecrated acts? We
find the only acceptable verbs in enunciations already transformed into
exchangeable objects without *pathos*. Except the pathos of reason, perhaps?
An irreversible reason? A universal one?

This science which claims to be the most scientific, or the only scientific,
science, is scientific only in the ethical absence of the subject. It can only
make claims to non-encroachment by the subject because it is deployed in
a world already constructed through and through. Already subjectivized?
But we're not supposed to know that. This kind of science leaves no room
for the unexpected, or for chance. All that's left are the views and perspec-
tives on the world of a subject who no longer even lives there.

Why would a subject not say: *I feel thus, I see such and such a thing, I
want* or *I can do this, I affirm that*? It's supposed to be a question of time?
Of a *control* over research? But this control no longer recognizes itself as
such, and claims to be the truth.

'I' is sometimes truer than 'one' or than 'it.' Truer because it admits its
source. And when science moves very quickly, the transmutation of 'I' into
'one' may make no sense. Except perhaps as an unavowed imperialism.

So all of this bowing down before 'one' and 'it' irritated me, and made
me laugh, because I was supposed to bow down as well. It is not proper to

say 'I' in certain research, certain publications. And deciding to say 'I' earned me bad grades in science. Which means that *science is a question of style* ... A type of discourse. An unavowed technique, which cannot distinguish itself from the so-called truth.

If I eliminate the 'ones' and the 'its,' those impersonal forms of proper scientific tone, I am often forced to use the *passive voice*, in order to admit to my feelings, to say that I am not an absolute subject, not pure action. I do not simply control; I am also controlled.

And my formation as subject results from the impact of other bodies, of matter that is foreign to me. In refusing the imperialism of the 'I' that is the paradigm of all speaking subjects, or of a neuter 'one,' or an impersonal 'it,' I acknowledge the ways in which I have been affected. Not always how I have been affected, but in which ways. No more undifferentiated, substitutable, universal subject. In changing, metamorphosing, and anamorphosing, does the subject not wonder about the resistance, or the insistence, of its own existence? Of its own body? Because either all of one's energy is reducible to scientific organization, and can be defined and regimented according to the norms and the tools of science, or certain dimensions, notably affective ones, and certain limits, notably bodily ones, are in conflict with that control.

In becoming, in accepting that it becomes, the subject must take into account its form and its sex. It cannot claim to be a universal without form. It has, and is, an incarnate form. It creates a morphology, and is one. The relation between the two is its story, with its projects, its generations, its loops, and its repetitions.

Up until now the form-giving subject has always been male. And this structure has, unbeknownst to itself, clearly given form to culture, and to the history of ideas. They are not neuter.'

We end up with this paradox: scientific studies prove the sexuality of the cortex, while science maintains that discourse is neuter. Such is the naivety of a subject that never interrogates itself, never looks back toward its constitution, never questions its contradictions. We learn that the left and right sides of the brain are not the same in men as in women, but that, nevertheless, the two sexes speak the same language, and that no other language could possibly exist. By what grace, or what necessity, is it possible to speak the same language without having the same brain? With what do we speak? Is the brain simply a center for processing information already encoded elsewhere? Where? With no traces of its coming into being? And this processing is then imagined, directed, or marked, by which sex?

Living beings, insofar as they are alive, are a becoming. They produce form. No becoming is morphologically undifferentiated, even if its source is chaotic. And the problem of sexual difference weighs in heavily, no doubt, on the side of the primary matter of nature, but also on the side of language. Do we still have something to say? Do we still have meaning to produce?

The female remains within an amorphous maternal matrix, source of creation, of procreation, as yet unformed, however, as subject of the autonomous word. The coming, or the subjective anastrophe (rather than the catastrophe), of the female has not yet taken place. And her movements often remain stuck in mimetic tendencies: whether it's a defensive or an offensive strategy, the female behaves *like* the other, the one, the unique. As of yet, she neither affirms nor develops her own forms. She lacks some kind of birth, or some kind of growth, between the within of an intention and the without of a thing created by the other, a passage from within to without, from without to within, whose *threshold* remains the prerogative of the subject that has always been. The female has not yet created her language, her word, her style. He, she, they [feminine case], I, are supposedly still the reservoir of the meaning, and the madness, of discourse.

How does the subject come back to itself after having exiled itself within a discourse? That is the question of any era. More pertinent to ours, perhaps? Language having become the language of technology, where the automaton is master, it is not always easy for the human subject to recognize its own path through the imperatives and circuits of machines. Has it lost space and time? There is a rupture between our own language, the language we program ourselves, and the one that comes back to us. Notably, when the information is transmitted to and through a certain number of mechanisms in different parts of the universe, in various sectors of society, in various languages, etc.

The thread has been cut, lost, propagates itself along electric, electronic, atmospheric, magnetic circuits. The sky, the earth ... Where are we coming from? To whom are we speaking? How do we manage not to get lost in all this? Outside the most generalized processes, the subject is cut loose, wanders adrift, goes astray. . . .

Why does it go on refusing any contra-diction, any face-to-face with the other sex? As yet unheard-of fecundity of and within sexual difference. The generation of a new culture that desire and the death drives would seek to postpone.

The analysis of language is a precious source of information and of foresight. It is also an effective aid for someone who knows how to use it: a word is as good as a chemical. But it has its toxins as well ... A discourse can poison, surround, close off, and imprison, or it can liberate, cure, nourish and fecundate. It is rarely neutral. Even if certain practices strive for neutrality in language, it is always just a goal, or a tangent, and never reached; it is always to be constructed. An ethics of neutrality can only be developed very slowly, and through rigorous analysis of discourse, and discourses.

This book is a questioning of the language of science, and an investigation into the sexualization of language, and the relation between the two.

It is also research into deviations, idiolects, neocodes, neoformations, and anomalous structures, in their relations to the most common, the most readily received, code. The strategy, tactics, and theory of enunciation can often be broached only through deviant practices. Unless one were able to find a subject who had happened upon a perfect distance with respect to its language, a metalanguage without dogmas or superimposed schemata? But that is virtually impossible. In order to theorize enunciation, we would need discussion among at least two or three interlocutors. And that never happens. Everyone chooses his or her own ideal perspective, makes the law in his or her own domain, hires assistants, and claims to have the first word, or the last. ... Or builds a house closed off to the other, to others.

Two sexually differentiated subjects would be one possible solution. However, this proposal is still dismissed as limited in scope, not really pertinent. Nevertheless, it could be the angle, the summit and the base from which we could protect language against the reign of a binarism which allows the subject to do nothing more than manipulate or weigh data, using divisions, oppositions, and contradictions that exhaust our reserves without creating anything new. Driven by already existing meanings, particles of significations. Oscillations or polemics of survival that do not engender new forms of life.

Discourse hardens up and closes off. In the subject itself. It loses its fluidity of communication, stiffens into pathological forms – pathogens that require the invention of strategies of observation, and of therapies for and through language. Psychoanalysis is perhaps the most astonishing of these: the most stratified experimental theater for the enunciation and for the pragmatics of language, revealing their impasses, their illnesses, their economic crises, their auto-logical circles, etc. This setting for the interpretation of language is not widely recognized as such. It is, nevertheless, unique as a scientific possibility. However, it depends on the aptitude of the subject for self-criticism and self-analysis *vis-à-vis* its most subtle and resistant determinations. This task is the task of the clinician and his or her patients, without witnesses guaranteeing some truth foreign to the scene. The tool is the speaking subject and his or her relation to the word.

I had sought to group these texts by theme, purpose, or goal. However, respect for chronological order seemed more interesting in its simplicity. Of course, requests or requirements on the part of the journals or institutions that inspired the research or meditation do interfere with this chronology. But, even if only to show the evolution of a style in the translation of thought, it is meaningful to leave the texts in the order of their writing. One reads in this the perplexity of the exposition of the work: complex, complicated, dependent at times on influences or subordinations, on the scientific oversimplifications required by publishing, or on a style that will sometimes be called literary or poetic, and which is often nothing more than the discovery of a mode of affirmation. All philosophers and thinkers are poets in the peaceful exposition of their message. But the strange economy of reason dictates that this style not be recognized, or that it remain unappreciated, until after the death of the writer. Who salutes the poet . . . in Aristotle, in Hegel, in Einstein?

A decisive contribution to the history of culture is signed *in* the text or the formula – the writing of a thought or of an equation cannot be separated from its expression. The existence of any creative work denies the opposition philosophy and science v. literature. Creation is writing just as much as it is a practice of objectivity, truth, or thought. It is both. Commentators and metalinguists believe that it is possible to dissociate, to differentiate, the two. For the one who creates, however, this opposition has no meaning, other than an artificial and paralyzing one.

How else can we understand the current effervescence centered around literature? And around writing as such? And how then can we understand the repeated claims by numerous scientists that science cannot be expressed poetically?

We are dealing with at least two phenomena: the interpretation of a story that is being read after the fact; and a period of transition where new meaning has not yet been discovered. The subject of science, or of the *episteme,* is dragged down, or swallowed up, by repetitions and formulas, by graphisms in which it does not recognize itself, but which control it. Too lucid or not yet lucid enough to create. Able to get to the bottom of certain things and not others? Affirming itself in maintaining the past order, and in repressing future discovery and research. This is domination by those who do not create.

There remains the still veiled horizon, which needs other instruments of translation. To go back to, or to finally turn to, 'I'? The *sexed* I. As yet unexplored discourse, especially in the sciences which refuse to confine themselves to metalanguage . . . It is extremely difficult, for anyone who does not affirm herself or himself as a sexed subject, not to remain blindly within the confines and the commentaries of the language, or the languages, of the other, especially the other sex. If science refuses the subject the right to affirm its sex, is the discourse it prescribes not confined to a generally neuter metalanguage, amputated of an important objective dimension?

The truth the subject believes about the world is still just a double of *his or her own* obscured, unrecognized truth. Without knowing it, she or he tells her or his own story, affirming as universal a truth that remains partial. No one, man or woman, inhabits his or her space in the postulation of norms valuable for all. Everyone, woman or man, has to negotiate varying degrees of freedom or confinement. Everything ends up being out of focus – discourse, words and gestures, whether taken together or apart. What is needed is an ethics for those who would build and inhabit their own territory, their own world, and who respect the other's, particularly the other sex's.

Strange days ... Where our truth is sought in the animal or in other domains. Science is interested in the homes and languages of animals, in vegetables and in minerals ... more than in human beings? Humans supposedly need an economy for life and one for speech, but no ethical link between the two realities.

II

Linguistic and Specular Communication
Genetic Models and Pathological Models

The reciprocal integration of the body and of language, origin of the imaginary, decenters man[1] in relation to himself, and marks the beginning of his wanderings. The ineluctable corollary of this is the impossibility of the return to the body as the secure place of his identity to himself. All he is is mediated by the word, and his trace can be found only in the word of the other.

In lived experience, the primary imaginary can be detected in the primordial phantasms forming the deep structures of human behaviors. The phantasm is the original specification of the imaginary in the submissive, passive mode, witness to the contingency of the coming into being of the subject – <I> – pierced by the world and by language from the beginning. Too closely defined, the phantasm changes into chains. Chance then becomes necessity, and possibility is reduced to linear reality. It is up to the word of the other to unleash what has been bound up. Retracing certain pathways, it reactivates all of their intersections, except when it acts as a boundary of immutable lines.

This word is sometimes the analyst's, but can also be the lover's, or the poet's. They all share the goal of getting back as close as possible to the initial integration of the body and of language, not in an endlessly retraced circular path, but in a spiral whose revolutions get closer and closer to the point of origin. Hence their incantatory power, and the fact that they temporarily liberate man from his phantasmagoria, making him the subject of all that, more essential than his story, is woven underneath his story, like his silence and his foundation itself.

At that time, man has no language. He is its plaything without power to play with it. He does not yet benefit from the signifier. But the discourse of the other leaves its indelible traces in him, constituting him as signifying matrix. A discourse of love whose content is provided by himself. And, in this primitive dyad that man forms with the other, he is by turns signifier and signified. But he is not yet structured as <1>[2] by the signifier, and *a fortiori* has not mastered the double face of the sign. That is to say that the subject has not been established in its singularity. The linguistic correlation of the phantasm is to be sought in the verb in its infinitive, impersonal, atemporal form: verb-substantive.

*

The effect of the third term on the relation of the <subject> to the other, of the <subject> to language, is decisive. At the introduction of the third party into the primitive relation between the child and the mother, <I> and <you>[3] are established as disjunction, separation. The initial *monologue* becomes the possibility of dialogue. However, this opposition of <I> and <you>, of <you> and <I>, remains <one>, without potential for inversion or permutation – the father being only another <you> – if the mother and the father do not communicate *with each other*.

In this dialogue between <you1> and <you2> – from which he feels excluded even though he is included within the communication – the possibility of communication through integration into the code is established for the subject, who is henceforth a being with/of language. It is through experiencing that the <you> that is for him the father – or the mother – is an <I> in communication with the mother, just as the mother is an <I> when she speaks to the father, and therefore that the <I> and the <you> are interchangeable, are relations and not terms, that the subject enters into the circuit of exchange.[4]

However, this requires that the subject has been constituted – the same as for the eventual permutation of the two other terms of the exchange – as a <he>. What is <he> at this point, if not <zero>, condition of the permutation of <I> and <you>, and in some ways empty form that guarantees the structure? Evocative of, without being similar to, that empty space in (draughts) or chess that allows one pawn to move into another's space. The status of <he0> is nothing like that of <I> or <you>, despite the ambiguity that reifies it and classifies it with the latter, the personal pronouns. It is nothing and nobody, but rather the possibility of identification and of permutation of <I> and <you>, of <the sender> and <the receiver>, the only terms that effect communication. Implicated in communication as its condition of possibility, this third, or, even more accurately, fourth number – <I>, <you1>, <you2>, <he0> – is a blank, a void, the space left by an exclusion, the negation that allows a structure to exist as such.

Situated in this space, the child is excluded from communication while at the same time integrated into it. This requires him to go through a first death, an experience of nothingness. The subject immediately constitutes itself as an I/0, if not a you/0, through identification with the father, or with the mother, senders or receivers of the exchange at which he is present.

The constitution of the circuit of exchange is none other than the positioning of the so-called Oedipal structure. The notion of castrating agent is thus reduced to a phantasmagoria, a misleading diachronic reification of a synchronic operation. In the same way, delegating its function to the father alone seems doubly excessive. The mother as well as the father is alternatively <I> and <you> in their exchange, and this is no doubt the origin of Oedipal ambivalence. In any case, the castrator, if he exists, is to be sought elsewhere, in the very conditions of the structure of communication.

These things can be considered differently. In their initial non-reversible relation, <I> and <you> make up <one>. Lack of differentiation of persons, of the identical and the non-identical, this <one> is already the possibility of their future disjunction. If a third term intervenes, <one> first divides up into:

[I = one] + [you1 = one] + [you2 = one]

This first division and the positioning of the persons translated by the +, addition and disjunction, leaves room for indeterminacy. <I> here is still <I + you1> or <I + you2>. Identification with the self merges with identification with the other. It is when it becomes <I + you1 + you2> that <one> becomes the possibility of disjunction and permutation. In the exchange between <you1> and <you2>, <one> comes to take the place of <I>, at the same time establishing identity to self as the interchangeableness of the locutor and the receiver of the message <one> witnesses.

There is analogy between the status of <one> and of <zero> in the functioning of the structure of exchange. To grasp this operation is to understand that *the unconscious can be founded as structure and not as content.*

At this stage, fictional of course, the functioning of the exchange is not yet linguistic communication. And this first structuring falls into the not-known, because it is not expressed; forever imperceptible to the subject and yet the basis of his behaviors as well as his words. The object of exchange is yet to be instituted, to be founded.

It will spring from the sleight of hand analyzed by Frege in reference to the engendering of the sequence of numbers.[5] <Zero> is counted there as <one>, <he0> as <he1>. <He1> is the signifying assumption of <he0>, constitutive of the referent.

The first object of communication comes into being as he1/he0. It is, for example, when he, excluded from the communication, is named in the father's and mother's dialogue, that the subject, the <zero>, becomes

<he1>. But it also occurs when he is designated as 'son,' 'man,' ,'woman,' or 'John,' in the words of the father, guarantor of the matrix of communication.

The proper name best represents the paradox of the engendering of '1' out of <zero>. Pure signifier of the <zero> of the subject, the proper name constitutes it as '1' by inserting it into the open set of '1' + '1' + '1,' etc., that is proper names.[6] It is never a closed set: another subject can be inserted into it, and the engendering of '1' out of <zero> is repeated for all possible subjects. However, this engendering is also the necessary condition for the ordering of the objects of communication, just as <zero> is the necessary condition for the ordering of the sequence of numbers. He1/He0 is not only the possibility of the inclusion of the world as object of exchange, but is also supported by being structured in organized sub-sets, always defined by reference to the <zero> of the subject. It is thus that one might represent the totality of animates and inanimates as (1) + (2); the sum of persons, animals and things as (1) + (2) + (3), etc. Such a structuring of the world, whose complexity is actually unequalled by the elementary picture painted above, is always modifiable, never truly finished or closed off, because it originated as <zero>.

The constitution of the object of communication, of 'he1,' is a death that is correlative to the structuring of the subject itself as signifier, finite, '1.' But this death is the condition of the insertion of the subject, of <zero>, into the chain, of its coming to, and its representation in, the order of the signifier. It exists here only as the place of the word of the other whose subject is object, and as such assimilatable to the world, to the inanimate. If it should name that other, the signifier would become the representative of its representation. This requires that the subject identify with the guarantors of the word, and it could then be symbolized as I/he1//he0/one. Thus in the back-and-forth movement from its structuring by the signifier to its mastery of it, the subject is born in its singularity.

Exclusion, the necessary condition for the establishment of the structure of exchange, has as its correlate finiteness, inherent in the object of exclusion. The double aspect of the nothingness and the finiteness of death is, for man, already inscribed in the very premises of communication. This is, no doubt, the source of his ability to anticipate death, since he lives it as soon as he is introduced to the symbolic order. All he has to do is to turn the origin into an ending.

'He1' corresponds more precisely to 'he' classified with 'I' and 'you' among the personal pronouns. However, unlike the latter, it already carries the mark of gender – 'he'/'she' – and of number – 'he,' 'she'/'they' – sign of its status as object of communication. The constitution of 'he1' allows the disjunction of 'I' itself into (I), subject of the enunciation, and 'I,' subject of the utterance. Even though the former underlies all utterance, it is not always expressed there, not always materialized. Ambiguous in this way, '(I) "I" desire' can be opposed to '(I) "You" desire' where the two subjects are clearly dissociated. But that is over-simplifying. (I) can be absent from 'I,' or can disguise itself as 'you,' or as 'he,' or even more effectively be represented under cover of the anonymous 'one.' The path is thus laid out for the deceits and deceptions of discourse, the subject's way to avoid the primary risk of finiteness, of reification, but also a proof of the impossibility of coincidence of (I) and 'I.' Thus the utterance can never be taken at face value, but must be taken as an enigma, a rebus, where the subject conceals itself. Knowing that, is one of the surest trump cards of analytic practice.

Allowing the subject to be absent from the discourse, 'he1' is also the condition of the inclusion or the exclusion of the world as possible subject of the utterance. It is also 'we' – 'I' + ('you' or 'he'), or 'I' + ('he' or 'you'), or 'I' + ('you' + ['they animate' or 'they inanimate']) – or else it is 'you plural' – 'you' + 'he.' We are not dealing here with the initial 'one,' the primordial lack of differentiation among persons, or between the world and persons. The marks of gender, and of number, carried by the grammatical forms attest to this. Persons here add up to specific disjunctive units, and the world is divided into animate and inanimate elements.

Although they are objects of the partners of the enunciation, 'I' and 'you' are not explicitly objects. Their function as subjects of the utterance can conceal the fact that they are already objectivized as those subjects. This remains true for the totality of utterances whose traces can be found, and whose science is founded, in analysis.

What is explicitly given as object is the object of the utterance; that is, 'me,' 'you,' 'him/her,' etc. As point of convergence for the subject of the enunciation and the subject of the utterance, 'me' becomes the partial and no doubt illusory possibility for the subject to master its objectivization, but is sometimes also the intentional transfer of objectivization to the other. <I see myself> is here opposed to <You see me>. In any case, 'me' is always a problematic and precarious appropriation. Turning oneself into an object always includes the risk of being possessed. Only the disjunction of 'himself'/'him' palliates this ambiguity. <He sees himself> but <I see him>. If 'him' is an object for the subject that I am, 'he' cannot really possess his own image constituted as an object for me in my role as subject. And even when he sees himself, it is still I who benefit from the spectacle. Thus, turning oneself into an object implies possible capture by the other.

More subtle is the mastery offered by <I please myself> where the utterance itself is taken up as object of the subject of the enunciation. It is (you) that it seeks to evict as the very space of all alienation. The discourse turns back in on itself, forms a loop. It envelops the subject, imprisons it in its own circularity and repetitions. (I) vacillates from having missed its call to (you). It doubles up its words, gets stuck in its utterances, the totality of which build up a <self> little by little.

Thus, the <*self*> that is named or displayed in the totality of the discourse is the objectivization of the subject, as well as its descent to the level of inanimate object: 'the self.' It is the 'me' cut off from its dialectical links to the subject, a trace of the subject, no doubt, but one that has fallen into disuse, where the subject subsists only as mute and opaque reification, just one among many objects in the world. Unless, failing to reestablish the link to (I), it is simply absorbed into the world. The 'self' is then the subject made world.

At every stage of the differentiation and lack of differentiation of persons we find <one>. The blending of identity and non-identity, it is the necessary condition of their disjunction. The negative pole. Thus it is noteworthy that the animate subject 'one' never becomes the object of the utterance. At the most it is the object of the partners of the enunciation, interchangeable with 'he1" or, more precisely, with 'someone' or 'no one' – asexual, non-countable. This usage is also ambiguous, because often within 'one' (I) or (you) can be concealed. 'One says' is not far from '(I) ... say' or '(you) ... say.' When the subject is included in 'one'[7] – 'We will be coming tomorrow' – it is indeterminate, not delimited for the other, without gender, or individual identity. Thus 'one' appears to be the last refuge of subjectivity, the closest possible position to the <zero> that founded it, or to the underlying unconscious.

The 'id' can be understood as the flip side of 'one' in the primitive disjunction of persons and things, animate and inanimate elements. Thus, in its possible substitution for 'one,' it is the reification of the unconscious.

In response to the imposition of the proper that which constitutes it as one/zero, the subject takes on the masked and fleeting appearance of the personal pronouns. Both the name and the pronouns have, according to linguists, a 'zero' signified – an ambiguous way of pinpointing both the coming of the subject into discourse, and the difficulty of delimiting it by linguistic means.[8]

*

The specular experience can be understood as the space of a possible reprise of the first integrations of the body and of language founding the subject. As such, it is a privileged moment for taking note of the assumptions, as well as the denials, the persistence and the inadequacy of the subject.

Specularization[9] is principally the perceptual experience of linguistic communication in its structure – <I>, <you>, <he0> – and its primordial object he1/he0. The unveiling of a second imaginary, it reveals the signifier constitutive of <he1>. It represents the engendering of <he1>, the paradoxical springing forth of the unit from the 'zero'. Hence the jubilation, but also the retreat, before this double aspect of identification, and even more of exclusion and finiteness, that the signifying structure implies. <You> is to be sought in those to whom the child turns.[10] For the subject, because of its split, things are not so simple. He1/He0 is still the <(I)> which benefits from its image, a gaze that can open or close at will upon the spectacle – unlike the ears which cannot refuse to hear – an evocation of future mastery over, indeed of future questioning of, the signifier. The fallen primordial <one> – in a word, the unconscious – remains. Non-specularizable, it is the guardian of specularization. Witness to its inadequacy, it ensures the return, the intervals and eclipses of the subject who, at all times, wants to vanish in order to reappear as <1>, in a repetition irreducible to any temporal continuity, or to an infinite that cannot be cut up into countable units, or an iterative sequence.

The specular image, visualization of the signifier, reveals its effects. Its structuring powers can be well illustrated in the neurological anticipation it allows the still immature child, anticipation made possible by the fact that he is constituted as <1> by the signifier. This unification, however ,is also a disjunction. The image unifies, but it also separates. As <1>, the child turns toward its mother, who has become an other. They had been merged; now they are juxtaposed, added together as '1' + '1.' The *Gestalt* of the image, like the discreteness of the signifier, institutes discontinuity. They have the same *splitting function*. Thus the specular image, like, and as, the signifier, is a carrier of death. It stands out as the correlate to structuring. Because life is in-finite outpouring. And this definite form of the self, of the specular *alter ego*, or of the proper name, fixes the real in determining it, cutting it out, cutting it off. The discriminating formalization of the second, diurnal, imaginary, which is tied up with death, is opposed to the primary nocturnal imaginary, the guardian of life.

Death is also found elsewhere. All structure presupposes *an exclusion*, an empty set, its negation, the very condition of its functioning. Down out of imaginary formalization falls a non-structured real. The signifier is always inappropriate to the signified. Faced with its image, the subject feels itself situated in the place of exclusion, not specularizable in its tripartite character – <I>, <zero>, <one> – and yet constituted as such by specularization. Thus the specular experience is reminiscent of the passage through nothingness required by the introduction of the subject into the order of the signifier, best represented by the imposition of the proper name.

This absence of the subject from its own image, as from its own name, undoubtedly explains their *power to make unreal.* It is where it is not that the subject is constituted as identical to itself. Thus is inaugurated for the subject the parade of captures by space, or by discourse, fascinating because the subject believes they hold the keys to its identity whose paradoxical engendering remains concealed. Undoubtedly, in turning toward the other, particularly toward the guarantor of communication, the subject will learn more about its fundamental alienation in the symbolic world, mediated by the tribute to the signifier. And yet ... The other has no power except insofar as he has conformed to the established order, as representative of the law to which he submits. Trying to get back to a first cause would be endless, and useless anyway, because the alienation is inscribed in the very principle of the synchronic functioning of the structure of linguistic exchange. The mirror seems to offer an escape from this social enslavement. Man seems to be able to attribute the signifier to himself, and become master of his own identity, freed from dependence on the word of the other.

Could we not then narrate this new version of the 'fall?' Man recognizes his own image in woman and thinks himself master of the universe. The day when Adam took a companion, not really other, but drawn from himself, is the day that he separated himself from God, and denied his subjection to the Word (it goes without saying that the manducation of the empty set did not promote the circulation of the signifier, any more than its metaphorization as a comestible object facilitated comprehension of what is at stake).

As seductive as it is, specular identification is nonetheless spatial alienation. In an initial moment, the mirror takes the place of the other, the first place of identification, all the more fearsome for being mute, immediate mediation, non-dialectizable. Thus specular identification is, for man, the unveiling of his freedom, but also the possibility of his madness. The most fascinating and the surest alienation.

This spatial alienation does not even avoid dependence on the other, as fundamental to specular identification as to the imposition of the proper name. For without the other's presence, the relationship of *my* image to *the other's* body which is established as I turn back toward the other, the spectacle of my image remains foreign to me. It is an other that I there encounter, but not really an other, because the other is merged with the world, and not any more established in his own singularity than I am in mine. It is the presence of 'you' that allows the exclusion of the world, constituted as empty set. From then on the structure that constitutes the relationship between *my* gaze, *my* image and *the other's* <body>, can function in the alternating commutation of the three terms. The gaze of the other – <(you)> – is thus the divided and necessary witness of my specular identification. The other's appropriation as mine – <for me> – remains ambiguous. For our respective gazes – <(I)> and <(you)> – our respective images are objects alternatively. In order for them to take on value as duplication of reality, our <bodies> will have to be, in their own turn, excluded, and our juxtaposed images become the common object of our exchange as possible subjects of our utterances. It is only as a final step that <you> itself will be constituted as an empty set, leaving as the only terms of the structure *my* gaze – <(I)> – *my* image, and the 0/one.

Thus I can feign possession of the specular image, bestow it or take it away from myself at will, and play at modifying it – in game-like prefiguration, similar to the syllabic games of the young child, of my power over the signifier. However, this mastery is ambiguous. The subject exhausts itself in a stereotyped reiteration, in the juxtaposition of metaphors which, even if they mime the possession of the 0/one, do not permit its real emergence into the linear signifying chain.

The image is a deceitful signifier. It looks from the start like a global, finished discourse. And the comparison of two specular images is rather more like the simultaneous presence of two autonomous representations of the same paradigm, than like the veritable relationship between one signifier and another. Nor does it resemble the establishment of a contiguity between signifiers that would be more than a simple juxtaposition, unable to constitute a specular utterance. I can try to articulate a total text by grimaces, the simulacra of utterances. These are then inscribed in an already given matrix; but when the first message is sent, the last is also sent. At the level of the specular text, A implies A and not Z, in maximum redundancy, total recursiveness. If, judging this iteration unbearable, the subject should mutilate its face, the text would, of course, be changed, but it would then be irreducible to the former text, a new set without relationship or link to the previous set. This is to say that the global signifier that is the image in the mirror excludes any possibility of temporal succession, because it cannot carry within itself the mark of the preceding image or of the one that will follow, any more than it can be associated with another image. Unlike the signifying chain of discourse. The subject does not find the way to carry out its own creation in this atemporal utterance?

Instability in the terms of 'communication' results from the totality of the text in specularization, because the gaze is constituted simultaneously as sender and receiver of the message. The image defines <he1>, but is still also a possible subject or object of the utterance – <I> or <me> – or even the subject of the enunciation – <(I)>. No doubt such permutations can be found in linguistic exchange, but they are carried out there in temporal succession. I can function as sender and receiver of the message only one after the other and not at the same time. This inscription of the utterance into duration is a function of the inadequacy of the signifier to the signified which requires the temporal unfolding of discourse. Thus, at the level of the terms of exchange, the diachronic instability of communication is opposed to the synchronic instability of specularization.

These different modes of specular <discourse> can be explained by the properties of the structure itself. It does not function due to the relative inadequacy of the signifer to the signified, but through a play of permutations of *two signifiers to one signified*, reset continuously in motion by the fact that the stakes are never engaged irreversibly. This can be ascertained through the fact that the subject appropriates its own image, its metaphor, as soon as it is constituted, but with no assurance of ever really seizing hold of itself there.

This type of structure can also be found at another level of linguistic communication – that of *writing*, which permits the specular duplication of the word.[11]

*

The avatars of specularization, and the distortions of language, can always be understood as expressions of a primordial absence, or at least of the precariousness of the empty set, of the <zero>, which underlies the structure of exchange and guarantees its functioning. If it has not been situated at the site of the <zero>, and if therefore it has not been able to assume non-identity to itself, the very condition of its identification, the subject, if it even exists at that point, cannot recognize the mirror image as the same and as other than the self, and cannot come into, even as it necessarily remains excluded from, the chain of discourse. The subject cannot exist merged with the signifier even in its negation or its denial, but it is also threatened if it refuses its effects or finds in them a too precisely appropriate representation of itself, or, indeed, if it wants to benefit from the signifier while eluding its law.[12]

For the psychotic, the deficiency is already to be found with the parents. He was, they say, his mother's partial object. That is undoubtedly to affirm that he was from the very beginning constituted by her as a reifying projection of her unconscious. Not having assumed her own non-identity to herself, she cannot consent to the status of alterity for her child. He will be the signifying medium of her desire, thenceforth destined to be partial. The same fate falls to the father also, unless he appears as the simple signifier of the law. Whatever the case may be, the relations of the mother to her man, as to her child, are structured within the permutation of two signifiers for one signified, reminder of the specular structure. The triangulation which presupposes, in the place of the partners of the exchange, two signifieds for one signifier, is never established here. This failure of triangulation means that the child never acquires the status of a distinct unit, and is thus deprived of the layering proper to the signified – he is given as pure signified object merged with the world – and of all possibility of representation in the signifying chain. Never having been constituted as he1/he0 in the first place, he is destined never to be anything but the representative of the desire of his mother, with no possible access to the function of representation for himself.

For the psychotic, the presence of the mirror signifies the confrontation of the pure signifier that he is, with that other, specular, signifier that duplicates him. The fact that he either turns the mirror around or turns away from it, or looks behind it for a trace of the signified, or sees his father in the image, shows how unbearable that confrontation is for him. The specular image presents itself to him as the place of a signifying deprivation, as he is left as nothing in front of the mirror which takes on his only right to existence. Unless, turning back to his mother, he lives the unsustainable contradiction of being at the same time himself and his opposite, signifying medium of her signified only, as well as its negation. Thus he comes face to face with the metaphoric layering of life and death rather than living their metonymic succession, which alone is bearable. The resulting anguish will not cease until the intolerable ambiguity is lifted. Merging into the image – going through the mirror – or denying it, and thus eliminating one of the terms of the contradiction, appear as the only possible ways out.

For the neurotic, the problem lies not in the formation of the system of exchange, but in the dynamic of its functioning. The structure of communication has a foundation here, but it has a tendency to jam up, freeze, and suspend exchange. These stases in the economy of the system can be understood in reference to the primordial experience of desired object on which access to the status of desiring and speaking subject depends.

The hysteric did not get enough love. Or at least that is his most fundamental phantasm. With respect to his mother's desire, he experiences himself as signifier marked by the sign of incompleteness, indeed of rejection, derisory because unable to sustain the comparison with the phallic signifier. The impotence and the abusive intolerance of the lawgiver father leave the mother in her immoderation and her refusal, or her inability, to symbolize her desire in some way, to focus it on some object, and thus allow her to change objects.

Thus for the hysteric, <he1> is always to be elaborated, to be deferred in its unifying virtue, the threat of exclusion from the field of desire that sustains him. His identity to himself will therefore always be precarious, and always feared. He does not accept himself as fragment, as facet of an always future unity, contested as soon as he feels himself taken in his totality. The subject suffers from this refusal, this fragmentation, of the signifier which should constitute him. He is always to be born, in the process of being born, halted at the metaphoric time of his structuring, which he relives over and over, exhausting himself being the ideal object, finally assumable because it conforms to the one he senses in the place of the other's desire. Sisyphean enterprise, because the other is never that first other who marked him with the sign, and whose fundamental dissatisfaction – phantasm or reality – he feels.

For the hysteric, the confrontation with the mirror is like the test of his insignificance. As the image unveils itself as the space of his unity, he rejects it as inappropriate to hold the gaze of the other. Ceaselessly outlined, only to be denied, the image inaugurates an inexhaustible series of sometimes confused sketches whose ending is dependent on vanquishing fragmentation, on the spatial reassembling of multiple, heterogeneous identifications, a unity desirable because postponed, and, in any case, impossible. For these specularizations, which claim to be partial, are also labile, lived in an instant, outside of all temporal contiguity which would authorize their summation. For the hysteric, beginning over again the metaphoric moment of his constitution ends up positioning <he1> as transcendence in the face of which all <he1'>, <he1''>, etc., collapse as derisory inadequacies. Avoiding the splitting function of the signifier, ceaselessly palliating his incompleteness, the subject misses the moment of his disappearance, but also the correlative moment when, excluded but involved, he could re-emerge in metonymic succession. That is to say that the image will be above all object – <he1> – for the other, the only true subject – <(I)> – and not taken up as representation of the subject himself – <me> or <myself>. If the image does take the risk of being the subject of the utterance, it is only on condition of leaving the responsibility for the utterance to the other. The question mark reveals this, just as, punctuating the grimace, smile or mask, it reveals the precariousness of their assumption by the subject. Never reducible to the empty set, without risk of evanescence for the subject himself, the other remains the immediate guarantor of all speech and of all desire.

The obsessive felt too loved. Therein lies his force and his tragedy. His mother found him too appropriate a signifier for her desire; as for him, he is marked by the sign of this comprehensiveness, or even excess. It is not that the phallic referent is totally missing, but that it is referred to some elsewhere, to some absent hero, whose death would be the surest guarantee of non-intrusion. Never incarnate in the person of a 'living' father, it leaves the child the certitude of being, in the present, the exhaustive answer to the desire of the mother, not subject to those polar inversions that are the risks of desire and the marks of its actual existence.

Naming is no problem for the obsessive, since it confirms him in his singularity as desired being. For him, his name will be the emblem, badge, and, no doubt, epitaph, of his phallic status. He experiences himself as too identical to himself, as the too exact adequacy of his signified to his signifier. In this stable equilibrium, the subject walls himself off, and, riveted to what he has been, is incapable of liberating himself for a perpetual becoming. The bar separating <he1> from the other participants in the exchange thickens, resulting in the stereotyping of discourse, the recurrence of utterances. If they can be heard as empty, it is not that the subject is absent. On the contrary, he duplicates himself there completely. However, in this metonymy of the self, detectable to the other in the loops of his interminable palavers, he seeks to recover himself without ever truly expressing himself. Stillborn.

The obsessive enjoys specular reflections. He likes to verify the permanence of his identity to himself and to reassure himself of his mastery over it. Specularization is for him without risks, established at the time when the image is contemplated – <me>, <myself> – and not invested – <he1>. In order to monopolize the spectacle more completely, he evicts all other gazes. <(You)> is the more easily excluded for being possessed in his desire at the level of the image itself. It is there that as <(you)> he can re-emerge, neutralized in his alienating functions, for a fictive dialogue. Alone, in front of the mirror, absolute master of the signifier, the obsessive will attempt to escape its power of fascination through meticulous examination, through an exhaustive inventory, imitations of a true temporal succession. In fact, these pure metonymies are inscribed in a spellbinding circularity, closer to the pacing of a prisoner than to a veritable progression. And the obsessive himself, always turned toward his past, is not fooled. Looking for what? The lost traces of the subject?

The fact that the subject is introduced into the signifying order as the representative of a system of connotations, and not as denotation, allows us to explain his future difficulties in sustaining the dynamic of exchange. That he was, as a first step, marked by either the + sign or the – sign, impedes the shuttling back and forth from exclusion to excess that is the condition of his effective emergence into discourse. The work of the analyst will be to restore his non-identity to himself, his identity to <zero> that permits the inversion of the sign. This requires that the analyst himself take up the wager and function as <zero>, the empty set, temporary guarantor of the free play of structure.

*

The specular image is the analog of the signifier, but not of language in its double nature. The signified is on the side of the non-specularizable. If we go back to the genetic fiction of the mirror stage, while the image represents the signifier, it is through the <one> that the signified is introduced; it is the <one> that will fall beneath the signifier in order to give it meaning. The gaze represents the subject who plays with the signifier. Thus the distortions of language emerge.

The schizophrenic, who lacks the back-and-forth from the mirror to his body, is the play of the signifier. His discourse is evocative of a new language of substitutions, of neo-forms that he claims are equivalences, but that are really pseudo-metaphors because they cannot be deciphered. The axis of contiguity vanishes. Like fireworks, his discourse fascinates with its freedom of creation, its playful offhandedness. That it has no meaning can be seen in the fade-ins and -outs of the intonation and of the articulation, as in moments of perplexity where the <subject>, listening, waits for language itself to pick up the ball. He is not really the sender of a message, just the carrier. Language, having become a free activity of generations and transformations, here holds the place of the subject of the enunciation.

For the delusional, things are different. His foreclosure of the specular image becomes the elaboration of a closed system, palliating the missing image. Language freezes into fascinating totalities where the <subject> alienates himself. Words no longer serve as a means of exchange. They are too similar to him and at the same time too inaccessible. Inaccessible because similar. The delusion represents an attempt at structuring the <self>, and the <subject> can be detected in the fragile and fecund part of the system, the stream where he nourishes himself.

The senile dementia patient – studies have been done showing the loss of recognition of the mirror image[13] – is pure object of the utterance. His irrepressible discourse spreads out along the chain, flat, very poor in vocabulary. He also is 'spoken,' not by language but by speech, or usage, hardened into a system of uncontrolled utterances. Hence that interminable succession of idiosemiological utterances which become more and more stereotyped as memory problems increase, and as the field of immediate experience diminishes.

Does one speak of language distortions in the neurotic? No, not really. And yet ...

The hysteric never runs out of words. Meaningful words, yes, but he takes them back immediately. That's never what he really wanted to say. Please don't take him at his word! It's his obsession. He takes up the stream of signifiers, selecting one in order to reject it immediately and choose another, which he denies as soon as it's out. There's no end to it. He can't tolerate his image, any more than he can pin himself down in discourse. The stream of signifiers and the stream of images, his zigzagging discourse, the masks he changes from moment to moment, all show his desire for a total discourse that would encompass all signifiers and for an image that would consist of innumerable contradictory facets. And then what? He gets lost in his utterances, doesn't recognize himself in his masks, suffers. 'Who am I?' 'What can that mean?' he worries, wonders. Lost, he turns to you. Because, finally, he senses the subject in his discourse. It's you.

How different are the prudent and formidable words of the obsessive. He delights in his discourse, touches it up, polishes it. He is the man of one single utterance, and of one unique image. He'll serve it to you over and over, prepared or presented differently. Don't be offended. He doesn't take you for deaf or stupid. He just ignores you. He talks to himself. You are merely a pretext, a spectator just barely admitted to the dialogue he carries on with himself, and which will go on in your absence. The less you show yourself, the better he'll feel, because he brooks no disagreement with his discourse or with his image. Only your silence, the suspension of your own desire, can one day interrupt the flux of redundant utterances, utterances of utterances, often, for the sake of prudence, empty. He interrupts himself: 'To whom was I speaking?' If you persevere, and resist the temptation to get a word in edgewise, scanning the silence when he finally speaks to you, his desire may be able to liberate itself from the capture of the gaze, from its too perfect appropriateness to the signifier, and open up a real dialogue.

Thus the distortions of language – aberrant prevalence of the signifier or the signified, of the image of the 'body,' fragmentation, over-investment, juxtaposed metaphors and frozen metonymies – are related to those of the specular experience. This is not to say that the specular experience merges into the experience of spoken communication. It represents it. One presupposes the other. And if one of the terms of specularization turns up missing, or vacillates, is the underlying discourse not the missing or vacillating origin?[14]

III

Negation and Negative Transformations in the Language of Schizophrenics

1

For an approach to schizophrenic language, psycholinguistics can use several types of functional models, depending upon the hypotheses adopted, or on the level of discourse targeted by the research.

It can study the utterance produced. In that case, textual analysis is applied to spontaneous or semi-induced discourse. The linguist uses a taxonomic model to carry out differential analyses of linguistic performances. Such analyses, done by Lorenz, for example, permit at best an elaboration of deviant grammars for schizophrenia. In this distributional perspective, the utterance can be studied only as a divergence from the norm, and can take on broader significance only when compared to the utterances of non-schizophrenics.

However, analysis can also take place at the level of enunciation – that is, at the level of the generation of messages. The methodology is adopted from generative and transformational grammars, which establish rules for enunciation, and for the transformations the utterance undergoes between its generation and its realization. Specific characteristics of enunciation can be detected in spontaneous discourse; however, linguistic models allow for experiments whose analysis brings the production of language to the forefront. For example:

- the production of sentences simulates the generation of utterances by asking respondents to produce a sentence integrating certain morphemes;
- the transformation of minimal sentences simulates the activity of the speaking subject by asking him or her to carry out linguistic operations under conditions where morpho-syntactical variables are limited, but which require the use of one or several transformations.

What can then be defined is not a deviant grammar, but a grammar specific to the schizophrenic, whose language can be seen as a whole, functioning independently of other languages, but using the same linguistic code. The compatibilities and incompatibilities of the lexemes used in the sentences produced, the ways in which messages are disambiguated, the resolution of semantic or syntactic anomalies, the relationship between the grammar of the sentences and their acceptability, the specific structure of the lexical classes where the choices are made – where the inclusion of terms is just as important as their exclusion – all permit the definition of the languages of schizophrenics as neo-structurings resulting, at the level of the generation of the sentence and its transformations, from singular, specific rules, definable in linguistic terms.

These two types of approach to schizophrenic language remain above all descriptive, even when they lead to the construction of functional models. The psycholinguist can try to get beyond distributional analysis of the utterance, and beyond generative and transformational analysis of the enunciation, by taking as explanatory hypotheses the structures of communication that underlie the generation of messages. She or he can study the modifications and perturbations in schizophrenic language, in order to determine the cause of the specificity of the verbal production of schizophrenics.

When the structures of communication are reduced to their three fundamental terms – subject: *I*; addressee: *you*; world: *he/she/it* – there are three levels where the relation between the partners of communication and its object or referent can be discovered.

(a) It can be studied at the level of the sentence, or of the utterance, in the interrelations among *'I,' 'you,'* and *'she/he,'* or their representatives. This will mean analyzing the relative frequency of the pronouns, and the dialectical relationships among sender, addressee and referent.

(b) At another level, the relationships among the partners of the enunciation and the referent can be pinpointed by specifying the types of transformation preferentially used or excluded by respondents. Thus interrogative transformations appear to be a way to leave responsibility for the utterance to the addressee, whereas emphatic transformations, at least when applied to the subject of the utterance, leave the world in the position of principal guarantor of communication. Finally, negative transformations can be carried out only by respondents capable of assuming responsibility for their own statements.

(c) The kinds of relationship established between enunciation and utterance also reveal the type of structures of communication preferred. The statements *I am hungry, I notice that I am hungry, he was hungry that day,* are all situated differently with respect to the process of enunciation. They can be qualified respectively as direct utterance, utterance of an utterance (or indirect utterance), and narrative. The indirect utterance, systematically employed, appears to be a means of eliminating the addressee, whereas narrative assigns responsibility for the utterance to the world, and not to the subject.

In this last type of analysis, utterances are not treated as texts where signifiers are studied in order to reveal the contents of a message; it is rather the linguistic forms that are taken as a means of locating the subject in the enunciation.

2

Linguistic perturbations and deficiencies were noted, among aphasics, in the realization of the message, and, among patients with senile dementia, in the generation of the message. What is problematic among psychotics, however, is the very existence of a dialectical relationship among the partners of enunciation and between the subject of the enunciation and his or her utterance, or the object of communication. Of course, this distinction must be made with caution, in the sense that the levels of language interact with each other. Isolatable in models, they merge in the realization of the subject's discourse, where they work together to determine its specificity. Nevertheless, it is useful to determine what type of analysis will be most fruitful, as well as which angle will allow us to explain most exhaustively, and to render explicit, the forms constituting the specificity of the discourse of a particular type of subject. It is from this perspective that I have chosen to center my research on the language of schizophrenics around the perturbations in the structures of communication.

3

I have just indicated, in a general overview, that variations in the structures of communication can be apprehended in several ways. Among these diverse types of analysis, I have chosen to deal with the problem of negative transformation, particularly its controlled realization in response to experimental exercises, because, even though only a small number of variables come into play, they allow us to examine the essential problem of schizophrenic language. Indeed, the results of the experiment, to which can be applied a distributional analysis determining the divergences between performances of schizophrenic respondents and those of so-called 'normal' respondents, or of other pathological groups, allow us to demonstrate the relationship between the subject of the enunciation and the subject of the utterance – or, if one prefers, between (I) and 'I' or 'you,' in a statement of the type: [(I) say]: 'I' love, or [(I) say]: 'you' love. The negative transformation, in fact, requires the ability to dissociate the subject of the enunciation, who generates sentences, from the utterances produced. It is only insofar as utterances are experienced as distinct from the subject, as objects proposed for communication, that transformations can be applied to them.

Of course, one might object that the process of dissociation is emphasized by the artificial nature of the exercises, and that, in any case, the utterance to be transformed is suggested by the researcher, which brings in new variables. However, despite their artificiality, the exercises do not create non-existent problems, because the spontaneous discourse of schizophrenics also raises the issue of negative transformations.

Respondents are asked to perform two different exercises in order to verify their aptitude for transforming a statement. In one of the exercises, I give the respondent a predicative sentence and ask him or her to apply a negative transformation, indicating the morphological procedure she or he will have to use: he/she closes the door → he/she *does not* close the door. In the other exercise, the opposites exercise, I ask the respondent to supply the opposites of given adjectives or verbs, active or passive. The adjectives used exclude morphological opposites – they are adjectives of the *wide/narrow* as opposed to the *polite/impolite* type. The same for the verbs; I exclude those of the type *do/undo*, or those that indicate an inversion and not an opposite: *to light up/to put out the light.*

The opposites exercise is based on the hypothesis that the lexical opposite (*big/small; to love/to hate*) is created, in the same way as the negation of a sentence (*he comes/he does not come*), from a negative transformation applied to a part of the predicate of the kernel sentence. It assumes the relative equivalence – with differences in the effect of the negation – of *he is not big → he is small;* or *not to love → to hate.*

Since the opposites exercise is much more easily manipulated (even for the so-called 'normal' groups of respondents) than the negative transformation exercise, the greater part of this study will be devoted to the analysis of results collected in response to it. Those obtained from the transformation of sentences will be brought in later.

4

Description of the exercise: the opposites requested are from two grammatical classes:

- ADJECTIVES: *grand, pauvre, chaud, doux, profond, beau, absent, vrai, pareil, comique, masculin,* etc. [big, poor, hot, sweet (soft), deep, beautiful, absent, true, similar, comic, masculine, etc.]

- VERBS: *naître, aimer, savoir*, etc. [to be born, to love, to know (knowing), etc.]

These words present different types of ambiguities:

- between several possible grammatical classes: *knowing* is both a verb and a substantive
- between words having different distributions – for example, *sweet (soft)* – or even between words and phrases: *to be born* can be heard as *not to be*;[1]
- between homophones distinguished only by the fact that some of them are associated with inanimates and others with animates: thus, *deep* can be associated with inanimates (*deep water*) or with animates (*deep mind*), or with behaviors or actions of animates (*deep text, deep gaze*). These divergent meanings result in two different types of opposites: *shallow* or *superficial*. This type of ambiguity is frequent on the list given to the respondent: *a warm spell/a warm person*; *a sweet dish/a sweet person*, etc.

Negative transformations require a disambiguation. In receiving the cue, the patient must, prior to performing the transformation, exclude certain types of distributions. The transformation cannot be carried out on an ambiguous term, but only after the word has been disambiguated. This will be emphasized in the behavioral reactions of the schizophrenics.

The instructions operate on two levels.

With the simplest instructions, the respondent is asked to give the opposite of a word – 'Give the opposite of the word *big*' – with no insistence on the fact that a negative transformation is expected. Such directions are usually sufficient to elicit the response.

If no response is obtained, the researcher proceeds to the second level, and the transformation is demonstrated using a morphological type of negation; the researcher leads the respondent to a lexical substitution through the execution of a transformation on a predicative sentence – 'If he is not big, he is ... ?'

One example is always given before the presentation of the first cue.

5

The respondent groups: the schizophrenic population was chosen by psychiatrists – Drs Daumézon, Boige and Melman – of the Hôpital Sainte-Anne. There were 45 respondents, 35 of whom were classified as paranoids, 5 as catatonics, and 5 as hebephrenics. Two control groups also responded to the exercises:

- The so-called 'normal' groups consisted of 15 respondents in the neuro-surgical unit at the Hôpital Sainte-Anne whose socio-cultural level was similar to that of the schizophrenics, and 49 students in humanities at the University of Tours. The performances of these two groups of respondents are convergent; the responses of the students, however, are more diverse, closer to those of the schizophrenics. The students therefore seemed more useful as a control group, a choice also justified by the greater number of respondents in the group.

- The pathological groups were patients with Parkinson's Disease, aphasics, non-aphasic patients with brain lesions and patients with senile dementia. The respondents were examined in the neurosurgical unit at the Hôpital Sainte-Anne, the patients with senile dementia by myself, and the other groups by J. Dubois and P. Marcie.

6

The schizophrenics' behavioral reactions to the instructions are specific.

(a) This type of exercise is well received by respondents, which can be seen in the limited number of refusals. For 45 respondents, there were three whose reactions showed confusion such as tears – and one absolute refusal to respond. This type of behavior is problematic, however, in that the 'normal' control groups do not show any such reaction to the exercise. On the other hand, the number of refusals is considerable among the patients with senile dementia – between 20 percent and 40 percent reject the exercise. The intolerance of the two groups would seem to be due to different causes. Among senile dementia patients, there is intolerance to any exercise carried out on language itself – metalinguistic operations, in Jakobson's sense. Also significant is the phenomenon of linguistic inertia which results in echolalic stereotyping of the refusal. Among the schizophrenics, the refusals seem to be caused by their inability to dissociate the subject of the enunciation from the subject of the utterance, or to distinguish the production of the sentence from the sentence produced. This can be observed in the stupefaction, or the confusion, respondents feel when faced with the exercise, and the justifications for their behavior they give afterwards.

(b) There were very few admissions of ignorance. There are some, however, in the responses of the various control groups, and even among the 'normal' groups, but not with respect to the same items as for the schizophrenics. Thus, *profond* [deep] results in 59 percent failure among the students, as opposed to 2 percent failure among the schizophrenics. On the other hand, *naître* [to be born] results in *mourir* [to die] 100 percent of the time among the 'normal' respondents, whereas 10 percent of schizophrenics respond: *je ne sais pas* [I don't know]. Similarly, *aimer* [to love] results in only 2.5 percent failure among the 'normal' groups, as against 11 percent among the schizophrenics; *savoir* (to know): 5 percent as against 18.5 percent. It should be noted that among the schizophrenics there are admissions of ignorance mostly when the opposite of a verb is requested, and in particular of verbs implying an animate subject – *naître*, *aimer*, *savoir* [to be born, to love, to know] – all verbs that have very strong connotations.

(c) Very often, a comment accompanies the response. The comments can *grosso modo* be reduced to two types.

(i) The comment expresses a modalization of the response: *on pourrait dire*; *par exemple*; *ça dépend*; *peut-être*; *je suppose*; *quelque chose comme ça* [one could say; for example; that depends; maybe; I suppose; something like that], etc.
Modalizations can be analyzed in various ways:

- They are not idiosemiological comments (of the kind one finds so frequently among the senile dementia patients) referring to the immediate context or to the past experience of the patient.
- They may signify the search for ambiguity at the level of the response itself, the reverse side of the ambiguity of the cue which the respondent does not wish to take responsibility for disambiguating; hence the relative aspect given the answer. The respondent may be insisting that the meaning given to the answer depends on the meaning the researcher gives to the question.
- They can also express a refusal to assume responsibility for the utterance, and the decision to leave the choice of response to the researcher. This explanation, although broader in its application, since it deals with the relation of the subject to her or his utterance, is related to the previous one, because the verbal behavior of the schizophrenic tends to leave the choice of response and the responsibility for eliminating the ambiguity of the message to the person giving the instructions.

This interpretation is confirmed by two behavioral reactions.

- If the given term is ambiguous or experienced as such, the respondent may ask the researcher to eliminate the ambiguity. The schizophrenic reacts by asking for the spelling of the word, for its use in a context that fixes its meaning, occasionally for a definition of the term: *Vous voulez dire par là? Comment le concevez-vous?* [What do you mean by that? How do you conceive that?], etc. This type of reaction is found very rarely among the 'normal' respondents or among the other pathological groups.

- Leaving the responsibility for the utterance to the researcher can also be expressed by a simple interrogative expression of protest that modalizes the response.

(ii) The comments show a questioning of the normal code, of the rules of language and of learned definitions, an attitude which lies at the origin of the neo-code schizophrenics substitute for the given one. This questioning may be expressed:

- through relativizing the learned code: *c'est relatif, c'est trop simple, apparemment c'est, j'aurais voulu mieux* [it's all relative; it's too simple; apparently it's; I would have preferred], etc.
- through a double response; or through insisting on the ambiguity: (the opposite of good?) m*auvais ou méchant* [bad or mean]; (the opposite of mean?) *Bonne ou aimable* [Good or lovable], etc. It also frequently happens that the schizophrenic gives a series of answers, refusing to stick to the one that is strictly related to the given item. These behaviors can be analyzed as the refusal to assume responsibility for a choice, or an utterance.
- through an explicit substitution, by the respondents, of their own arbitrary codes for the normal code: (The opposite of true?) *Dans l'état actuel des choses, je dirai irréel* [In the actual state of things, I would say unreal].

7

The results of the survey: in comparison to the responses of the 'normal' and the other pathological groups, the principal characteristics that stand out at first glance in the responses of the schizophrenics, can be grouped under several rubrics.

(a) Diversity of responses: for example, the opposite given for *beau* [beautiful] is *laid* [ugly] 100 percent of the time among the 'normal' respondents, and 48 percent of the time among the schizophrenics, who also answer *moche* [tacky] (19 percent), *vilain* [nasty] (14 percent), and *mauvais, mal, désagréable à voir* [bad, evil, disagreeable to see], etc. *Naître* [to be born] results in *mourir* [to die] 100 percent of the time in the 'normal' group and 33 percent of the time among the schizophrenics, whose responses cannot otherwise be classified: *décéder, disparaître, crever, flageoler, tituber, se pâmer, renaître, ne pas venir au monde, qui n'est pas, mort, décès, absent, le néant* [to pass away, to disappear, to croak, to sag at the knees, to stagger, to pass out, to be reborn, not to come into the world, that which is not, death, decease, absent, nothingness], etc. *Bon* [good] induces *mauvais* [bad] 78 percent of the time in the 'normal' group and 48 percent of the time among the schizophrenics, *méchant* [mean] 16 percent of the time in the 'normal' group and 10 percent of the time among the schizophrenics; the normal group gives no response 6 percent of the time, whereas all the schizophrenics give an answer, 42 percent of which are *haineux, cruel, mal* [hateful, cruel, evil], etc. The opposite of *savoir* [to know] is *ignorer* [to be ignorant] for 90 percent of the 'normal' group, who also respond *méconnaître* [to be unaware of] (5 percent) or who give no response (5 percent); only 22 percent of the schizophrenics give *ignorer* (to be ignorant); the others respond with *ne rien savoir, être sot, être illettré, l'ignorance, le néant, ignare* [not to know anything, to be stupid, to be dumb, to be illiterate, ignorance, nothingness, ignoramus], etc., or give no response (15.5 percent). The opposite of *aimer* [to love] is *haïr* [to hate] for 59 percent of the 'normal' group, who also give *détester* [to detest] (36 percent), or *mal aimé* [unloved] (2.5 percent), or make no response (2.5 percent); the schizophrenics respond with *haïr* [to hate] 30 percent of the time, *détester* [to detest] (22 percent) and *mourir, vomir, se garder à soi-même, insociable, froid, stylé, indifférence* [to die, to loathe, to keep to oneself, unsociable, cold, trained, indifference], etc.; 11 percent give no answer. *Doux* [sweet [soft)] can have many opposites, and provokes diverse responses even in the 'normal' group; however, in their 49 responses, there are only 11 different terms, whereas the 45 schizophrenics give 28 different terms.

(b) Systematic quantification through negative hypertransformation: the first rule of schizophrenics seems to be to give a stylistically marked term, and in particular a term quantitatively marked by the '+' sign. They set aside the neutral term. Thus they give as opposites of *grand* [big]: *nain, minus, minuscule* [dwarf, minus, minuscule]; as opposite of *pauvre* [poor]: *opulent* [opulent]; of *bon* [good]: *haineux* [hateful]; of *doux* [sweet]: *brutal, violent, cruel, coléreux, intransigeant, revêche, une brute* [brutal, violent, cruel, irascible, intransigent, surly, a brute], etc.; of *chaud* [hot]: *glacial, terrible, austère* [glacial, terrible, austere], etc.; of *beau* [beautiful]: *moche* [tacky]; of *masculin* [masculine]: *efféminé, délicat, frêle, fragile* [effeminate, delicate, frail, fragile]; of *aimer* [to love]: *vomir* [to loathe]; of *savoir* [to know]: *être bête, être sot, être illettré, ignare* [to be dumb, to be stupid, to be illiterate, ignoramus], etc.; of *pareil* [similar]: *opposé* [opposed]; of *se lever* [to get up]: *s'écrouler* [to collapse], etc. This tendency is not found in the 'normal' group. Among them, *pauvre* [poor] → *riche* [rich] (100 percent); *grand* [big] → *petit* [small] (100 percent); *masculin* [masculine] → *féminin* [feminine] (100 percent); *chaud* [hot] → *froid* [cold] (100 percent); *bon* [good] → *mauvais* [bad] or *méchant* [mean], etc.

(c) Preference for animates: when the suggested term could belong to two classes, one associated with animate and one with inanimate terms, the schizophrenic almost always chooses the metaphoric or figurative term; that is, the one associated with the animate class. Thus, *doux* [sweet/soft] has for the 'normal' group the following opposites: *rugueux, rêche, amer, aigre* [coarse, rough, bitter, sour]; the schizophrenics prefer: *rigide, coléreux, cruel, austère, intransigeant, brusque, revêche, brutal, une brute* [rigid, irascible, cruel, austere, intransigent, brusque, surly, brutal, a brute], etc. As opposite of *chaud* [hot], the 'normal' group gives *froid* [cold] (100 percent); the schizophrenics give *froid* [cold] (ambiguous as to its lexical class) 70 percent of the time, but their other responses are associated principally with animates: *terrible, repoussant, austère, sévère, agresif, glacial* [terrible, repulsive, austere, aggressive, glacial]. For *beau* [beautiful], the schizophrenics give *vilain* [nasty] (14 percent), a term referring mainly to animates, and, moreover, stylistically marked, as is *moche* [tacky] (15 percent); these responses are not found in the 'normal' group who all answer *laid* [ugly]. The schizophrenics give as the opposite of *comique* [comic]: *triste, taciturne,* or *sérieux* [sad, taciturn or serious], rather than *tragique* [tragic], the former associated with animates, the latter with inanimates. This tendency to prefer animates, to understand the terms figuratively, also explains the divergence between the 'normal' group and the schizophrenics in response to the word *profond* [profound]. Of the 'normal' respondents 59 percent give no answer; 12 percent give *peu profond* [not very deep], 6 percent *creux* [concave], 5 percent *plat* [flat], 5 percent *bas* [low], and 14 percent *superficiel* [superficial]. Only one schizophrenic claimed not to know the opposite of *profond* [profound]: the answers given were: *superficiel, futile, léger, artificiel* [superficial, futile, light, artificial], etc., all either ambiguous or applicable to animates.

(d) Affectation of stylistically marked terms: this shows the desire, found also in the negative hypertransformations, to give the response affective connotations. Thus, *naître* [to be born] provokes *absent, stérile, le néant, flageoler, tituber, se pâmer* [absent, sterile, nothingness, to sag at the knees, to stagger, to pass out], modalizations of the verb *mourir* [to die]. *Aimer* [to love] provokes *insociable, froid, stylé, flegme, indifférent* [unsociable, cold, trained, phlegm, indifferent], etc.

The stylistic mark also has the effect of placing the term on a particular linguistic level:

- either familiar: *moche* [tacky] for *laid* [ugly]; *crever* [to croak] for *mourir* [to die]; etc.;
- or elevated, literary, administrative: *déceler, disparaître* [to detect, to disappear] for *mourir* [to die]; *délicat, frêle* [delicate, frail] for *féminin* [feminine]; etc.

(e) Predominance of the signifier: responses show homophonic analogy with the cue word. There is rhyming play between the cue and response. For example, the opposites given for *naître* [to be born] are: *renaître, ne pas être, dispaître* [to be reborn, not to be, to disappear.][2] When this tendency is too strong, it can provoke aberrant, or even schizophasic, responses: one respondent gives *le pot* [the pot] as the opposite of *pauvre* [poor].

The privileging of the signifier appears to explain the exceptional consistency of the schizophrenics' responses to the cue *absent* [absent] (also found for the cue *masculin* [masculine]). They give *présent* [present] 90 percent of the time, and among the other responses we find *présence* [presence]. *Present/absent* do show a certain homophony. It should be added that *present/absent* are principally associated with animate terms.

(f) The tendency to operate across several lexical classes at once, with a preference for adjectives and substantives: negative transformation divides the terms into two classes, and their grammatical function is of only secondary importance. From two classes related only by the negation, the schizophrenic often chooses adjectives and nouns as opposites for verbs, and sometimes nouns as opposites for adjectives. Thus for *naître* [to be born]: *le décès, le néant, la mort, absent, stérile* [decease, nothingness, death, absent, sterile]. For *aimer* [to love]: *insociable, froid, stylé, flegme, indifférence, indifférent, stérile* [unsociable, cold, trained, phlegm, indifference, indifferent, sterile]. For *riche* [rich]: *la mendicité* [begging].

Since the first words proposed in the exercises are adjectives, one might conclude, at least in the case of the verbs, that inertia plays a role in the choices made by the patient. However inertia is much less obvious among the schizophrenics than among the aphasics, the Parkinson's Disease patients, or even the senile dementia patients, whose discourse shows massive signs of inertia, not even comparable to what is found in the schizophrenics' discourse. It would seem then that inertia alone is not at issue, but rather the predominance of semantic correlation over grammatical integration. There is a relative indifference on the part of the schizophrenic to syntactical and morphological categories as compared to the attention devoted to the establishment of semantic relations.

(g) Schizophasic responses: at least two different meanings must be assigned to the word schizophasia:

• it can mean singularity, or improbability, in the correlation established between a suggested term <a> and the given opposite <a-1>: *vrai/irréel; chaud/agressif; masculin/frêle; profond/artificiel; naître/tituber, se pâmer* [true/unreal; hot/aggressive; masculine/frail; profound/artificial; to be born/to stagger, to pass out], etc. Such slippages in meaning, interpretable in the context of the study, are the origin of the elaboration of neo-codes and can appear as neologisms in the freer context of spontaneous discourse.

- it can be understood as the creation of neo-forms elaborated from phonemes, or syllables, in the learned code, that are not part of the lexicon. One single response of this type was given: [*kats*] as opposite of *poor*. The stability of the class of opposites, and the artificial nature of the study, undoubtedly helped minimize the creation of neo-forms among the respondents whose spontaneous discourse contained many more.

(h) The tendency to substitute morphological negation of the predicate for lexical negation is found among certain catatonic or hebephrenic respondents. *Naître* [to be born] is assigned the opposite *pas naître* [not to be born] (8 percent); *savoir* [to know]: *ne pas savoir* [not to know] or *ne rien savoir* [to know nothing] (22 percent); *aimer* [to love]: *ne pas aimer* [not to love] (9 percent). Once again the verbs are the terms selected for this procedure. It can be attributed to inertia – the response that takes up the cue and the predicative negation are very frequently employed – and to the economical character of this type of negative transformation. It is not actually necessary to find a term from the lexical class A-1, but simply to add the quantifier *no/not* to the given term. This type of response, not found among the 'normal' respondents, is found among the aphasics and even more frequently among the senile dementia patients.

(i) A relative lack of differentiation in the types of transformations can at times be found among catatonic and hebephrenic respondents. It would seem to be explained in the same way as the responses using the morphological negation of the predicate. Inertia induces a patient to give *belle* [beautiful] as the opposite of *beau* [handsome]; *masculine* [masculine {feminine form}] as the opposite of *masculin* [masculine form],[3] *la vérité* [truth] as the opposite of *vrai* [true], etc. The responses of the catatonics and the hebephrenics show similarities in this area to those of the senile dementia patients and of certain of the aphasics.

8

An interpretation of the collected results leads first of all to the conclusion that there is no one grammar for all types of schizophrenics. Sticking to psychiatric nosology, one must distinguish between the grammar of paranoids, and the grammar of catatonics and hebephrenics. The former is characterized by the importance of neo-structurings, the latter by a deficiency evocative of deterioration. That is still simplifying too much, however, because one can go on to isolate several different grammars for paranoids alone.

Furthermore, the most frequent responses and their dominant characteristics allow us to conclude that what differentiates the responses of the schizophrenics from those of the 'normal' group or from the other pathological groups, is the relation between the subject of the enunciation, the subject generating and producing the sentences, and his or her text, the utterance produced. What the exercises require of the schizophrenic is that she or he experience the researcher's utterance, and her or his own, as proposed objects of communication, objects on which transformations can be carried out. However, one constant distinctive feature of the responses of the schizophrenic seems to be the difficulty of assuming responsibility for the utterance produced.

This can be detected in the way that schizophrenics leave to the researcher the task of resolving ambiguities in the exercises presented to the respondent, as well as in the messages they themselves produce in response, which comes down to leaving the responsibility for the utterance to the researcher.

Regarding texts for which responsibility is not assumed, another interpretation is to consider them as a play of signifiers, possible only insofar as respondents do not invest in them as their own. The responsibility for the statement is left to language itself, viewed as a free activity of generations and transformations. This also explains the schizophasic neo-forms elaborated according to patterns of language freed from rules of derivation, suffixation, etc.

Modification of the relationship between the subject of the enunciation and the subject of the utterance is also perceptible in the way schizophrenics modalize their statements. The almost constant modalizations can take different forms: questioning of the code or of the utterances of the addressee, hypertransformation, using stylistically marked terms, using attenuating modal expressions, etc. Whatever the means used, the goal is always the privileging of the moment of enunciation.

The schizophrenic preference for human animates is also due to an inability to dissociate the producing subject from the utterance produced. The schizophrenic identifies the answer with its production, and has great difficulty positioning the text as a finished product subject to objectivization, which is somewhat easier to do in the case of a sentence with a non-animate subject. Metaphorization of the utterances appears thus to be the result of the predominance of the subject of the enunciation who mediates all lexemes.

The lack of differentiation of grammatical classes, and the predominance of nouns over adjectives, seems to result from the fact that, at the time of the generation of the messages, it is the semantic components that determine the sets of words from which the appropriate terms will be selected.

The fact that *naître* [to be born] → *absent, le néant* [absent, nothingness]; *aimer* [to love] → *froid, stylé, indifférent* [cold, trained, indifferent]; *savoir* [to know] → *nul, l'ignorance* [nil, ignorance], etc., do not belong to the same grammatical classes does not bother the schizophrenic because semantic correlations take precedence over grammatical correlations. It is enough for the schizophrenic if the terms are related semantically. In the experimental production of sentences, the schizophrenics reject semantically inappropriate utterances [*the horse sees red*] and produce semantically correct sentences, requiring great grammatical complexity, and even anomaly. 'Normal' respondents, on the contrary, prefer syntactically correct and simple sentences, accepting any semantic anomalies. These results, which seem curious at first, can be explained by the subordination of syntactical patterns which are part of the utterance produced, to the establishment of semantic relations at the level of the enunciation.

9

Analyses of performances of schizophrenics raise the question of their ability to carry out negative transformations. In fact, since schizophrenics do not assume responsibility for their utterances, transformations of utterances become problematic. What does the use of these morphological methods mean? How can these apparently negative sentences, generated in the same way as affirmative sentences, be explained?

The experimental transformation of predicative sentences can be used to verify that what occurs is not actually a negative transformation of the utterance, but the generation of a new utterance. For example, when schizophrenics are given the sentence *he ate apples*, and asked to carry out a negative transformation, with specific indications about the morphological procedures for doing so – *did not* – they invariably respond: *he ate bananas*; *he ate pears*; *he ate oranges*; etc., despite the examples given and the insistence on using the morphological procedure. In fact, the respondent generates a new sentence characterized by a relation of exclusion to the given sentence, the researcher's utterance. Such responses can be found in the 'normal' group or in other control groups, but are not common – far from it. Their consistency among the schizophrenics can be explained by the fact that, in response to the directions to make a negative transformation, the schizophrenic generates another utterance, with which he himself is in a direct relation of enunciation. This sentence can then take on the appearance of a negation, insofar as it excludes the researcher's utterance, and perhaps even the researcher as well.

10

It would be appropriate in this context to raise the question of negation itself. Three different levels where affirmation and negation are opposed should be distinguished. Both affirmation and negation have, at each of the three levels, a different purpose, and yet we erroneously designate them all as the same concepts.

The utterance, and even the behavior, of the subject can signify inclusion or exclusion of the world. At the first level, 'yes' and 'no' are implicit. They can be revealed through analysis of the message and of the attitude of the locutor, but are not given as such in the utterance, which is situated with respect to the subject of the enunciation in a direct relation of immediacy, or even of affirmation. The subject is merged with the utterance, in pure inclusion or pure exclusion. The 'yes' and the 'no' are absolute, mutually exclusive, and permit no dialectical play of acceptance and refusal, which becomes possible only when each is able to turn into its opposite without canceling itself out.

At the second level, 'yes' or 'no' are explicitly expressed in the statement, and they mark the assumption, by the locutor, of his or her acceptance or rejection of the world, in particular as it appears in the utterance of the addressee to which the subject refers. The actual presence of affirmation or negation in the utterance allows the subject of the enunciation to distinguish herself or himself from the utterance produced, and not to merge into the movement of inclusion or exclusion of the world expressed therein. This first dissociation of the subject who produces the message from the message produced is correlative to the distinction of the subject from the world, and of the subject from the other. This can be seen particularly well in the fact that (I say) *yes* or (I say) *no* presupposes the possibility of (*I do not say yes*), (*I do not say no*), demonstrating the ability of the subject to sustain himself or herself beyond an immediate adhesion to or rejection of the world, and beyond the addressee's utterance. Out of the subject's distance from the utterance comes the ability to carry out partial dialectical inclusions and exclusions of the world, expressed notably in (*I say*) *yes and no*. It should be noted that at this level the acceptance or the rejection have the world as their object as it is manifest in the utterance of the addressee.

The negative transformation – in the form of morphological procedures using *no/not*, and lexical opposites and inversions – would constitute the final level. With the negative transformation, the subject actually turns the utterance into its opposite or its inversion. The transformation does not really represent acceptance – either implicit or explicit, total or partial – of the world, but rather the expression of the relation between subject and utterance. It demonstrates even more clearly the dissociation of the subject who produces the message from the generated utterance, a dissociation that is not just a simple instantaneous drawing back from the world, but the manifestation of the split between the subject of the enunciation and the subject of the utterance. The latter appears as one manifestation, among others, of the speaking subject that can be modified with time, or even inverted, and presupposes, at the moment of speech, the possibility of turning into its own opposite. Thus, *I love* requires the possibility of *I do not love*, and vice versa. It is only with this potential reversal in place that the subject can truly assume the statement as an actual sanctioned choice.[4]

11

With respect to the utterance produced, the schizophrenic always appears to be situated in a direct relation of enunciation, incompatible with the assumption of responsibility for the utterance as such, a necessary condition for the realization of a true negative transformation. Affirmation and negation are present in the schizophrenic's discourse only in the form of immediate inclusion or exclusion of the world, of an implicit 'yes' or 'no.' Just because the schizophrenic is capable of using the morphological or lexical processes of negation does not mean that when she or he does so, they are being used to express a negative transformation of the utterance.

Certain sentences taken from schizophrenics' spontaneous discourse are significant from this standpoint: *Que l'on mange ou que l'on ne mange pas, c'est la même chose* [Whether one eats or doesn't eat, it's the same thing]; *Que tu paries ou pas, c'est la même chose* [Whether you bet or not, it's the same thing]; *Que l'on soit ici ou que l'on soit ailleurs, ça sera pareil* [If one is here or somewhere else, it'll be the same thing]; *Qu'on sache ou non, c'est la même chose* [If one knows or doesn't know, it's the same thing]; *Il veut m'interdire que j'en parle ou que je n'en parle pas* [He wants to forbid me from talking about it or from not talking about it]; *C'est une thèse que je dois défendre ou pas défendre* [It's an idea I have to defend or not defend]; *Un faux geste, même si c'est un geste régulier, il m'est interdit d'en parler* [A false gesture, even if it's a regular gesture, I am forbidden to speak of it]; *Je peux parler ou le contredire, dire cette vérité ou ce mensonge* [I can speak or contradict him, tell the truth or tell this lie]; *Ce que je peux aussi bien supporter chez moi que chez vous, ici qu'ailleurs* [What I can stand just as well at my place as at your place, here or somewhere else]; etc. Such statements, where negative phrases are posited as equivalent to positive phrases, demonstrate clearly that the morphological procedures of negation are represented principally as a formalistic play of signifiers, as a deployment of the virtualities of language, or as concretized ambiguities which ultimately carry no message besides the one for which the addressee might care to take responsibility.

Aside from raising questions about all negative transformations, such an attitude on the part of the schizophrenic *vis-à-vis* the utterance produced suggests a problem concerning the structures of communication. It is the referent, the world as it is supposed to be assumed by (I) and (you) in their utterances, that regulates the exchanges of the partners of enunciation. This third term seems to have no basis for the schizophrenic, and the rules attempting to define it are always contested. This justifies our thinking that the relationship of (I) and (you) – barely distinct at this level – can be reduced to the play of mutual inclusion or exclusion, beyond, or foreign to, that which we call linguistic communication.

IV

Toward a Grammar of Enunciation for Hysterics and Obsessives

Analysis of linguistic forms decodes, behind the message the neurotic explicitly seems to want to send, another message revealing the real import of his or her discourse, despite the fact that the carrier of this second message is unaware of it. Beyond the impressions of a first reading or a first listening, analysis can uncover the true identity of the subject who assumes the utterance, the identity of the addressee, and the nature of the proposed object of communication. Who is speaking? To whom? About what?

Distributional analysis of utterances is insufficient to shed light on the schema of communication underlying the discourse of the speaking subject. Utterances should be approached through their dialectical relations with the partners of enunciation, insofar as they constitute a means of apprehending the subject in the very act of enunciation. In other words, it is not another grammar of the utterance that is needed, but *a grammar of enunciation.* Such a project, requiring us to rethink the grammar of 'normal' subjects, will be sketched out here in reference to neurotic languages. I will attempt to show that the functional systematizations found in the singular structures of the languages of neurotics can be interpreted in terms specific to a grammar of enunciation.[1]

*

Reduced to three fundamental terms, the schema of communication can be understood as an exchange between the partners of enunciation – (I), (you) – about an object, the world or the referent – (he/she/it). It is important to emphasize that the three basic terms of enunciation cannot simply be assimilated to their realizations in the utterance. The subject generating the message cannot be equated with the subject of the message produced. This appears clearly in such statements as (I say) *you love,* or (I say) *he loves.* On the other hand, confusion is possible when the subject of the utterance – I – seems to refer to the sender of the message. In fact, the subject assuming the message can be inferred only from an analysis of the discourse in its totality, notably in the transformations the utterance under-goes prior to enunciation. For example, the interrogative transformation can turn the one who, in the utterance, is the designated addressee, into the sender of the message. It is necessary to work back through the chain of transformations in order to designate the addressee of the message and its object. The point is to reduce discourse to its essential model, and uncover the form of the kernel sentence and of its constituent parts hidden by the play of transformations; a kernel sentence revealing the structure of communication: (locutor?) ← (NP1? + V? + NP2?) ← (addressee?).[2] I will attempt this analysis using two corpora of spontaneously produced language: one hysterical, the other obsessive.[3]

From a text approximately 20 pages long produced by the hysteric, I extracted at random three fragments of 42 lines. To begin with, I analyzed each clause as a whole, and broke it down into its constituent parts. The classifications established were: NP1, V, NP2, NP3, adverb, adjective. The goal was to find out how the hysteric filled in the categories, and if it would be possible to distinguish, for him or for her, the specificity of the constituent parts and of their dialectical relations, permitting the establish-ment of a model of the utterance.

Regarding NP1 – the subjects of the utterance – *I* and *you* play almost equal roles in the hysteric's discourse, with *you* being somewhat more numerous, however (40% > 34.5%). If *I* is the subject, the responsibility for the utterance can still be left to (you), either due to the interrogative form, or to the fact that the subject of a completive subordinate clause is *you* and the real utterance is expressed there. I will come back to this. In a dream narra-tive, which is part of the corpus, it was noted that the predominance of *you* over *I* was even more marked. In the dream, or at least in the telling of it, *you* appears to be virtually the only subject of the utterance: *vous aviez votre vrai visage; vous me racontiez ça; vous aviez un mari; vous aviez un apparte-ment; vous avez sorti une fourrure* [you had your real face; you were telling me that; you had a husband; you had an apartment; you took out a fur], etc. Other subjects of the utterance can be divided up into 5.1 percent human animates, 5.1 percent non-human animates (animals), 6.5 percent concrete inanimates (material objects: dresses, coats, rose, paintings, etc.), 6.5 percent demonstrative pronouns (this, that) expressing a precise situational reference, and 2.55 percent relative pronouns referring to a material object. The deter-minants and the linguistic or extra-linguistic contexts allow us to conclude that the representatives of the world are mediated by (you). In fact, it's all about *votre mari, le furet, le renard* [your husband, the ferret, the fox], evoked by an animal skin belonging to (you), *vos robes, vos manteaux* [your dresses, your coats], etc. (You), whether explicitly stated or masked as *it/she/ he*, animate or inanimate, dominates as subject of the utterance.

The verb phrase, in the hysteric's discourse, has specific characteristics. Action verbs are frequent, especially in the cases where *you* is the subject of the utterance: *vous aimez*; *vous restez*; *vous avez*; *vous faites faire*; *vous demandez*; *vous mettez*; *vous regardez*; *je supprime*; *j'achetais* [you love; you remain; you have; you have made; you ask; you put; you look at; I eliminate; I was buying], etc. In addition, incompleteness prevails over completion, which can be seen in the morphological procedures as well as in the choice of verbs; the present or the future are more common than the past, the active than the passive, action verbs than verbs of being. When the verb expresses a condition, it most often appears to be either in process – in the process of elaboration within *I*, brought about by the actions of *you*, rather than established, stable, or the result of a prior development – or presented as established without reference either to a development or to an agent. The narrative, utterance of the utterance, although morphologically marked by the past tense, translates incompleteness: *vous racontiez*; *vous parliez*; *j'écoutais*; *vous mettiez* [you were telling; you were speaking; I was listening; you were putting], etc. The action is ongoing, not complete. Only rarely would an action or a condition be shown as definitively over and done with. It should also be noted that transitive verbs predominate significantly over intransitive verbs.

The object of the utterance is often integrated into the minimal sentence in the hysteric's discourse as NP2. The most remarkable feature is the chiasmus established between subject and object with respect to the partners of enunciation. When *you* is the subject of the statement, *me* comes in as direct object, and even more often as indirect – *vous m'aimez* [you love me]; *vous me racontiez* [you were telling me]; when *I* is the subject of the statement, the object is *you*: *je vous écoute* [I listen to you]; *j'ai rêvé de vous* [I dreamed about you]. Frequently, (you) can also be implicitly reintroduced into the sentence because the animate and non-animate NP2s are related to (you). Among non-animate direct and indirect objects in the analyzed discourse, 80 percent refer to (you). The insertion of *she/he/it*, of the world, into the hysteric's discourse, appears to be directly dependent upon the partner of enunciation, as if the hysteric had no objects of his or her own, as if the world only presented itself as mediated, possessed, valorized by (you), even merged with (you). This evidently raises the question of the referent in the hysteric's discourse. What object of exchange can be proposed to the addressee if the world is neither assumed nor assumable by the hysteric? It should also be noted that the referent/world shows up in the hysteric's discourse more frequently as concrete inanimates (75 percent), than as abstract inanimates (25 percent). The world is actualized in the form of material objets, always exterior to the subject of enunciation, whose character establishes an equivocal relationship of possession. A dress, an apartment, these are not so much possessions as they are worries in the hysteric's discourse.

Adverbial phrases, NP3, also introduce the world into the statement. The hysteric most frequently uses precise spatial references (62 percent): *dans le métro; dans une grande maison; dans une pièce très claire; dans un fauteuil* [in the metro; in a big house; in a very light room; in an armchair], etc. Explicit or implicit reference to (you) is found in this context as well, because it is all about *votre bureau, votre appartement* [your desk, your apartment], or, at the least, *la pièce très claire, le fauteuil* [the very light room, the armchair] appear only insofar as they evoke, or as they can be compared to, *your* lodgings or *your* furniture; it is as if the hysteric had no spatial references besides (yours), and as if she or he were trying to orient herself or himself in space with respect to the addressee. Most of the other adverbial phrases (28 percent) express temporal references, which are precise in cases where they are related to moments of exchange with the interlocutor – *la nuit dernière, l'autre jour* [last night, the other day [of the preceding meeting)], etc. – and very vague in all other cases – *de temps en temps, il y a x temps* [from time to time, x amount of time ago].

It is noteworthy that the hysteric's adjectives most frequently describe the object NP2, although they can also come in as attributes of a concrete inanimate subject. Adjectives specify the object quantitatively and always suggest a comparison with another object, or with another condition of the object itself: a *grande* [big] house; *aussi net, aussi rangé* [as clean, as neat] as here; a *pareil* [similar] coat (the same length), *assorti* [matching]; a *tout petit* [tiny little] fox; a *très claire* [very light] room; etc. Other adjectives convey either quasi-sensorial qualities of the object – *soyeux, doux* [silky, soft] – or, in the rare cases where they refer to an animate entity, qualities relating directly to the partner of enunciation – *sympathique, attachant, intéressant* [nice, appealing, interesting] (for you). As for the adverbs, they also express quantitative or comparative modes of verbs of action or being: *trop, très, aussi, tout, beaucoup* [too much, very, also, all, a lot].

After analysis of isolated clauses, each considered as a whole, I moved on to analysis of larger fragments of utterances, like sentences, in order to reconstitute, through reduction of transformations, the minimal sentence.

Completive subordinate clauses occur mostly in cases where *I* is the subject of the utterance of the main clause. The completive's subject is *you*, and it carries the message, the main clause being not really much more than a dictum introducing the subordinate – *je me dis que vous aimez les roses* [I say to myself that you like roses] – or a modalization of the statement giving it an interrogative nuance – *j'ai vu que vous deviez aimer le jazz* [I saw that you must like jazz] → do you like jazz?; *j'ai l'impression que vous êtes debout* [I have the impression that you're standing up] → are you standing up? The chiasmus of the subjects of the two clauses ends up reproducing the order NP1 = *you* → NP2 = *me*. The division *into* two clauses appears to be an attempt to establish mediations between *I* and *you*: *j'ai peur que vous partiez en voyage* [I am afraid you'll go away on a trip] → your departure frightens me; *j'ai peur que vous preniez de l'importance pour moi* [I am afraid you're becoming important to me] → your importance worries me; *ça m'agace que vous aimiez le jazz* [it irritates me that you like jazz] → your liking for jazz irritates me; *ça ne me plaît pas de vous sentir là* [I don't like to feel your presence] → your presence bothers me. It is significant in this context that in the dream narrative, the nearly consistent order NP1 = *you* → NP2 = *me* is undisguised; *you* is explicitly the one who assumes the statement and carries out the action, *me* being its object. In cases where *I* is the subject of the completive clause, the main clause is reduced to a modalization expressing either constraint – *il faudra que je passe par là* [I will have to come to that]; *il faut que je me retrouve* [I will have to find myself] – or the virtual and incomplete character of the action, evoking in turn an outside obstacle or pressure – *ça me plairait de faire le foutoir ici; je voudrais envoyer vos feuilles en l'air; j'avais envie de dormir* [I'd like to make a real mess in here; I would like to throw your papers around; I felt like sleeping].

The object is expressed with clearly significant frequency in the form of an indirect interrogation: *je me demandais pourquoi vous m'en parliez; je me demande si je vous suis sympathique ou si je vous suis antipathique; je me suis demandé s'il y avait longtemps que vous étiez mariée; je ne sais pas si vous me l'aviez donnée ou si je l'avais prise* [I was wondering why you were speaking to me about it; I wonder if I am agreeable to you or if I am disagreeable to you; I wondered if you were married a long time (if it had been a long time since you were married); I don't know if you had given it to me or if I had taken it], etc. It seems as if the first clause is there only to conceal the indirect interrogation which would more explicitly leave to (you) the responsibility for the utterance, and if necessary, the assumption of the negative transformation. When (you) does not intervene to make decisions, alternatives remain balanced in never-ending oscillation, the perplexed subject being unable to make a choice, which consequently means that the action or the condition remains incomplete: *je ne sais pas si je dois me coucher ou si je ne dois pas me coucher; je suis incapable de savoir si c'est un truc à acheter ou pas* [I don't know if I should go to bed or if I shouldn't go to bed; I can't tell if it's something to buy or not.] It is interesting to note that in the dream (space for the expression of desire?), it is (you) who asks the questions, positioning *I* as subject of the utterance: *vous me demandiez si j'aimais les bijoux; vous me demandiez ce que j'en pensais* [you were asking me if I liked jewels; you were asking me what I thought about it]. Would the fundamental project of the hysteric, always concealed in ordinary discourse, be to get himself or herself recognized as valid subject of the utterance?

Subordinate relative clauses often specify or make explicit the relations of the object – NP2 – representative of the world – to (you): *tout ce que je peux deviner de goût que vous pouvez avoir; dans votre métier, vous devez avoir des gens qui vous sont plus ou moins sympatiques, qui vous attirent plus que d'autres; j'aime vos tableaux, sauf celui qui est sur votre bureau* [all I can guess about what tastes you might have; in your profession, you must have people who are more or less agreeable to you, who appeal to you more than others; I like your paintings, except the one that's on your bookshelf]. Determinative rather than qualifying relative clauses predominate, specifying above all the conditions of the object's existence, its spatio-temporal co-ordinates.

Conditional sentences are found in the form: if A then B, with the chiasmus of the subjects already pointed out, the action of *you* appearing as a necessary and even indispensable condition allowing *I* to carry out an action or experience a condition. This tendency to make *you* responsible for all actions and conditions is even more exaggerated in the cases where potential or hypothetical actions on the part of *you* are presented as what could have avoided actions or conditions for *I*: *si vous aviez mauvais goût, je ne me sentirais pas d'affinités avec vous; si vous faisiez comme X, j'aurais moins peur de m'attacher à vous* [if you had bad taste, I wouldn't feel an affinity for you; if you did as X, I would be less fearful of becoming attached to you].

In cases where causals show the chiasmus of *I* and *you*, they can be reduced to the same schema as the conditionals, leaving *you* the responsibility for *I*'s condition or action. Otherwise, they indicate the motivation which causes the subject to defer action or to leave it unfinished: *je ne le fais pas parce que ça coûte cher; je ne pouvais pas parce que je ne voulais pas; je ne dois pas m'acheter ça parce que je m'apercevrais que c'est une erreur* [I don't do it because it is expensive; I couldn't because I didn't want to; I must not buy that for myself because I would realize that it's a mistake].

The impact of comparatives is often similar to what was noted for adjectives; they create a parallel between two objects, less frequently between two conditions, one of which is related, either directly or indirectly, to *I*, and the other to *you*, or to a *he/she/it* assimilatable in some way to *you* (husband, colleague, etc.): *ça (votre vie) me paraît plus intéressant que ce que je peux penser ou faire; si vous aviez de vieilles peintures comme celles qu'a ma tante; vous avez la même que j'aurais voulu avoir* [that (your life) seems more interesting to me than anything I can think of or do; if you had old paintings like the ones my aunt has; you have the same one I would want to have].

Adverbials of time most often express an attempt at orientation on the part of the subject with respect to the temporal co-ordinates of (you), notably to the moment of his or her speech: *quand vous me dites au revoir;*

avant de vous rencontrer; avant que vous me parliez [when you say good-bye to me; before knowing you; before you spoke to me].

*

The most frequently used subject in the obsessive's utterance is *I*; explicitly 66 percent of the time, or disguised as *she/he/it* or *who/that* 4 percent of the time. It is remarkable that *you* is never represented as subject, at least in the three fragments (of the same length as those taken from the hysteric) that were analyzed. Other subjects can be divided up into 3.6 percent human animate indefinites (*quelqu'un, on, les auteurs, le monde des gens nerveux* [someone, one, the authors, the world of nervous people]), 10 percent abstract non-animates, distinctive also because of their general, indefinite character (*des choses, quelque chose, un grouillement, un mouvement, la notion, la distinction* [some things, something, a seething, a movement, the notion, the distinction]), 10 percent demonstrative pronouns (this, that) and 6.4 percent relative pronouns. It should be noted that the abstract non-animates, or their pronoun substitutes, are for the most part related to (I). They allude to (I)'s condition, or else they are notions mediated by (I)'s conceptual system.

The obsessive's verb phrases do not express any action regarding the world or the addressee, but rather the enunciative process itself, or a condition of the subject: *je me disais; je me suis demandé; j'ai entendu dire; j'ose à peine affirmer; je suis étonné; je me suis libéré; je ressentais* [I was saying to myself; I wondered; I heard tell; I hardly dare state; I am surprised; I freed myself; I was feeling]. Most of the verbs indicate completion, marked by morphological means – a good many of them are in the past tense – or by the paradigm class they belong to. They are verbs of condition. For the most part, verbs of that class express a passive state and have no direct object. One is immediately struck by the number of pronominal verbs included in the discourse of the obsessive. Looking closely, one might even say that the pronominals have often been turned back into reflexives: *je me suis trouvé gêné; je me suis trouvé bien; je me demande la raison d'une telle évolution; je me demande si vous viendrez; je me sens libéré; je me sens une envie de chanter* [I found myself troubled; I found myself well; I asked myself about the reason for such an evolution; I ask myself if you will come; I feel myself liberated; I feel myself wanting to sing]. It should be noted also that a significant number of verbs carry the morphological mark of unreality or potentiality.

The object of the utterance is more frequently found to be a completive clause than a word integrated into the kernel sentence. If it is represented as NP2, it does not introduce the world itself in its materiality, but an imprecise abstract image of the world (74 percent): *un monde de notions; mon discours; des difficultés; le réflexe; ma possibilité; mon désir; l'impression* [a world of notions; my discourse; difficulties; the reflex; my possibility; my desire; the effect; the impression]. Moreover, these abstract conceptions of the world are most often related to the subject, or at least mediated by him (66 percent). It is all about *his* desire, *his* possibility, *his* impression, the affect on *him*, etc. Ultimately, it is always a question of his own image, relayed through an image of the world, and thus more elaborate, more carefully concealed. And even this image is presented imprecisely so as not to convey any clear information about the subject himself, or about his apprehension of the world, and so as not to appear to be a veritable object of exchange. The subject can be objectivized as *me* in NP2 (24 percent). However, this occurs only in clauses where the subject is *I* or a non-animate, never *you: je me sens comme libéré d'une tutelle; je me suis trouvé assez gêné; ce qui me frappe; ce qui m'ennuie* [I feel as if I'm liberated from supervision; I found myself rather troubled; what strikes me; what bothers me]. In the case of non-animate subjects, the obsessive still manages, through passive transformations, to put *I* back in its place as subject of the utterance: *I am struck; I am bothered.* It should be mentioned that *me* is used more often as indirect than as direct object of the utterance, notably with verbs expressing the process of enunciation itself: *je me demande; je me dis; je m'interroge* [I ask myself; I say to myself; I question myself]. Thus, *you* appears neither explicitly nor implicitly as addressee, and the subject designates himself as receiver of his own message.

NP3, another possible space for the appearance of the world, can essentially be reduced, in the obsessive's discourse, to temporal indicators situated in the past, the reference point always being the moment of the subject's own discourse: *les deux derniers entretiens; tout à l'heure; depuis quelque temps; il y a quelques jours; en classe de philo* [the last two meetings; in a moment; for a while; several days ago; in philosophy class]. That is to say that the world actualized in NP3 is still the world of the subject, mediated, interiorized by him, and related to his conditions or enunciations. This is opposed to social time, but even more opposed to spatial references, which always presuppose a certain exteriority with respect to the subject.

Adjectives specify conditions or attitudes of the subject, in cases where they are not specified in the verb phrase by a passive voice or a verb of being: *sceptique; nerveux; fier; embêté; malade* [skeptical; nervous; proud; annoyed; ill]. When they qualify a non-animate, it is still in relation to the speaking subject. In particular they mark the relations of the subject to the object, and sometimes even the evolution of those relations, implying a comparison with a time gone by: *je la trouve plus difficile; tout cela me paraît plus compréhensible* [I find it more difficult; all of this seems more comprehensible to me]. Adverbial expansions show up most often as modalizations of the utterance, aimed at softening its decisive character, either through the introduction of doubt – *peut-être*; *sans doute* (maybe; no doubt) – or through attenuating expressions – *tout au moins*; *à peine encore*; *petit à petit*; *enfin!* [at the very least; hardly yet; little by little; finally!] – or through negative transformations, or through temporal references signifying that even if the utterance had been assumed at some moment in the past, that is no longer necessarily the case, and even if it is assumed at the present time, that is not definitive either, and could be called back into question. All of these modalizations fundamentally express doubt, and a questioning of the utterance, the only means the obsessive has of preventing himself from being completely objectified in the utterance, and of keeping open the possibility of getting the discourse moving again.

In the obsessive's discourse completive clauses often constitute the object of the utterance. Not integrated into the minimal sentence, completives take the place of NP2. Frequently they carry the message, and actually constitute the utterance itself, which was introduced by a clause that was nothing more than a representation of the process of enunciation, usually not made explicit in the discourse of others: *je dis*; *je demande*; *j'interroge* [I say; I ask; I question], etc. This objectivization of the enunciation, almost always found in the obsessive's discourse, gives it its deferred or indirect character, and reveals the steps interposed between locutor and discourse, as well as those between the sender and the eventual receiver of the message. The latter is often even bypassed by the reflexive form of the introductory clause: I say to *myself*; I ask *myself*; I question *myself*, etc. The obsessive's utterances begin as an objectivization of the enunciation, and then continue by referring to the subject of that enunciation. In fact, the subject of the completive is still *I*, and the verb expresses a condition, most often passively experienced, of the subject of the enunciation. The subject takes note of this fully accomplished condition in the way a spectator would, not as one who is or was the agent: *je suis poussé par*; *j'éprouvais*; *j'avais tendance*; *j'ignorais*; *je me sentais obligé* [I am pushed by; I was experiencing; I had the tendency; I was ignorant of; I was feeling myself obligated], etc. The completive thus expresses a quality of the subject that he would like to be the unique witness to and beneficiary of. It is not proposed to the interlocutor, to (you), as a term of exchange, as an *it*, an object of communication. The object expressed in the form of indirect interrogation shows the same characteristics. The subject questions himself and reserves the right to respond. The question is not formulated for the partner of enunciation who has been evicted, as already indicated, by the transformation of the pronominal into the reflexive: *je me suis demandé ce qu'était ce truc*; *je me demande si c'est ça qui ...* [I asked myself what this thing was; I ask myself if it's that ...].

Conditionals are another type of subordinate clause in the obsessive's discourse that have distinct characteristics. They do not take the form: if A then B, but rather indicate the possibility that the realization of the condition remains hypothetical, suspended. Confusion between the potential and the unreal is maintained. This is another way for the obsessive to express doubt, and its function is to keep the utterance open, not closed in on itself. All the more so since this potential-unreal is proposed as that which would allow the obsessive to say, to affirm, to think, what is given in the text. The decisive assumption of the message thus remains problematic, susceptible to eventual remanipulation. The interlocutor has no grounds to contest that which the sender reserves the right to call into question. The hypothetical character of the condition can be expressed by *as if*, which accentuates the nuance of unreality. *As if*, as substitution for *because*, also serves to call the condition of the subject into question: *je me suis trouvé mal à l'aise comme si se produisait une sorte de grouillement interne*; *je me sentais gêné comme si je ressentais une panique devant toutes les possibilités* [I found myself uncomfortable as if there were some sort of interior seething; I was troubled as if I was feeling panic faced with all the possibilities]. The rare causals are generally introduced by *as*, rather than *because*, or *since*, which attenuates their constraining character: *comme la notion avait l'air appuyée par des auteurs valables* [as the notion seemed to have the support of valued authors].

There are a large number of subordinate relative clauses in the obsessive's discourse. Their function, and that of most of the adjectives as well, is to relate the subject of enunciation to non-animate subjects or objects, and to specify the type of relationship he has with them. In other words, relative clauses do express qualities of the world, but they are dependent on the subject of enunciation, and are only valid insofar as they express an interaction between him and the world. They translate a personal imagery of the world, preserved in its singularity, and, as such, relatively incommunicable: *je découvre un monde que j'ignorais*; *un grouillement interne que j'aurais du mal à comprendre*; *je me souviens des notions que j'avais sur ça en classe de philo*; *ça me paraît quelque chose de très grave et qui a du mal à passer* [I discover a world I was ignorant of; an internal seething I would have trouble understanding; I remember notions that I had about that in philosophy class; that seems to me something very serious I would have trouble getting out (= I have trouble saying)].

Temporals in the obsessive's discourse convey the attempt to situate, most often in the past, the utterance, or his own condition, in relation to another: *il me venait des choses tout à l'heure avant que j'arrive* [things were coming to me just now before I arrived [= before I began to talk to you)]; ... *depuis que j'ai commencé à vous parler* [... since I began to talk to you]; ... *quand ça allait bien* [... when things were going well]; ... *lorsqu'il me vient une image et que j'essaie de passer* [... when an image comes to me and I try to move beyond it (=not to tell it)].

*

It becomes clear from this rather brief analysis, which will be developed further elsewhere, that specific models of enunciation correspond to the discourse of hysterics and obsessives. The typical utterance of the hysteric is: (I) ← *do you love me?* → (you). The hysteric leaves it to the addressee to assume the utterance, the interrogative form making the message ambiguous, incomplete, in a word, non-assumed. It is the *yes* or the *no* of (you) that underlies the message, and constitutes the addressee as the only subject of enunciation. Responsibility for whatever is expressed in the utterance is also left to its subject, *you*. The subject apparently producing the message only intervenes as possible object of the addressee, an object which is not the point of convergence for the two partners of enunciation, not an object of exchange, because the unique subject is (you). The typical statement can have such variants as: *I love what you love.* We should not be taken in by the *it* (what) in this example. Whatever it may seem to be, it is the object only of (you), and is not the hysteric's own object, any more than the action expressed by the utterance was the hysteric's own action. Even in cases where the utterance is not in interrogative form – *I love what you love* – the fact that the world, the referent, appears as mediated by (you) implies that the utterance is only a carbon copy, a duplicate, of an implicit or explicit statement of (you).

The typical statement of the obsessive would be: (I) ← *I tell myself that I am loved* → (you), which can also take the form of a double negation (I) ← *I don't tell myself that I am not loved* → (you), the expression of a doubt that will eventually show up as: *I tell myself that I am perhaps loved*; *I wonder if I am loved.* The statement here appears to be assumed by the locutor, accompanied nevertheless by the quasi-constant precaution of a doubt that authorizes questioning and reworking, and is in a way a kind of incompleteness. However, incompleteness also shows up elsewhere in the lack of agent. The locutor is not the problem here, but rather the addressee. His or her function as receiver of the message is in fact called into question by the reflexive character of the enunciation, and by the fact that the object of communication is so utterly mediated by (I) that it is relatively incommunicable. In addition, the addressee is also left out of the utterance where she or he functions neither as subject of an active verb, nor as agent of a passive verb, nor as object.

Incomplete with respect to either the locutor or the addressee, utterances of the hysteric and the obsessive raise the problem of the differentiation of the two poles of enunciation. (I) and (you) are distinguished from each other through their individual relationships to the world, transmitted in the message. However, the hysteric is shown to be lacking his or her own experience of the world, while the obsessive lives his experience in a way that is so elaborated by his own imagery that it cannot be directly understood. This does not mean that we are back to a total confusion of (I) and (you), a hypothesis valid for psychotic languages. We do, in fact, see a kind of differentiation interior to (you) itself or to (I) itself – (you') → (you); (I) → (I'), a system of mediations which becomes the basis for the future emergence of (I) and of 'I' in the hysteric, as well as of a resurgence of the past (you) in the obsessive. The trace of such a system of mediations can be detected at the level of the partners of enunciation, and at the level of the proposed object of communication.

No doubt the objection will be made, with reason, that what were sketched out here as models of enunciation for the hysteric and the obsessive are still very close to models of the utterance. Although the enunciation is conveyed through the utterance, it cannot be considered isomorphic to it. The enunciation is asymmetrical to the text, and this asymmetry may even go so far as to require that these models be reversed. Thus, one cannot exclude the hypotheses that the hysteric might be afraid to grant reality to the addressee, and that the obsessive might be the pure object of the addressee, and unable to assume an utterance as its subject.

It would be necessary, in order to come to a conclusion, to analyze larger corpora, collected over a period of time. Study of a large body of texts will clarify the rules governing them, rules that, from the structuring principle specific to discourse, to its deficiencies and lacks, will allow us to construct models of enunciation. It is also conceivable that analysis of the discourse of phobics, or even of psychotics, will be necessary in order to refine the models proposed for the hysteric and the obsessive. They would then undoubtedly lose their almost caricatural antithetical character.

V

On Phantasm and the Verb

In the utterance, discourse fails as realized structure; in the enunciation, it is always infinite, unfinished. The inadequacy of utterance to enunciation makes all discourse incomplete, unendingly taken up and taken back, unstable in signification. Enunciation is not a system of relations among defined units, but rather a relationship among structures – subject, code, world, co-locutor. It is the permanent questioning of already spoken discourse. As dynamic articulation underlying the programming of the utterance, it can never be totally realized therein; nor can it ever be perfectly isomorphic to it.

IN THE BEGINNING IS THE VERB ... [1]

Postulating the existence of a relation, verbs dominate the enunciation, whereas substantives, the becoming-explicit of terms, govern the utterance. What corresponds most precisely to the structuring that founds discourse is the *verb in the infinitive*, not that it designates the act of enunciation, but rather that it functions in the space of enunciation itself. Devoid of any mark of person or number, the verb in the infinitive expresses only the establishment of a relationship, the existence of compatibilities. It implies neither subject nor object, but rather defines their place and the way they function, and establishes the type of relationship that unites them.[2] Furthermore, the dissociation of subject and object has not yet been finalized. The subject, at this level, does not really carry out an action, contemplate a spectacle or articulate a discourse; the subject is included within the action, the spectacle, and the discourse themselves. We are indeed at the stage of *phantasm*.[3]

And yet, at this point, the 'subject' is already specified, marked by anterior discourses – the other's, and the world's. It is acted as much as actor, structured as much as structuring. That is no doubt why the articulation of the utterance varies from one <subject> to another. This is not to say that the <subject> is substantialized in some way, but that, through its most irreducible phantasm, it is situated in a system of relations constraining the realization of its discourse. Thus the various types of verbs that are given as examples should be considered not for their meanings, but to the extent that they presuppose a specific structuring, a unique mode of interdependence.

Listening to various types of discourses in psychoanalysis leads to the hypothesis that, for each individual, at the site of enunciation, a phantasm governs the realization of the utterance. An *effaced* verb in the infinitive corresponds to that phantasm: *to live, to grow, to grow up, to absorb, to eat, to breathe in, to reject, to give, to communicate, to retain,* etc. This enumeration has only exemplary value and makes no claim to exhaustivity. A linguistic analysis, even a summary one, of these different verbs, reveals what types of subject–object relation they presuppose.

To live implies an animate subject, not necessarily a person, who would undergo the activity more than carry it out. *To live,* in fact – as well as *to exist, to grow, to grow up* ... – can be taken as a passive form.[4] It expresses a condition that the subject experiences, that she or he might take responsibility for, or assume, but with respect to which she or he would not, strictly speaking, be the agent. The status of the subject means that a partner of enunciation is not in position, at least not in his or her individuality and actuality.[5] Undoubtedly it can be inferred as 'subject' of an anterior utterance, necessary cause of the current action or condition. It can also be assimilated to all that will not be the subject, to the world not yet defined as such. But it does not at this stage appear to be differentiated as co-agent or co-locutor. Furthermore, to live excludes all action, or all transference, of the subject onto an object. It is intransitive, and incompatible with the existence of a relation between a subject and any given animate or inanimate playing the role of object, direct or indirect.

To absorb – or *to eat, to breathe in, to consume* – usually takes a human animate subject, or at least a metaphorically animate or personified subject (the sand absorbs the water). The action appears to be actively accomplished by the subject. An individualized unit in the world carries out the action on an inanimate or a metaphorically inanimate object. To absorb excludes any relation between the human animate functioning as subject, and another animate functioning as object. To absorb implies that something in the world, exterior to the subject, is brought into its sphere, or its space. What was exterior and foreign becomes interior and part of the subject, assimilated by the subject. The inanimate becomes animate insofar as it is identified with the subject. The partner of enunciation can be merged with the world, an object to be absorbed. In that case it is inanimate, or non-differentiated, as least as (you). If it has animate status, it will eventually be the one under whose gaze the action takes place, and who participates in it – *to co-absorb* – or favors it – *to give (oneself) to be absorbed, to be eaten.* If the partner of enunciation more effectively resists letting herself or himself be reduced to an inanimate object than the subject itself, this co-agent could remain as the only agent, and *to absorb* changes for the subject into *to be absorbed.* The action actively assumed is always liable to transformation into a passively undergone condition, due to a link of dependence between the inanimate and the animate. Finally, at the level closest to the differentiation of enunciation from utterance, closest to the co-locutor, (you) will be the one to whom the action is reported. But the status of (you) as such is still insufficiently defined, relatively fluid, oscillating between that of an object-world capable of being incorporated, and that of an animate co-actor, or even of the unique agent or subject of the enunciation.

To give – or *to communicate, to transmit, to give back* … – also presupposes a human animate subject who would assume the action in question. The action is more elaborate than is the case for a verb such as *to absorb*, and puts a more complex system of relations into play, since it moves an inanimate or metaphorically animate object-world out of the sphere of the subject into that of another animate entity – *to give something to someone.* It is a question of a transfer from interior to exterior which presupposes an anterior moment when the subject would have appropriated the object. The simple opposition subject–world, in evidence for *to absorb*, becomes an act of transformation of a previously defined object-world. In the present, *to give* establishes a relationship between two animate entities with respect to an inanimate object. The identity of the partner of enunciation is difficult to establish, at least unequivocally. Strictly speaking, the partner of enunciation is the one to whom the action will be announced, for whom the utterance itself would be the transferred object. But that would already be marking a clear-cut separation between enunciation and utterance. At the level of the infinitive, the partner of enunciation would more likely be the one to whom one gives, *to give* expressing the dynamic interdependence between two possible actors. However, (you) can also be identified with the one – assimilated to the world – from whom something has been taken, or with the one who was constituted as object capable of being possessed. Hence another system of relations between the one who is supposed to have formerly participated in the action, and the one who is actually included in it in the present.

As verbs in the infinitive, and expressions of phantasms, *to live, to absorb, to give* express above all a dynamic and not a true temporality. However, while *to live* seems incompatible with a temporal scan, that is not the case for *to absorb* or *to give*. *To live* implies a constant actuality that cannot be assimilated to a present whose existence is thinkable only through the separation from a past or a future. The action is always in the process of happening; the condition is always in the process of coming about. Neither is ever repetitive or able to be anticipated, because neither is ever complete. *To absorb* and *to give*, as infinitives, do express incompleteness, but they are not incompatible with a temporal scan related to the object. It is the presence of the object that means an action can be considered complete, and therefore repeatable, and predictable. It also means that the action can be contested, modified by a questioning of or a change in the object. What is important is that the space of the object be marked out, that its function be required by the verb. The possibility of the existence of a present, past or future character of an action is posited only on that condition. What appears to be the impossibility of rupture or of reiteration in the pure dynamic of *to live* comes from the absence of the object. On another note, the temporal movement of *to absorb* differs from the one implied by *to give*. Incompleteness is suggested more by *to absorb*, in that what is expressed in it is above all a tension between the present and the future. The act would be in process, with no assurance concerning its eventual accomplishment. Only from its repetition do we gather that it has been accomplished. *To give* presupposes a double temporal reference, from the present to the future, since a transfer of an object must occur, and from the present to the past since that would be possible only thanks to a prior appropriation of the object. In the case of *to give*, it is undoubtedly the anterior functioning of the object that makes the temporal scan more obvious, evoking a quasi-ongoing present, the accomplishment of a quasi-immediate action.

Another trait, related to the existence, or lack thereof, of the object, and to the status of the subject, individualizes these three types of verb. No transformation can be carried out on the verb *to live*, except in the metaphorical, or figurative, sense of the term. Regarding the negative transformation: to live or not to live are not really alternative choices. That is not the case for *to absorb* or *to give*. Not to absorb something, to refuse to give some object to someone, or to refuse to give an object to such and such a person, are possible choices. One can even differentiate further, in the sense that while not to absorb anything is not a viable option, that is not the case for not to give anything, which brings us back to a previous time when the subject–world relation was already articulated.

These characteristics relative to temporality and to negative transformations clearly distinguish between *to live* on the one hand, and *to absorb*, *to give*, on the other; one could point out other distinguishing characteristics: for example, passive/non-passive, injunctive/non-injunctive, emphatic/non-emphatic. One could sum up by saying that *to live* is comparable to *to be*, whereas *to absorb* and *to give* belong to the domain of *to have*: tendency toward having, or toward acting in order to have, in the case of *to absorb*; and transfer of a 'had' thing, along with the possible constitution of another as 'having,' in the case of *to give.*

... IDENTICAL AND NON-IDENTICAL TO THE SUBJECT

Whichever one of these verbs underlies the discourse of a subject in psychoanalysis, it has an effect on the structuring of this discourse. There are specific characteristics in the utterance which demonstrate this. What is at stake here is the dynamic of enunciation which, either converging with or diverging from what is actually said, is actualized in transference.

It would seem that what has been theorized about transference, and even what has been improperly called counter-transference, has been elaborated almost exclusively using the verb-phantasm *to absorb*. The transferential dynamic can no doubt be clearly detected and analyzed with respect to the verb-phantasm *to absorb*. In the case of so-called positive transference, the analyst functions as an object to absorb, to eat, either as a whole, or in certain of her or his attributes or productions that are preferentially delegated for absorption. This transferential phantasm can call up an echo in the analyst: phantasms such as *to feed, to stuff with food, to be eaten, to wean*, etc., often accompanied by the specification of that which, on his or her part, would be particularly appropriate to be given up to be absorbed, or to be threatened with being devoured. This phenomenon can converge with, but at times also diverges from, the unconscious aims of the analyst. It is therefore appropriate to speak of transference on the part of the analyst. When that transference does occur, what may prevent the development of a positive transference in the analysand,[6] is the connotation of the analyst as something bad to eat, something poisonous, or the fear of the 'law of an eye for eye,' dictating that *to absorb* implies the possibility of being absorbed. Resulting in the refuge in anorexia, or even in the attempt, on the part of the analysand, to reverse the phantasm, *to feed* the analyst. Feed the analyst what? All the already assimilated objects. That, however, is nothing more than an avoidance decoy, and it reverts back to giving oneself to be eaten, to be absorbed.

The analysis of transference is relatively delicate, in that both the analyst and the analysand, rightly or wrongly, feel directly implicated in it. The action is *transitive* and without the mediation, or at least the actualized mediation, of an object of exchange. That is where the risk occurs of getting stuck in what can be called the co-phantasm, a type of behavior not symbolized by those involved, whatever words they use to conceal it. The traditional principles of interpretation of transferences of the *to absorb* type are well known. One supposedly proceeds to locate and then to analyze the object. Who or what is it? Not I; it is he, or she. Why good? Why bad? Etc. In the end, that means nothing more than the elimination of an artificially born transference neurosis. Or possibly the naming of the object included in the phantasm, creating obsession where there was anxiety. It is the phantasmatic dynamic itself that requires attention, minus the permutable object that the subject–object relation unavowedly makes out of discourse. Interpretation would need to be applied to the junction of the enunciation and the utterance, and would articulate the link between them, the movement back and forth from one to the other. The analyst is an object to be eaten, at the site where the patient is not yet the <subject> of her or his speech, and is still spoken more than speaking. Playing on silence and the word, his or her own and not that of some doctrine, the analyst marks the passage from phantasm to utterance, from acting to saying, raising the question of the status of the object. The analyst interprets, through multiple comings and goings from the state of object to be eaten to that of speaking subject, creating the patient as co-locutor, and not exclusively as absorbing subject or as object to be absorbed. Thenceforth the utterance can function as object of exchange. Interpretation thus conceived is work, action, and not just speech. But this action takes place inside the laws of discourse. The phantasm is irreducible to the word; it is acted out in another register from the utterance. Made from language, it understands it not. The word of the analyst would go unheeded, a dead letter or a swallowed letter, if it were only spoken, and not also acted, as articulation, from one register to the other, from enunciation to utterance.

If the phantasm underlying the analysand's discourse is of the *to give* type, the structuring of the transference is different. First of all, it presents as bifid. *To give* presupposes a dynamic relation between the subject and the one to whom the subject gives, but also between subject and gift object. This relation must be analyzed, unfolded, differentiated within a network of relations. Although transference seems less problematic because the object already has a status, and because the third term has already been established, it is complicated by the multiplicity of relations implicated. It is also made difficult by the apparent symmetry between the phantasmatic structure and that of linguistic communication. In both cases, an inanimate object is transferred from one human animate to another. The artificial character of this analogy calls for analysis. Although the object does exist, it is not easily exchangeable, since it is partially identified with the <subject>, and is an object-world integrated into the subject's phantasmatic universe: an object whose symbolization escapes the subject – lived as non-mediatable, non-verbal, not even capable of being verbalized. The human animate implied in *to give* is also caught up in an imaginary network, and not positioned as <subject>-addressee. He or she can undoubtedly be experienced as co-actor, as the one who wants to take, the one who asks, who is ready to accept or to reject, who appears as possessive rival, as demanding beggar, as dangerous ravisher, or as indifferent, belittling everything proposed. This transferential experience is capable of calling up in the analyst complementary opposed phantasms, in counterpoint. The action of *to give* is structured in a unique global field, according to the types of organization of the phantasm. Subject, object and partner are caught up in this unique construction. The analyst will have to work at breaking it up. The laws of discourse, and of all symbolized exchange, imply fragmentation. If the speaking <subject> tends to produce a global utterance as the metaphor of this phantasm, she or he is forced, in order to be understood, to accept its suspension, its splitting, its metonymic postponement, of which the code, the world, and, most of all, the co-locutor must be the guarantors. Interpreting this verb-phantasm comes down to coming in out of synch, off the beat, not in the space of the cause of the gift, where the phantasm of the analysand expects someone, but rather in the space of the guarantor of the metonymic movement of the utterance, where the analysand awaits no one.

The phantasm which, in analysis, causes the most problems, is certainly *to live*. It effectively excludes all transitive action on an object, and indeed all objects, which is the same as saying all transference, if one defines the latter as an objectival relation. The subject is caught up in a phantasm that is closed in on itself, without dynamic striving toward an outside pole, at least a differentiated one. If the subject comes to analysis, he or she has been brought in by a word. This type of subject expects nothing, asks for nothing, seems a stranger to the meaning of, or even to the possibility of, taking such a step. They speak sometimes, but in the same way as one lives or grows, a solitary expression without any particular appeal to the other, any definite relationship to the world. Speaking becomes the equivalent of *keeping quiet*, prior to any alternation with the word. Or better yet of *murmuring*, pure manifestation of life. Undoubtedly nothing would happen without the profound anguish such a <subject> inspires in the other, in the analyst, for example. In the register of *to have*, the register of the object, which is familiar, and where the analyst is forewarned and awaits the patient, nothing is requested of the former. He or she feels useless, non-existent. It is now the analyst's turn to be disconcerted, unless he or she defends himself or herself by taking the analysand as object, as *had*, thereby aborting for the latter any possibility of access to actively assumed action, or discourse. Perhaps that is the only function the analyst is asked to have. However, when the latter accepts this anguish and lives this transference, he or she will be confronted with death. Not only familiar death linked to objectivization, against which the analyst is relatively armed, and which she or he might happen secretly to call upon to escape from herself or himself, or to give free rein to her or his own aggression. Not even death implied by the divisible character of the object. The death in question here is death that is loss of all identificatory process, the fall into the unrepresentable, where the unique mysteries of birth and death can be felt in ways both undefinable and heavy with meaning. Having come through the silence that founds his or her story, through that intimacy with his or her own death, and not the always contestable death imposed by others, the analyst can find the patient. The analyst must summon the patient to an encounter with death. Not in some acting out together, where the analyst would be executioner or victim. It is not the latter's place to put to death, or to be put to death, but to recognize death and to have it be recognized as the first master. The acceptance of death designs for each of us a unique and solitary destiny. For the indefinite, for the passively undergone, for *to live*, it substitutes the contours of one's own life, to be assumed or rejected. It makes the living being into a <subject>. Perhaps the register of *to have* will remain inaccessible or indifferent to that subject. That does not stop her or him from being brought to act, even to make something, an object perhaps, or at the very least to transform her or his life into a work. The only valid non-deadly transference for such <subjects> is sympathy, provided it excludes all merging together of individuals, and all pity.

There are many diverse verb-phantasms underlying discourse. I could isolate verbs implying non-individualized objects – *to breathe*; cite those that exclude any transitive action between subject and object – *to please*; differentiate those implying an animate object from those implying an inanimate object – *to seduce/to make*. An exhaustive study would also allow us to analyze and formalize the links of interdependence between subject and object, and the typical transformations corresponding to them.

The case of *to desire* is different. *To desire* should be interpreted above all as a modalization – such as *maybe, no doubt* – or as a modal verb – such as *to want to, to be able to, to have to*. Of course, it seems to be the primordial modalization, the trace of the appearance of the speaking <subject> itself, negation of an accomplished present, and assertion of a non-accomplished future. For this reason, it should not have to be analyzed in isolation. It should be treated as *to desire to absorb, to desire to give*. In the case of *to live, to desire* would be situated in the place of enunciation, exterior to the <subject>, to whose marking it would submit, or whose marking it would assume. Whatever the case may be, this desiring can be interpreted as the site of interrogation of the always possible functioning of the other, the partner of enunciation.

VI

Linguistic Structures of Kinship and Their Perturbations in Schizophrenia

The lexical micro-system of words designating kinship relations within a linguistic community lends itself well to the type of componential analysis whose principles were established by H. Conklin ('Lexicographical treatment of folk taxonomies,' *International Journal of American Linguistics*, April 1962), and effectively applied to kinship by Lounsbury ('A semantic analysis of the Pawnee kinship usage,' *Language*, 32, 158–94). The essential factor in the success of this type of analysis is the potential to produce, within a limited field, conjunctive definitions of a body of terms, an exhaustive list of which can then be constituted.

The fundamental problem posed by these structural analyses is to distinguish what belongs to the register of linguistic structure and its use by the 'speaking subject,' from what belongs to the socio-cultural structure formed by kinship relations among members of a defined community. There is the risk of describing the social structure, i.e. the structure of the signified objects (*denotata*), rather than determining the system of lexemes themselves. Thus, linguistic analysis must take care to discriminate between the two levels, and to base itself on the morphological rules governing the lexical structure of kinship terms.

Obviously, this linguistic structure exists only because it is used by speakers; it is defined by the way it functions in discourse. Problems of linguistic description are inseparable from their use by speaking subjects. In this field, as in others, the study of dysfunctions can constitute one approach to the analysis of linguistic functioning. Description of the lexical organization and usage sheds light on 'types of errors,' and on the psycholinguistic hypotheses that can be formulated concerning senile dementia (cf. *Le Langage des déments*, Paris: Mouton, 1973) and schizophrenia.

DESCRIPTION OF THE LINGUISTIC STRUCTURES OF KINSHIP

Lounsbury's principles and method will be used as theoretical reference for the analysis of kinship vocabulary in French. It is important to note that this linguistic structure is defined not only by a limited number of semantic dimensions, but also by reference to the speaking subject.

REFERENCE TO THE SUBJECT AS FOUNDATION OF THE SYSTEM

The system is founded on the referential subject, *ego*, who is actually using the linguistic structure. Kinship terms refer to *ego* implicitly. *Ego* has no fixed place in the linguistic kinship structure, but, without *ego*, the structure does not exist. It is therefore the speaking subject who founds the system and gives meaning to the relations established among the terms. The basic question in the study of kinship structures is: how does *ego* situate himself or herself as reference point in the linguistic structure, of kinship in particular, and how does *ego* convey this referential function in discourse?

Furthermore, it should be noted, from the standpoint of the lexical micro-structure, that for *ego* there is a fundamental double opposition:

- ego, as opposed to relatives within the kinship structure;
- ego and relatives included in the structure, as opposed to strangers.

   These fundamental oppositions bring out:
(a) referential ambiguity at work in the kinship structure:[1] thus, the French word *parent* can designate any type of kinship relation, and it also has a specific referent in the structure: the parents of a child.
(b) Semantic ambiguity: the same term can apply in several different lexical structures (that is, it can have several different distributions), or within the same structure at different levels of specificity. The same example can be used again: the polysemy of the term *parents*.

THE STRUCTURAL DIMENSIONS

The system of kinship names is founded on several dimensions, used in French either jointly or separately, whose pertinent traits constitute the relationships defining the morphological structure. Each dimension can be represented technically by a dichotomous operation. The structural dimensions of the system of kinship names are:

(a) consanguinity: the group of family members united by bonds of blood, as opposed to the group of relatives united by alliance;

(b) generations: within the system defined by the differentiating trait of consanguinity, generations – that is, the relationship instituted among parents and their children across ascending and descending generations – constitute the fundamental dimension of the French system;
(c) Sex: male as opposed to female;
(d) collaterality: within each generation, with respect to *ego*, there is an opposition between immediate family relations (direct) and non-immediate family relations (indirect) that constitutes the dimension of collaterality; for example: father as opposed to uncle, son as opposed to nephew;
(e) relative age: the relative age dimension characterizes age differentials between persons corresponding to the same basic designation. It is limited, in the French type of kinship, to immediate consanguineal relations in the direct line; for example: eldest son as opposed to youngest son.
(f) generic terms: generic terms are those that, in one of the previously indicated dimensions, neutralize or suppress one of the other dimensions, in particular the sexual dimension. Thus *parents* designates father and mother, *children* designates sons and daughters.

Remarks concerning the linguistic specificity of the kinship structure of French have been developed in Luce Irigaray and J. Dubois, 'Les structures linguistiques de la parenté et leurs perturbations dans les cas de démence et schizophrénie,' *Cahiers de lexicologie*, I: 8.

THE PSYCHOLINGUISTIC SURVEY

In order to study the types of error in the manipulation of kinship structures found among patients with senile dementia and among schizophrenics, a survey was drawn up giving respondents definitions of kinship relations and asking them to supply the corresponding term. They are asked: What do you call a sister's husband? The expected answer, and the only one possible according to correct usage, is *brother-in-law*.

The survey includes several questions:
- What do you call a sister's husband?
- What do you call the children of someone's children?
- What do you call a brother's child?
- What do you call an uncle's children?
- What do you call the children of two brothers?

The survey given to a control group (neurological ward patients at the

Hôpital Sainte-Anne who had no mental problems or problems with language) was completed without errors.

The instructions and examples presented as illustrations included the precision that the answer given was to be the kinship term, and not the name of a person who was related to the respondent in that way (Peter, Paul, etc.).

In cases where the general instructions did not elicit an appropriate first response, further directions with increasing linguistic precision were brought in. Precision is increased through references to the pragmatic context:
- emphasizing the relation with *ego,* and references to the actual situation of the respondent: What is your sister's husband's name? What do you call your children's children?
- emphasizing relationships defined in the survey by dividing each of the distinctive traits into a separate question, always referring to the pragmatic context. For example: Do you have a sister? Is she married? What do you call her husband? Etc.

For the schizophrenics, since the results of the first survey indicated that almost all their errors concerned the generational axis, a second survey was elaborated where certain items from the first were differently formulated, deliberately emphasizing the generational dimension, and in particular the relationship of *ego* to *father.* The point was to study the relative stability of the term 'father' in relation to *ego,* and vice versa, as well as the ability of *ego* to identify, if necessary, with the term *father* in the structure.

The questions are formulated as follows:
- What is your father's father to you?
      your mother's father?
- What is your father's brother to you?
      your mother's brother?
- What is your father's wife to you?
- What are your father's children to you?
- What are your children for your father's father?

Refer to Table VI:2 for the results of this study.

ANALYSIS OF RESULTS AND TYPES OF ERRORS

REACTIONS TO THE INSTRUCTIONS

(1) This exercise is not so well received by respondents as exercises permitting a metalinguistic type of response. In this case, the speaking

subject is implied as privileged reference point of the structure in question, which makes it more difficult to answer using the merely formalistic play of language. There is more reticence, a longer period of hesitation. There are reactions of astonishment, irony, and non-comprehension, and sometimes even reponses of 'I don't know,' more indicative of refusal than of ignorance.

(2) The questions on kinship structures, implicating *ego*, intersect with the family history of the respondent. Hence, in this exercise, the far greater prevalence of 'hallucinatory' comments interfering with the response. The other exercises make simple language games easier, and leave the 'hallucinations' to spontaneous or to semi-induced language.

(3) Metalinguistic comments take a specific form. Respondents call into question the validity of kinship denominations, the stability of family structure, the way *ego* comes into the structure, etc. Along the same lines, one observes responses illustrating what could be called a neo-code of the familial micro-structure, as well as attempts by the schizophrenic to restructure an individual language.

(4) In most cases, respondents know the term that answers the question, but first responses are often inexact, in the various ways analyzed below.

TYPES OF ERROR

Preliminary remarks

In 30/60, or 50 percent, of the cases, the incorrect responses are corrected by the respondents, and end up as correct answers after one or two repetitions of the question. It is possible that there is not a higher percentage of error corrections because, for a certain number of respondents, the question was not repeated, and there was only one answer given.

Counting all responses obtained – all responses to each repetition of the question – there are 79 'right' answers and 79 'wrong' answers; the latter also consist of comments on the instructions, on kinship structures, etc. Out of 79 incorrect answers, 53 (53/158) can be considered errors, the others being comments of various types.

Generational errors

Most of the errors (36/53) concern generations. The respondent makes a mistake about generations, 'skipping' one or two. Two, sometimes three, generations can be merged. *Ego*'s and his or her father's generations, sometimes those of *ego*'s son and her or his father, are not distinguished.

For example: A brother's children? *Des cousins* [Cousins]. An uncle's children? *Des neveux et/ou des nièces* [Nephews and/or nieces]. The children's children? *Des frères* [Brothers]. The children of two brothers? *Neveux* [Nephews]. Your father's brother to you? *Un frère; un beau-frère* [A brother; a brother-in-law]. Your grandfather's grandchildren to you? *C'est mon fils* [It's my son]. Your father's nephew to you? *Petit-neveu* [Grand-nephew]. Your children to your father? *Ils seraient ses enfants* [They would be his children]. Your mother's father to you? *Un beau-père* [A father-in-law]. Your father's father? *Un père* [A father].

Some might want to object that the incorrect responses are due to the difficulty of these genealogical or familial subtleties. However, besides the fact that the respondents themselves often correct their own answers, it should be noted that there are not fewer errors when the questions are easier, and imply only the direct filial relation. On the contrary. For example: 'What is your father's wife to you? or 'What is your mother's husband to you?' seem to be difficult problems to solve for schizophrenics. One obtains responses such as 'A wife,' 'I don't know,' etc. And the respondent is perplexed by such questions as 'What are your father's children to you?', questions concerning in particular the father → *ego*, ego → *father* relation.

Confusion about distinct kinship lines

Alliance and collaterality
A sister's husband? *Un oncle, un cousin* [An uncle, a cousin]. An uncle's children? *Les petits-fils, mes filles* [Grandsons, my daughters]. Etc. This can be interpreted to mean that collateral relations by alliance are confused with consanguineal collateral relations, the latter often preferred in the response. It should also be noted that this error is accompanied by an error in generations.

Generations and collaterality
Your father's father to you? *Un oncle* [An uncle]. The children's children? Your children's children? *Des frères* [Brothers]. Your mother's father to you? *Un oncle* [An uncle]. Collaterality seems to prevail over generations here, or more precisely, it seems that responding with collateral relations offsets the difficulty of having to position oneself in the genealogy. Two responses, however, contradict this interpretation: Your mother's sister to you? *Une grand-mère* [A grandmother]; response subsequently corrected to: *tante* [Aunt]. A sister's husband? *Gendre* [Son-in-law]; subsequently corrected to *Beau-frère* [Brother-in-law].

Neutralization of distinct kinship lines, or response with a generic term
A relatively rare type of error, whose low frequency can be compared to its high frequency in the responses of brain-damaged patients or those with senile dementia (cf. *Le Langage des déments*). For example: Your father's children to you? *C'est des enfants, et puis c'est tout; je n'en sais rien, c'est des enfants* [They're children, and that's all; I don't know anything about it, they're children]. Your father's wife? *Une épouse* [A wife]. Your father's children to you? *Des filles* [Daughters]. Etc. Extremely simple questions, from the standpoint of the manipulation of kinship structures, result in such responses as this because the respondent is implicated very seriously in direct filial relation: relation either to the father or the mother. The problem does not lie in the difficulty of producing the appropriate terms, because it can be verified elsewhere that the respondent can recall them.

Designation type responses

These responses show confusion about the relation between the structural terms and their content, or even their attributes, and confusion between the designation and its various possible realizations. For example: The sister's husband? *Robert, André* [Robert, Andrew]. The responses are modified after repetition of the question. It cannot therefore be the result of ignorance of the appropriate term.

Neo-code of kinship structures

One might hesitate between rubrics 4 and 5 in classifying these responses. They have been put into a category suggesting remanipulation of the kinship structure – the same type of restructuring of the mother tongue that has been observed in other areas – because the response provided does not correspond to the name of the person in question, but corresponds to what might be called a symbolic overdetermination of the requested term. The respondent is really manipulating the code here, and elaborating a sub-code for kinship structures. For example: Your father's father to you? *Abraham* [Abraham]. Your father's brother? *Caïn* [Cain]. Your father's child to you? *Esaü* [Esau]. These are answers given by one respondent. Also from the same respondent: Your father's father? *C'est Judas* [It's Judas]. Your father's brother's children to you? *C'est Judas* [It's Judas].

The following responses can also be interpreted in the same way. Who are you to your father? *Bouillastre, un truc comme ça* [Bouillastre, something like that]. Your children to your father? *Des poussins* [Baby chicks]. Your mother's brother to you? *Un Dieu* [A God]. Your sister's husband? *Un beau-frère . . . et un frère quelquefois. Quand c'est un vrai beau-frère, c'est un frère.* [A brother-in-law . . . a brother sometimes. When he's a real brother-in-law, he's a brother].

Errors in the direction of genealogy

For example: What are your children to your father? *Ben, c'est le grand-père* [Well, he's the grandfather]. What are your father's brother's children to you? *Ah ben, c'est mon oncle* [Well, he's my uncle].

It's the same type of mistake that makes one respondent answer: 'Great-children' for 'grandchildren,' a response that shows confusion about the morphological marks of ancestry and descendance. This mistake was corrected by the respondent.

Schizophasic or aberrant responses

The children of two brothers? *Des ormeaux* (Elm striplings). This response can be understood as a paraphone of twins,[2] a kind of schizophasic neologism.

INTERPRETATION OF ERRORS

(1) Schizophrenics know the terms for kinship structures. They can summon them easily as terms of the language, often with an excess of precision and of information. For example, the precision of '*first* cousins,' or of *two* genders given for a term instead of the generic response (nephews *and* nieces),[3] etc. They experience no deficiency with respect to the lexical micro-structure.

(2) Most of the errors concern the generational dimension. Two, sometimes three, generations are confused. The supplemental survey (cf. Table VI:2: another series of questions formulated after the first responses) indicates that the problem for the schizophrenic lies in the *filial* relation. The *ego*–father relation.

Responses given as comments on the proverb '*Tel père, tel fils*' [Like father, like son] confirm that it is direct filiation that is perturbed in the manipulation of kinship structures. For example: '*Le père et le fils sont pareils,*' '*Le père est semblable au fils,*' '*Tel père ressemble à tel fils,*' '*Papa et Guy* [= *ego*] *sont des frères,*' '*Le père, c'est le fils; le fils, c'est le père*' ['The father and the son are similar,' 'The father is like the son,' 'Such and such a father resembles such and such a son,' 'Papa and Guy [= *ego*] are brothers,' 'The father is the son; the son is the father'] etc. (cf. the comments on proverbs in 'Idiolect or Other Logic'). In utterances like these, the filial relation is denied, inverted, neutralized, or flattened out. Spontaneous or semi-induced discourse also contains affirmations such as *'Dans ma propre personne, je suis père'* ['In my own person, I am a father']. One particular respondent indicates his father's date of birth as his own. One effect of this perturbation in the filial relation is to destabilize the fundamental dimension of the kinship system in French – the generational axis. It also problematizes the referential function of *ego*.

(3) The question that is apparently the most difficult for the other respondents, 'What are the children of two brothers to each other?', is the one to which schizophrenics respond with the most ease. This seems to be due to that fact that it implies a lesser degree of involvement on the part of *ego*, and to prove that the problem is not the integrity of the lexical micro-structure, but rather the way *ego* functions in the relation of enunciation to utterance, in relation to the conversion of linguistic forms into discourse, into asserted utterances. The above question is paradoxically easier for them than 'What is your mother's husband to you?'

(4) Concerning the lexical micro-structure, one notes reactions parallel to those shown for the language function: questioning the learned, or imposed, structure (cf. the comments, for example), attempts at neo-structuring, neo-formation of the kinship organization, a kind of neo-code which can consist of symbolic overdetermination of the existing structure (cf. responses given in B5), but which can be just as incomprehensible as certain schizophasic neologisms if the cipher, the key, is too cryptic or too inconsistent.

(5) As for the question of the relation of the schizophrenic to kinship relations in general, and specifically to genealogical relations, some elements appear in the analysis of spontaneous and semi-induced utterances about family, relatives (or parents), children, birth, etc.

Table VI.1   Kinship structures

Respondents	A sister's husband?	A brother's children? A sister's children?	The children's children?	An uncle's children?	The children of two brothers?	Comments or remarks
Baro.	That's an uncle//*I thought that it was an uncle. My relatives, I've never seen them. // Cousin ... I don't know.	Second or third cousins ... // Nieces and cousins // Cousins or nephews.	Great-children ... // Yes, rather than 'great', 'grand'children.	Great-nieces and nephews. (C).	They're cousins.	Commentary on how this relates to the family tree: difficult to do if the relatives are dispersed, if they are dead.
Bege.	A brother-in-law.	Cousins.	Brothers (C).	First cousins.	Uncles and nephews/ nieces// First cousins. They're first cousins.	That's related to the last sentence. Don't you think?
Beno.	A brother-in-law.	Nieces and nephews.	Grandchildren.	First cousins.	They're first cousins.	
Bria.	–	–	–	–	–	
Cabr.	–	–	–	–	–	
Carr.	–	–	–	–	–	
Cayr.	–	–	–	–	–	

Note
*// indicates an additional presentation of the cue. C indicates a comment in response.

Table VI.1   Kinship structures

Respondents	A sister's husband?	A brother's children? A sister's children?	The children's children?	An uncle's children?	The children of two brothers?	Comments or remarks
Cham.	I have the feeling that I should say nothing, absolutely nothing.// (C) // (C).		... // Hmm. I'm their mother. // They're my grandchildren. Anyway, clearly there are males. I don't know anything about it, am abstaining to do it.	Theoretically, I don't have an uncle any more. I've only got an aunt. (*Some aunt?*). There's only one of them (C).		Frenetic commentary.
Chan.						
Char.	—	—	—	—	—	
Chol.	My brother-in-law	My nephew.	My grandchildren.	My cousins.	?	
Cohe.	—	—	—	—	—	
Dali.						
Daud.	A brother-in-law.	Nephews.	Grandchildren.	Nephews.// No, cousins.	Hmm ... hmm ... cousins.	
Dave.						

Table VI.1 Kinship structures

Respondents	A sister's husband?	A brother's children? A sister's children?	The children's children?	An uncle's children?	The children of two brothers?	Comments or remarks
Deno.	That's the son-in-law.// That's the son-in-law.// The son-in-law, i.e. my brother-in-law.	Ah well, they're nephews.	They're ... grandchildren.	They're cousins.	They're elm striplings.[1] They're called cousins, aren't they?	Commentary about consanguinity.
Desc. Dhui. Fabr.	— That's more complicated, that // Cousins[2] ... cushions[2]. Baby chicks[3] ... I don't know ... You could take it much further ... Chickens// I can't find the word.	—	—	—	—	
Fleu.	A brother-in-law.	Nephews (C).	My grandchildren.	My cousins ...	... You see, that's the same again.// Well, first cousins.	Frenetic commentary.

Table VI.1 Kinship structures

Respondents	A sister's husband?	A brother's children? A sister's children?	The children's children?	An uncle's children?	The children of two brothers?	Comments or remarks
Foug. Graf.	(C)// I could never figure out how fam...ilies work. I couldn't get my head round my sister having the same cousin as me ... I wanted to have him all to myself. Nobody ever managed to make me understand that we had the same relatives.// I hope that it's the brother-in-law ... because I don't call him that anymore.	In other words, a nephew.	(C) I hope they're grandchildren.	Mustn't ask me too much because I'm the source// Nephews and nieces, there are both.	Oh, that that's asking me too much. OK, they're nephews, they're all the same.	Frenetic commentary.

Table VI.1 Kinship structures

Respondents	A sister's husband?	A brother's children? A sister's children?	The children's children?	An uncle's children?	The children of two brothers?	Comments or remarks
Hard.	The brother-in-law.	Nephews and nieces.	Grandchildren.	Female cousins.	Nephews again, nephews and nieces. // cousins.	
Hare.	The brother-in-law ... and sometimes the brother. When he's a true brother-in-law, he's a brother-in-law.	–	My grandchildren.	Nephews.	Cousins.	Commentary about his uncle.
Here.	... brother-in-law.					
Héra.	Make a sentence out of it? Make the sentence longer?// I don't know anything about it, an uncle, obviously.// That's a brother-in-law.	I don't have a brother.// They would be my ... nephews.	They would be my grandchildren.	They would be ... my nephews as well. // Cousins.	They have to be cousins.	

Table VI.1 Kinship structures

Respondents	A sister's husband?	A brother's children? A sister's children?	The children's children?	An uncle's children?	The children of two brothers?	Comments or remarks
Kame.	The brother-in-law.	The nephew. Nephews and nieces.	Grandchildren.	Nephews.	Cousins? Cousins.	
Lebr. Lecl.	–	–	–	These are our nephews or nieces or male or female cousins.	–	
Lesu.	What do you call a sister's husband? ... I don't understand// I don't know. I've never visited my family. // A brother-in-law.	–	–	–	I don't know.// I don't know.// I haven't got a clue, a family?	
Marc.	–	–	–	–	–	

Table VI.1 Kinship structures

Respondents	A sister's husband?	A brother's children? A sister's children?	The children's children?	An uncle's children?	The children of two brothers?	Comments or remarks
Migo.	*My* sister's husband, you mean? André// Hmm ... a brother-in-law.	–	So that would be the cousins from ... Brittany. Our cousins' cousins. Still, there our cousins' cousins are our cousins. Not always though, since there are many who claim to be cousins but aren't.	Nephews.	The children of two brothers? Also nephews.	
More.	That's the brother-in-law.	Nephews and nieces.	Grandchildren.	Cousins.	First cousins.	
Pers.	Robert.// A brother-in-law.	Ah, well ... // I don't know, nephews?	Grandchildren.	An uncle's? Cousins.	The children of two brothers? // Cousins.	
Pier.	That's my brother-in-law.	That's my daughters ... my nephews.	That's my grandsons.	Cousins?	Brothers-in-law? No. Hmm, I don't know// Cousins.	

Table VI.1   Kinship structures

Respondents	A sister's husband?	A brother's children? A sister's children?	The children's children?	An uncle's children?	The children of two brothers?	Com-ments or remarks
Pill.	–	–	–	–	–	
Porc.	–	–	–	–	–	
Preb.	–	–	–	–	–	
Quer.	… Moses …	–	–	… Esau …	–	

Note
[1]*Translators note*. The words "*ormeaux*" (elm striplings) and "*jumeaux*" (twins) rhyme in French; their English translations do not.
[2]*Translators note*. The words "*cousins*" (cousins) and "*cousins*" are clearly closer in sound and appearance than their English Counterparts.
[3]*Translators note*. "*Poussins*" (baby chicks) is one step further in the word play link from "*cousins*".

Table VI.2 Kinship structures (Part I)

Respondents	Father's father? Mother's father?	Father's brother? Mother's brother?	Father's sister? Mother's sister?	Father's children?	Grand-father's grand-children?	Father's nephews? Mother's nephews?
Asse.	Grandfather.	... That's my uncle.			That's my son ... the grandson, that's my son// Ah, no, that's me, well ... my father ... no, it's me.	My mother's nephew? That's a little nephew, I think ... a cousin// A cousin.
Dave.	Grandfather.	Uncle ... I don't like that uncle because ... That's a brother.		Brother and sister.		Little cousin ... cousin to be more precise.
Fabr.		An uncle.		Brothers and sisters. That's a brother.		
Foug.	An uncle. My mother's father is a father-in-law// That's a grandfather.					
Lesu.	Oh, that? Those are uncles// That's the uncle// Ah, that's the grandfather.		Well, it's the same// It's grandmother? Your mother's sister ... Ah, that's an aunt.			

Note

// indicates an additional presentation of the cue. C indicates a comment in response.

Table VI.2   Kinship structures (Part I)

Respondents	Father's father? Mother's father?	Father's brother? Mother's brother?	Father's sister? Mother's sister?	Father's children?	Grand-father's grand-children?	Father's nephews? Mother's nephews?
Preb.	My father's father? My grandfather.	I've always got mixed up with that. I didn't understand anything about it// I don't know anything about it. That has to by my father-in-law.// I don't know how close a relation that is. I've never put that question to myself.		I know absolutely nothing about that. They're children and that's that. I don't know how closely they're related// I don't know anything about it. I swear to you// I don't know anything about it, they're children. What do you want them to be?		
Quer.	Abraham.	. . . Cain.	. . . Adelaide?	(Long silence, 15 seconds)// 5 orders// Girls.		

Table VI.2 Kinship structures (Part I)

Respondents	Father's father? Mother's father?	Father's brother? Mother's brother?	Father's sister? Mother's sister?	Father's children?	Grand-father's grand-children?	Father's nephews? Mother's nephews?
Cohe.	It's a particular Judas (C) // (C) // Well, it's the grandfather.	The father's brother? The brother ... my uncle who's in Israel and who's a great guy, that's my father's brother.		*My father's?* // he laughs // My father's children, but because it's my father's child it could very well, he will say: I am ... for example, Habib, and there you have it.		
Hebe. Lecl.	... Grandfather. That's my grandfather.	... Uncle That's my uncle.		My father's children ... wait ... well, my father's children, that's us! thank you very much.		

Table VI.2 Kinship structures (Part II)

Resondents	Your children for your father?	Brother's children? Father's children?	Father's wife? Mother's husband?	Mother's brother for the father?	You for your father?	Comments and remarks
Asse. Dave. Fabr.	If I had children. Well, that's the grandfather // The great-great-children.			. . . a God // a God.	Bouillartre, one like him. // I don't know. Oh yes . . . a little baby chick.// Me, I'm his son.	
Foug.	The grandfather, the godsons between the grandchildren.	That's a nephew, that's a little nephew.				
Lesu.			Husband? // your mother's husband . . . // I don't understand // the mother's husband? . . . father?			
Preb.						To the question about the your mother's brother, respond immediately with an uncle.

Table VI.2 Kinship structures (Part II)

Respondents	Your children for your father?	Brother's children? Father's children?	Father's wife? Mother's husband?	Mother's brother for the father?	You for your father?	Comments and remarks
Quer.		Esau.	A wife. // A wife // That depends on that person's fidelity.			
Cohe.	Oh boy, that's because I didn't have any (C) // For which father? Ah, for *my* father. Ah, well, they would be his children.	My brother's children? // My father's brother's children. Well, I've already lost one of them. But I do have another // Something like Muriel // Oh, yes, Judas, or Lissia.				Commentary about his relations to members of his family.
Hebe. Lecl.	Grandchildren. . . . // Hmm, well, it's their grandson or their granddaughter, it's my boy.	. . . Cousins.				

VII

Sentence Production among Schizophrenics and Senile Dementia Patients

In order to establish models of performance for sentence production among patients with senile dementia and schizophrenics, analysis should, strictly speaking, be done using spontaneous, as opposed to induced, utterances. However, divergences among spontaneous utterances are so great that they do not allow for easy isolation of the various factors contributing to the singularity of the sentences produced. Therefore, a survey was created using linguistic material that is restrictive and standardized, and allows dissociation of the various factors at work in the production of utterances, particularly the attitude of the speaking subject *vis-à-vis* the competence model. Indeed, giving such a survey to respondents presupposes the inevitability of a common competence model, even if it means taking note *a posteriori* of its non-integrity, or dysfunctionality. The underlying hypothesis of this study, a hypothesis that has proved pertinent, is that particularities or perturbations in the utterances produced, are, for the most part, a function of the subject's use of the combinative linguistic function. The variations in performance, corresponding to the diagnosis of senile dementia or of schizophrenia, do not invalidate the stability of the competence model, but rather can be explained as divergent behavioral modes *vis-à-vis* linguistic rules, and as diverse strategies adopted *vis-à-vis* the model of competence.

*

In the sentence production study, two, three or four morphemes were presented to respondents in a definite order, along with the instructions to integrate them into a minimal sentence pattern: 'Make a sentence, the shortest and the simplest possible, with the words I give you.'

The given terms correspond to various syntactic functions, belong to different lexical classes, and can be combined with varying degrees of ease or difficulty. The exercise requires that three types of linguistic rules be put into play: syntactic (intuition of the minimal sentence, with possible

expansions); lexical (respect for syntactic–lexical correlations, disambiguation of the proposed morphemes, and possible selection of a functional
verb); and semantic (understanding the compatibilities and incompatibilities between the given morphemes and certain messages, and among the
given terms themselves).

The cue is always accompanied by an example demonstrating the
minimal sentence, and implicitly suggesting that the respondent rectify any
possible agrammaticality or anomaly in the message constituted by the cue
words. Thus, for the item *door–nurse*, the response 'The nurse opens the
door,' re-establishes the canonical order animate → inanimate, which is
not demonstrated in the cue.

The items are: *maison–mère*; *enfant–hôpital*; *maison–chat*; *lampe–lumière*;
père–enfant–absent; *feuille–détacher–voler*; *rouge–voir–cheval* [house–mother;
child–hospital; house–cat; lamp–light; father–child–absent; leaf–detach–fly;
red–see–horse], etc.

*

The groups of respondents were chosen by neurologists or psychiatrists
using extra-linguistic criteria: confinement due to behavioral problems,
clinical examination, or various psychometric tests. The population of
senile dementia patients includes 52 respondents: 32 in the neurosurgical
service at the Hôpital Sainte-Anne (Drs H. Hécaen and R. Angelergues);
and 20 examined in the university psychiatric clinic of Geneva (Hôpital
Bel-Air: Drs Ajuriaguerra and Richard). The schizophrenic population –
45 respondents, paranoids for the most part – was studied at the Hôpital
Sainte-Anne (Drs Daumézon, Boige and Melman).

*

The strategy adopted by the speaking subject *vis-à-vis* linguistic rules can
be analyzed in two ways: explicitly, in the behavioral reactions to the
exercises, and implicitly, in the analysis of the actual responses.

How do senile dementia patients react to instructions to make a
minimal sentence integrating the imposed terms? Just as for all other
exercises carried out on language-as-object (for example, word or syllable
repetition exercises, transformation exercises), senile dementia patients
frequently respond with reactions of silence, refusal, opposition, protests of
inability to carry out the instructions, or of having forgotten the cue.
Negative reactions to the cue also show up in paraphonic or semantic
confusions of the terms, for which more familiar terms tend to be substituted. The most consistently observed reaction is the 'idiosemiological
comment': the patient relates the terms of the cue to a familiar situation,
integrates one, or at the most two, of them into previously transmitted

discourse, and tries to situate the morphemes in a familiar context. For example: '*Ma mère n'est pas ici, elle est aveugle, elle est dans le milieu de la France;*' '*Quand nous étions petits, ma mère mettait la soupe sur la table pour mes soeurs et moi*' ['My mother is not here; she is blind; she is in central France'; 'When we were small, my mother put soup on the table for my sisters and me'] (for *house–mother*); or '*J'ai trois enfants*' ['I have three children'] (for *child–hospital*); etc.

The various types of reactions to the instructions show the inability of the senile dementia patient to perceive the proposed morphemes and the syntactic models as linguistic objects to be manipulated. Patients in the state of advanced senility seem incapable of metalinguistic behavior, of establishing enough distance from linguistic rules to assure their mastery over them, or to play with them to generate messages. This interpretation can be easily verified through repetition exercises. Although the senile dementia patient is willing to repeat items consisting of meaningful words, either sending them out as messages or integrating them into utterances, he or she refuses to repeat meaningless syllables – pure phonic objects.

Analysis of sentences actually produced by the senile dementia patients also allows us to determine the attitude of these respondents *vis-à-vis* linguistic knowledge.

In the recorded performances, one notes that syntactic patterns are resistant to change. Phrasal schemata are carried out properly, syntagmatic sequences most often respected, and the parts of speech correctly used. Therefore the syntagmatic and transformational models appear to be intact. However, there are frequent incoherencies. The laws of implication, inclusion, exclusion, and even of non-contradiction, underlying grammatical categories, are no longer respected, which results in unacceptable, anomalous messages that look syntactically correct as minimal sentences. The correct usage of the syntactic rules raises the question of whether what we see is automatic functioning of patterns of previously produced utterances, or linguistic material actually used for the purpose of generating new messages. The inappropriate intervention of transformations, even of what appears to the receiver to be their lack of differentiation, can be explained according to the same principle. It should be noted that the *sentences* produced by the senile dementia patients are syntactically complex. Although the instructions make specific reference to simple linguistic models, the senile respondent does not respect them, and his or her utterances take on the appearance of an idiolect. Insistence on action and on references to personal experience most frequently explain the multiplicity of transformations and the length of the sentences produced. Also noteworthy in the responses of dementia patients is the difficulty they have in putting syntactic programs into operation. If at least one of the terms of the cue cannot be easily integrated into an idiosemiological discourse, the initiation of the utterance is often left to the researcher. This initiation is most effective when it eliminates the syntagmatic constraints, and thus almost automatically produces the rest of the discourse.

Since the studies of J. Seglas (1892), K. Goldstein (1933), and M. Critchley (1964), we know that the lexical stock available to the patient with senile dementia diminishes in proportion to the degree of deterioration, the first terms affected being proper names and highly specific terms. However, analysis of recorded performances also illustrates loss of lexical stability. Words, for the dementia patient, do not seem to be defined by systems of correlations, by dependencies that differentiate them, put them into opposition with each other, or specify them with respect to other units of language, but rather seem to have variable meanings which would be a function of the situation or of the idiolectical context where they appear. Their meaning is essentially determined by previously produced or heard discourse, or by lived experience. The lexicon no longer appears to consist of the defined units of a code that can be appropriately mobilized and manipulated with a certain distance. Hence, the difficulty in establishing relations of compatibility among the morphemes proposed by the researcher: the responses of the dementia patients frequently seem like a series of clauses, each one of which integrates one of the terms of the cue into a familiar context. For example: *'Je suis allée chez le docteur et, quand j'étais chez lui et que j'étais assise, je voyais que c'était bien'* ['I went to the doctor, and when I was at his office, and I was sitting down, I saw that it was'] (for *docteur–fauteuil–asseoir* [doctor–armchair–sit]); *'Dans la cour, il y a des arbres qui sont bien verts et on voit très bien à l'intérieur'* ['In the courtyard, there are some trees that are quite green, and one sees very well inside'] (for *arbre–vert–feuille–voir* [tree–green–leaf–see]); etc.

Because the lexemes are reduced to only some of the semantic traits that constitute them, one can conclude that they are relatively undifferentiated. It is the neutralizing of distinctive traits that, in fact, explains semantic or syntactic–semantic anomalies resulting from the patient being unable to recognize ways in which the morphemes can, and cannot, be combined. For example: *'Le cheval voit rouge'* ['The horse sees red']; *'L'arbre vert met sa feuille au printemps'* ['The green tree puts out its leaf in the spring']; *'Le crayon écrit sur une feuille'* ['The pencil writes on a sheet of paper']; etc. The fact that the words are defined only by association partially explains this type of error. Since associations vary from one patient to another, and are furthermore dependent upon the extent of the loss of lexical availability, the elements of the lexicon have no stable reference points which would allow them to be grouped together, substituted for each other, or appropriately combined.

Although utterances transmitted by dementia patients are ambiguous due to the absence of any precise reference to the language, the ambiguity and potential polysemy of the terms given in the cue for the sentence production exercise seem to escape the respondent. Thus, to give a very simple example, when the researcher proposes the morpheme [*mer*] to be integrated into a minimal sentence pattern, none of the dementia patients notices that he or she could choose *sea*, *mother*, or *mayor*.[1] The automatically chosen term, undoubtedly the only one heard, is 'mother,' clearly because it belongs to the idiosemiological context of the respondent.

The availability of terms of the lexicon varies according to which grammatical class they belong to. Verbs, especially auxiliary or generic verbs, pronouns, and linking words, are more resistant to deterioration than nouns or adjectives. In senile discourse, words expressing a relation, those that are more closely correlated with the syntactic function, subsist. On the other hand, the selection of terms capable of bringing specific content to a *current* message is perturbed. This results in serious semantic and syntactic-semantic anomalies when the components are, like adjectives, related less to norms of syntactic integration than to rules of selection. In senile dementia, the framework of the utterance is intact, but the patient cannot make use of it easily, manipulate it in order to generate new messages. The rules in operation in the production of sentences subsist, but the senile dementia patient has no more than a relative mastery over them.

The lack of distance between respondent and linguistic knowledge can also be detected in the points of intersection between subject and code, or between subject and utterance, in particular in the analysis of the shifters and of the modalizations of the text.

It is the pronoun 'I' that holds the subject position in the sentences of the dementia patients, which points up the minimal distance between the subject producing the message and the utterance produced. Indeed, the context indicates that it cannot be the generic 'I' of the speaking subject, but is rather an 'I' demonstrating the adherence of the locutor to her or to his own experience, which hinders the process of formalization, or abstraction. The generic subject 'he' that refers to the class of human animate subjects never appears. As for other subject noun phrases, they consist of human animates or specified inanimates (mother, child, pencil, etc.) whose position in the idiosemiological or pragmatic context of the speaking subject is emphasized by the determinants used: *my* mother as opposed to the mother; *this* child as opposed to the child; etc. The shifters and the types of subject phrases used in the sentences of the dementia patients show a lack of aptitude for formalization, a minimal distance between subject and linguistic production.

Modalizations such as *maybe, no doubt,* etc., traces of the relation between speaking subject and text produced, are not found in the analyzed utterances. The only modals used specify a situation – *often, always* – or mark adherence to the context, rather than demonstrate the subject's ability to distance himself or herself from both the utterance and the actual experience.

Analysis of sentences of senile dementia patients seems to demonstrate that the means of production or of reception of utterances do subsist as materials subordinated to the message, and, more specifically, to previously transmitted messages.

*

The reactions of the schizophrenics to the instructions to make a sentence are very different from those noted among the senile dementia patients. There are almost no refusals, no opposition to the instructions, no negative reactions. On the other hand, comments are very frequent, and also very specific. Comments by schizophrenics often emphasize the ambiguity of the received message. For example: *'Le maire ou la maman?'* ['The mayor or the mama?']; *'Le maire? Une mère ou la mer? Parce qu'il y a maire de la ville et il y a mer, l'océan'* ['The mayor? A mother or a sea? Because there is the mayor of a city and there is the sea, the ocean'] (for: *maison–mère* [house–mother]);[2] *'Père? P-è-r-e?'* ['Father? F-a-t-h-e-r?'] (for: *père–enfant–absent* [father–child–absent]); *'Volet? Le volet ou le verbe?'* ['Shutter? A shutter or the verb?']; *'Ça peut être les feuilles d'un arbre, ça peut être des feuilles de papier, ça peut être bien différent'* ['That could be the leaves of a tree, that could be sheets of paper, that can be very different'] (for: *feuille–détacher–voler* [leaf–detach–fly]); etc.[3] These comments seem to indicate that the schizophrenic is leaving responsibility for the content of the message to the researcher. The respondent underlines its ambiguity and non-acceptability, and asks the researcher to disambiguate it, to fix the contents. In addition, the response itself is often accompanied by such comments as: *'Par exemple'* ['For example']; *'On pourrait dire'* ['One could say']; *'Comme ça, c'est en ordre'* ['Like that, is that in order?']; *'C'est banal, non?'* ['That's banal, no?']; *'Disons ça'* ['Let's say this']; *'Un truc comme ça vous suffit?'* ['Is something like that good enough for you?']; etc. These comments seem to indicate that the schizophrenic's message is transmitted as a game played with linguistic rules; the sentence constitutes an object that the speaking subject does not assume as message; its content, therefore, is never made clear. This attitude on the part of the schizophrenic, *vis-à-vis* the text produced, can also show up in the interrogative transformation, which explicitly leaves the message to the researcher, or in a series of transformations on the first utterance transmitted that seem to demonstrate that, for the schizophrenic, the sentences are, above all, a manipulation of the linguistic function and have no significant specific or stable content. Thus: *'Ma femme a une récompense si elle a un enfant. Elle récompense l'enfant* ou *L'enfant a une récompense'* ['My wife gets a reward if she has a child. She rewards the child *or* The child gets a reward']. Even more obviously: *'Détacher la feuille d'un volet?* ou *Les feuilles s'attachent au volet'* ['Detach the leaf from a shutter? *or* The leaves are stuck on the shutter']; *'Le père louera les petits enfants absents* à moins que ce ne soit le contraire: *les petits qui loueront plutôt le père absent'* ['The father will praise his absent children *unless it's the opposite*: rather the children will praise their absent father'].

Analysis of sentences produced by schizophrenics demonstrates the durability of syntactic schemata. However, grammatical rules are used in specific ways. Thus, unlike the utterances of the senile dementia patients where syntagmatic constraints appear to determine the contents of the message, schizophrenics' sentences often aim at defining classes of equivalents, and even, at times, at creating some, whether it be equivalences between lexical morphemes, between phrases, or between clauses. For example: *'La mère est la reine de la maison'* ['The mother is the queen of the house']; *'Le chat est le gardien du foyer'* ['The cat is the guardian of the hearth']; *'L'enfant peut être une récompense de l'amour'* ['The child can be a reward for love']; *'Avoir un joli bébé est une récompense'* ['Having a pretty baby is a reward']; etc. Verbs of attribution replace the action verbs, more appropriate to reporting lived experience, preferred in the sentences of the senile dementia patients. Unlike the utterances of the senile dementia patients, which are long, narrative, and most often unfinished, constituting only part of an idiosemiological context, the schizophrenics' sentences are like utterance-discourses; they are composed of paradigmatic elements, and are sometimes reduced to a single word–word-discourses: *'Chapiteau,'* *'Tabellion,'* *'Infanticide,'* *'Maison–mère,'* *'Stylo-bille'* ['Capital,' 'Legal Eagle,' 'Infanticide,' 'House–mother,' 'Ballpoint pen'], etc. The relational elements are fragile here, or, more precisely, less prevalent. Sentences without verbs or determinants are found: *'Mère absente de la maison'* ['Mother absent from the house'], *'Feuille rouge'* ['Red leaf'], etc. On the other hand, the emphasis is on nouns and adjectives. The schizophrenics' sentences include fewer transformations than the senile dementia patients', but the pronominal and negative transformations in particular serve to resolve the problems of compatibility and incompatibility established in the cue, which require the mastery of the formal schema itself: *'Le tiroir du bureau s'ouvre'* ['The drawer of the dresser opens'], *'Je ne vois pas un cheval rouge'* ['I do not see a red horse'].

From the lexical standpoint, the insistence on specificity contrasts with the use of generic terms in the sentences of the senile dementia patients:

'On va donner à la mère la table d'orientation' ['They will give the mother the orientation table']; *'La lumière doit être diffusée par une lampe assez douce'* ['The light must be diffused by a rather soft lamp']; *'Les lampes phosphorescentes donnent une lumière assez douce'* ['Phosphorescent lamps give a rather soft light']; etc. However, this insistence on specificity could signal the rejection of the banal message of the researcher, or the refusal to transmit a banal message, or the intention to create a beautiful or surprising sentence. It is not caused by concern for the appropriateness of the message to lived experience. It is the rejection of banal messages that also explains, in the schizophrenic, the fact that the sentences produced are far from being modeled on the minimal sentence pattern required by the instructions: *'Dans la maison, il y avait un chien et un chat siamois'* ['In the house, there were a dog and a Siamese cat']; *'La maison au bord de la mer est très ensoleillée'* ['The house by the sea is very sunny']; *'La feuille s'est détachée et elle volait dans le ciel et elle a disparu avec les rêves'* ['The leaf came off, and it was flying up in the sky, and it disappeared with the dreams']; *'Prendre un crayon et décrire une chose réelle'* ['To take a pencil and describe something real']; etc.

Schizophrenics do notice the ambiguity of the morphemes proposed by the researcher. This has already been observed in their reactions to the instructions, and their requests for disambiguation. Furthermore – contrasting with the responses of the senile dementia patients – for the cue: *house–mother*, the schizophrenics produced sentences where the terms were understood as *sea* and *mayor*.[4] The term *mother* even seems somewhat neglected. This can also be understood as a rejection of banality, or as the refusal to give the sentence a too personal content, or as the rejection of affective connotations: the latter two hypotheses are in any case related.

Do we find neologisms, schizophasic expressions, in the sentences produced? There are very few neoforms: *'Je ne crains pas le mur du son, sonade'* ['I do not fear the wall of sound, *soundage*']; *'Avenue, temporaire, subsistaire, partial'* ['Avenue, temporary, *subsistary*, partial']; for example. It should be noted that these two neologisms are elaborated from an existing foundation, according to linguistic principles of derivation and suffixation. They appear to be a formalistic game played with the categories of language. On the other hand, singularities and improbabilities in semantic compatibilities, in established syntactic–semantic correlations, are more frequent. Such slippages in combinations of terms, which can more easily be interpreted within the framework of the study, are undoubtedly at the origin of neo-codes, and can appear as neologisms in the freer context of spontaneous discourse. It would be tempting to relate these singularities of word association or selection to the instability and lack of differentiation of lexemes found in the discourse of the dementia patients. However, what demonstrates lesser mastery of the language model caused by degeneration in the senile dementia patients, appears to be, among schizophrenics, an effort to stand out, to transform, even to reconstruct the code itself.

Subject noun phrases are most often specified animates in the schizophrenics' sentences; however, respect for the instructions almost always exercises control over selection of terms. These subject noun phrases are not determined by the possessives and demonstratives *my, this,* that one finds in the utterances of the dementia group, but rather by definite and indefinite articles: *the, a, an.* The preferred shifter is still 'I,' but it cannot be interpreted as adherence or reference to a lived personal experience. Accompanying comments that attenuate or even annul the utterances demonstrate this: *'J'écris sur une feuille blanche avec un crayon bleu, je dis ça mais je n'écris pas du tout'* ['I am writing on a sheet of white paper with a blue pencil; I say that but I am not writing at all'], etc., as do the types of sentences introduced by 'I,' and its eventual transformation into impersonal 'one.'

Modalizations in the sentences produced differ from *maybe* and from *no doubt,* ways of expressing the way the subject of enunciation assumes the utterance; they can be interpreted as a sign of the radical exteriority of the speaking subject with respect to the message sent: *'Par exemple,' 'On pourrait dire,' 'Eventuellement,' 'Probablement,' 'Je dis comme ça mais je pourrais dire autrement'* ['For example,' 'One could say,' 'Possibly,' 'Probably,' 'I say it this way, but I could say something else'], etc.

*

After analysis, it is possible to conclude that there is minimal distance from linguistic knowledge in the sentences produced by the senile dementia patients. Although the rules underlying the production of discourse seem to be resistant to degeneration, the senile dementia patient cannot manipulate them as objects, master them to elaborate new messages. They are only material for idiolectical messages already transmitted in the past. The adherence to experience, to the content of the utterance, determines the functioning of discourse. At the most extreme, the senile dementia patient is no longer an active subject of enunciation; she or he is spoken by language, and is only the passive emitter of a corpus of already completed verbal productions. But that is a limit case. The fact that sentences are produced from the imposed morphemes bears witness to the ability to receive and send new utterances, provided that they carry well-known, familiar messages. What governs linguistic production in the senile dementia patient is the message itself.

The attitude of the schizophrenic *vis-à-vis* linguistic knowledge is practically the reverse. For schizophrenics, there is not – this is also the limit case – any content in the message beyond a formalistic play on the linguistic rules. Their language is no longer a set of rules or laws serving to transmit experience; it itself is legislator, creator, a language-object. Whereas the dementia patient has no distance from the message, and is pure object of the utterance, in the schizophrenic, the subject of the enunciation and the utterance do not intersect, and what is said can be understood as manipulation of the code itself.

*

Analyses of sentences of normal respondents (cf. Dubois and Irigaray, 1966) – assuming all the caution required by the notion of a norm – demonstrate the use of a double strategy *vis-à-vis* the model of competence: one strategy considers language as the pure material of a message the subject wants to transmit; the other, more formalistic, consists in considering language as object to manipulate, a set of rules the speaking subject can master and play with. The passage from the first strategy to the second takes place for children around the age of 15 years (Dubois, Assal and Ramier, 1968). Nevertheless, the two strategies always remain available to a 'normal' locutor. The systematizations and singularities, and even the perturbations, detected in the verbal productions of senile dementia patients and schizophrenics should consequently be understood as the result of exclusive recourse to one of these strategies, the other strategy having been lost through lack of, or deficiencies in, the model of subjectivity, or through having become unavailable, due to a dysfunctional relationship between the speaking subject and the addressee, or the world.

AUTHOR'S BIBLIOGRAPHY

Critchley, M. (1964) 'The neurology of psychotic speech,' *British Journal of Psychiatry*, 110, 353–64.

Dubois, J., G. Assal and A. M. Ramier (1968) 'Production de phrases dans une population d'âge scolaire,' *Journal de psychologie normale et pathologique*, 2, 183–207.

Dubois, J. and L. Irigaray (1966) 'Approche expérimentale de la constitution de la phrase minimale en français,' *Langages*, 3, 90–125.

Goldstein, K. (1933) 'L'Analyse de l'aphasie et l'essence du langage,' *Journal de psychologie normale et pathologique*, 30, 430–96.

Irigaray, L. (1973) *Le Langage des déments*. The Hague: Mouton.

—— (1967) 'La Production de phrases chez les déments,' *Langages*, 5, 49–66.

—— 'Négation et transformation négative dans le langage des schizophrènes,' included in this volume, Chapter III, 'Negation and Negative Transformations in the Language of Schizophrenics.'

Seglas, J. (1892) *Les Troubles du langage chez les aliénés*. Paris: Rueff.

VIII

The Utterance in Analysis

Psychoanalysis can be a technique for subverting the utterance. In several different ways.

- Even taken literally, the utterance is always understood as a symptom of some particularity in the function, or the dysfunction, of the structuring of discourse.
- The definition of *an* utterance, constituted as object of analysis, implies the possibility of isolating it as a discourse-unit. Psychoanalysis simultaneously insists on both the fragmentation of the text, *and* its insertion into a network, into networks, of utterances, from which it cannot be isolated. Always contested as a unit, the utterance in psychoanalysis is interpreted according to its polyvalence, its ambiguity, its plurality.
- Any analysis of the utterance refers more or less explicitly to a typology. Various types of discourse come to be expressed in psychoanalytic treatment; however, their forms and figures are called into question as forms and figures, uncovered as metaphors on which the speaker is dependent.
- Finally, analysis of the utterance, its formalization in models, makes use, either intentionally or unintentionally, of the schemata of communication. And the analyst, even as she or he utilizes these schemata, must question them as possible phantasmatic correlates of the one defining them. Because the phantasm[1] is irreducible to discourse, discourse turns out be *in-communication* [non-communication], with the speaking subject unable to express what he or she means, with the interlocutor unable to understand what the utterance conveys. Nevertheless, all kind of efforts are made in order to work out, or to work up, the unreceivable non-said, or the mis-understood, mis-heard. Even when denied, the phantasm reveals its importance.

Whoever practices psychoanalysis must therefore target the production of discourse. Psychoanalysis, a situation of experimental enunciation unavailable to linguists and psychologists, puts the analyst in the position of being able to zero in on phenomena the former two are unable to isolate; in psychoanalysis, everything is actually set up so that the very production of discourse can be investigated. Whatever functions as variable in 'worldly' discourse – referent, addressee, context – is defined (to the extent that this is possible) as invariable in the psychoanalytic situation;

this allows us to grasp the functioning – always covered over, always hidden – of enunciation itself. How then is the analysand's enunciation articulated within this elimination of the 'worldly' context, which corresponds to a removal to another scene, the scene of analysis?

*

Patients are no longer naive. Should we mourn over it? Rejoice in it? It matters little. That's the way it is. As soon as the trappings – or lack thereof – of psychoanalysis are in place, patients take up their life story, illustrating it with sexual landmarks. They are hardly at all disconcerted or concerned about doing this. They inscribe themselves into what they believe to be the project of analysis, of the analyst. They speak from the position of an other, or of a theory, leaving the decision about what to say to the analytic field. They perform no act on their own, but insert themselves into the analytic act. And this *debriefing* does indeed provide a certain satisfaction, a certain comfort, eventually translated into reduction of symptoms.

They avoid action in another way: by uttering what has already been uttered. For themselves, they pose as a he, a she, or an it, exhibit themselves as a he, a she, or an it, presenting themselves deliberately as alienated within an anterior, and relatively mastered, intentional discourse. They play around a bit with the already said, the already thought, going back over the same paths whose traces they have (re)covered, a kind of treasure hunt, a challenge for the perspicacity, or rather for the complicity, of the analyst. But all of that is nothing more than avoiding speaking.

At this stage, waiting for something to say, punctuating it, interpreting it, establishes a kind of connivance in deception. The first dupes are the patients, caught up in their alibis, believing in the illusion of gaining access to a meta-discourse, to a meta-story, in a place where they certainly cannot be suspected of any crime, being outside the domain where acts are carried out. If encouraged even ever so slightly in their duplications, their retrenchments, they end up with 'logorrhea,' or at best with a case of logomachy, changing their forced takeover by articulation into the pseudo-struggles of arguments and quibbling. Good talkers, good souls, happy to be getting off so easily, they are completely taken in.

However, there was something taking place in this discourse that was, in spite of the patient, worth listening to – its emptying. Because utterance of utterance – retelling oneself, retelling the other – hems in if taken up as text, but reopens and empties out, if received by another ear, an ear that solicits, or, rather, as fallen 'object' does not solicit, but functions only as pre-text, small change in a parsimonious economy of death. Undoubtedly, repetition as such does have an effect on the repeater, for the reason that it is, in fact, impossible, and that from this impossibility results abreaction. It is repetition only for whomever wants to think of it that way, and not for the analysand whose only intent is to master it in narrative, utterance of utterance. Taking the time to look for some lost text, some unheard fragment, in what is re-cited, would be the way to make this exchange at a profit.

As for sex, so lavishly provided in the discourse, it merits questioning, not in its forms, particularities, or aporia, but rather insofar as it, like enunciation, is produced in a dehiscence of the utterance. Silent questioning. Because the speaker is not about to hear. She or he speaks from the place of analysis, and listens with the analyst's ears.

In other words, the utterance itself may here evoke its cause, its stress point; the patient, however, is busy denying it, burying it inside. It is the silence of the analyst that will bring this enterprise toppling down. That silence is the act, neutral insofar as the poles of enunciation[2] remain undifferentiated – *ne-uter*, neither the one nor the other – that could be the pledge of a redefinition, or, more exactly, of a remodeling of their economy.

One day, this lack of differentiation becomes obvious to the analysand as being the threat of a death more implacable than the one he or she is trying to annul; promise of infinitude, maybe, but also effacement of all limits, and abolition of all form, articulation, and representation. A death by drowning, where some envelope, some pocket, some air bubble protects the speaker from total fusion, confusion, at the same time as it isolates, or even puts him or her to sleep ... A turning inside out of the very thing whose exclusion, rejection, or splitting ensures the discontinuous functioning of the speaking subject; metaphor of the mythical unity, continuity, identity to itself, of the lost subject, or better yet the impossible subject ...

Here the pathways diverge. In reality, that's the way it has always been. And pathway is already saying too much. Any linear discourse about analysis implies that it cannot be used to mark off a path, but only at best to indicate motion. Predicting the figures of enunciation – some of which will be evoked here – runs the risk of becoming a more or less concerted effort of indoctrination, of suggestion, of subjugation, from which patients must be protected, occupied as they are with seeking it out, preferring any form of centering at all, no matter how cumbersome, to their own irreducible decentering.

Will patients speak from the bathyscaphe? From beyond the grave? Unknowingly rearticulate the discourse that marked them? Addressing it to the Other, the great inscriber presumed scriptable, the one in charge, the accomplice? Or will they try to inscribe this scrawl onto the inert, virgin expanse, the opaque continuum that surrounds them, trying to animate it, bring it to life, appropriate it as lost flesh, missing skin, stolen text? Good for plugging up all orifices, for the restitution of the integrity of the body and of discourse. Or they might impute this enveloping explicitly to the analyst, chalk it up to indifference, only possible representation of the analyst's neutrality, of his or her non-difference; transforming the support into an obstacle.

Whatever the case may be, and it could be otherwise, some act, different from avoidance or emptying, is shaping up, and some other is taking shape. The point is that the patient perceives the place where she or he is called, sought, denied as other. That is not to say that the patient responds in any way to the inquiry, but that he or she discovers his or her right to be implicated in it.

Since deceitfully we have to spin some yarn, to fake some story, let us suppose that the patient takes the very silence of the analyst for a story, that the patient takes the latter to task for the non-sense of her or his own utterance, evanescent since it apparently produces no effect at all on the one who is listening. Forgetting that up till then nothing has been addressed to the patient at all, that all he or she has received from analysis so far are some pretty theoretical and impersonal ears (maybe not even ears at all), on the outside of a supposedly circular discourse.

However, the utterance of utterance is interrupted. We move on to another figure. *Interpellation, interrogation, prayer* even. Experienced as all the more formidable for having been eliminated up until then, and thus situated right where the impossible loop doubles back on itself, the analyst is requested to begin to speak. Not in just any terms, it's true. The analyst is not asked to tell her or his own life story, or challenged to see where that might lead, but rather to assume another role with respect to the functioning of the discourse. Confronted with the precariousness of the status of 'speaking subject,' even as he or she tries to reassure himself or herself about it with 'I already said, or did this, so I am,' the patient would like to leave it to the analyst to revive the utterance, now emptied out. It is an interrogation, however formulated, that conveys this abdication, an interrogation whose subtlest form will be to impute it directly to the other. Not only, 'What do you think of it?', 'What do you have to say about all this?', or in other words: 'Can you take the position of the guarantor of the discourse, take the role of the "subject," so that we can co-produce an utterance?'; but even more so: 'What do you want me to say?', 'What precisely are you asking of me?', or: 'Point out an "object" for my remarks, "your" object that I will make the thread of my discourse, that I will envelop with my statements.'

This bargaining, although it seals the failure of the allegedly solitary production of the discourse, seems to define the roles a bit too clearly not to be covering up some trap. What is at stake here, if not the preservation of unity in the locutor, at the price of being willing to function as supposed subject and object of a unique discourse whose verb would be provided by the transference? In doing this, patients miscalculate the extent to which they are committing themselves; or, at the least, they evaluate the profitability of this operation at too short a term. Because once put in place, this operation irreversibly dramatizes the split in the speaking subject. Even if it is articulated at the very heart of the sentence, it will one day fracture the cohesion of the fabric of discourse, in the same way that it will puncture the sentence.

The analyst is always silent – neutral. Which could be understood as *ne utra pars*. As for requests – the analyst has none to make, except the one already expressed for payment, all the more extrinsic to the functioning of the discourse for being in some ways parallel to it, relaying it, linking it up somehow to the outside, a transition between the within and the without of the scene. But ... should the analyst not express some opinion, some judgment, concerning the utterances already transmitted, given that the patient appeals to what she or he knows, or to what she or he has, or to what she or he sees?[3] The request that the analyst enter into the circuit of production of discourse is also an invitation to quit the register of the word, and to enter into the domain of the gaze, where, whatever the premium that has to be paid, the speaker is assured of receiving a certain form, coherence, or unity, truncated to be sure, but unity nevertheless, that no ear would ever be able to guarantee, except if desired as or desiring to be eye or ... mouth, or hand. Interrogated, or at least implicated within the field of interrogation, the analyst has no business responding.

The aim of the analyst's apparent non-receptiveness is to carry the questioning right into the heart of the utterance of the patient, without his or her knowledge; the patient's questioning might take the form of a silent scanning, or of a quavering voice, or of a fade-out in intonation, or even of a suspension of the discourse. The assurance of the re-citer fails; the utterance loses its coherence. And sometimes the discourse stops, freezes up, comes up against the opacity of a question, a silence, a question that cannot be translated, except as real silence.

The analyst might have to intervene and bring the patient out into the open with 'What comes to you?' or 'What are you thinking about now?', displacing the silence in order to open up the possibility for it to be articulated in the discourse.

Thus taken by surprise, you can bet that patients will produce some such utterance as: 'This wall is white,' 'Your painting is beautiful,' 'I was listening to the children playing,' 'I wonder what that noise is,' 'I wonder if I am intelligent,' etc., in a vexed, even an aggressive, tone of voice. Because they think that responding beside the point is breaking the analytic rule. But one is always inevitably within the domain of some discourse, and it is enough to hear, to point out, where the utterance is functioning, to get it to develop or to change directions.

In reality, the patient speaks from several positions. At the simplest level, at the first listening, the analysand is producing an assertion about the world, indicating an object in the world, naming it, perhaps describing it, affirming that a thing is, or, eventually, how it is. That is the most common type of statement in worldly exchange, the type that in some ways even constitutes its framework and support. But with another ear, the analyst can hear how the patient is reassuring, and even defending, herself or himself. Through a judgment expressed about such and such an object in the world, through the designation of its reality, the analysand is making sure of his or her right to speak, of his or her own existence, and of his or her own existence as speaker. This time, it is the world, and neither the story nor the analyst, that the patient takes as guarantor.

To hear is not to intervene. Focusing on the reality of the world, or on anyone's aptitude to judge it, would run the risk of provoking a quarrel where the analysand would be only too happy to come back to what she or he actually knows, and provoke an only too intentional confrontation. The analyst – who will so often be asked to be guarantor of a deception – has no business confirming, or invalidating, the exactitude or the veracity of an utterance, nor even judging its acceptability. The analyst's role is to play on the ambiguity of the text, to emphasize its irreducible polyvalence, its equivocations, its density, and not to examine the so-called referent of the utterance, or its constitution as message, except to take note of their status, and the status their designator, their producer, would like, through them, to enjoy.

The analyst is really there to investigate the very structuring of the utterance. In the articulation of the forms of discourse something is expressed without the knowledge of the one who speaks. 'This wall is white,' 'Your painting is beautiful,' 'I love this room,' 'They're shouting in the courtyard,' would be inaccurately interpreted, or grouped together, as direct, and in some way isomorphic, utterances. The category of 'direct' utterances is a mythical one, in any case, and it here creates deceptive groupings. As subjects, 'this wall,' 'one,' 'I,' 'your painting' imply different articulations between enunciation and utterance, in each case a more or less complex shuttling back and forth from enunciation to utterance, from the weaving of the discourse to the grammatical grid, and to the implied discourse of the analyst or the world. Furthermore, the enunciation does not insist[4] within, or delegate itself to, some personal or impersonal other, or to the utterance constituted as object, or to the world, all at the same time. One could on several accounts oppose 'They are shouting' to 'I love'; 'this wall' to 'your painting'; 'white' to 'beautiful'; and also 'is' to 'love' or 'shout,' where the prevalence of the complete over the incomplete signifies a particular mode of integration of the always infinite, unfinished process of enunciation, with the defined structures of the utterance – not to mention the inaugural function of 'is' in the coming of the speaker to discourse.

This type of utterance, where the patient was hoping to be on firm ground, on some foundation, and not on shifting sands, must be understood as a series of transformations whose order and suspensions deserve some attention. By the same token, the analyst will have to collect utterances which at first seem more complex, more deferred, or indirect: 'I was listening to the children play,' 'I wonder what that noise is,' 'I wonder if I am intelligent,' etc.

Moreover, it cannot escape the analytic ear that certain patients may have become, at least for a time, all ears, or that others may have become all eyes, or all affect, nor that patients imagine that, speaking in that way, they will be able to leave the domain of treatment, transgress its boundaries. Where do they mark off that space? How? For whom? If they cross over some line, what do they say while doing it? Are they imitating what they perceive as the analyst's response?

Thinking furtively to recover coherence through simply designating or naming a unique object in the world, the analysand is thrown back upon her or his complexity, upon the plurality of networks interfering in that one utterance, upon the multiplicity of sequences woven together there, themselves evoking other texts, either already transmitted, or potential, waiting to be produced. The patient had been resigned to being an indicator, even an index – but for whom? or for what? – and finds he or she is a network, summoned by the analyst – neutral, *ne uter* – at each junction, each crossroads, each fork in the road. The patient intended to answer off the subject, and is shown that when it comes to discourse, it cannot be otherwise, that whatever one tries to say is always irreducibly off the subject. What will the next retrenchment be?

At times, patients end up holding forth in the recitative mode, in the past tense or the present, all the while watching over their own utterance, commenting on it, criticizing it, pointing out mistakes, peculiarities and contradictions. Even making a case against the utterance, re-uttering the utterance, rearticulating it. They act out, in their own way, the interventions of the analyst that have hit the target. And that is what must be understood. Most often, they are on the watch for a meaning, a message. It is meaning they want to discover, uncover.

As they watch for coherence in the text, try to stretch it out, refine it

under the gaze of the analyst, their talk takes refuge, converges, in certain
words that repeat, insist, intervene in unedited contexts, crossroads of sense
and non-sense. Marker words for the analyst, who has to track them down,
and can punctuate, underline, question them. Thus 'to know' can hide
'too, no,' or 'two, no;' and to know what? For whom? 'Understand,' is
'stand under,' and who stands? Who is under? 'Guilty?' No doubt, but gilt
on what?[5]

After a period of defeat, of wandering, patients turn toward language
itself, ask for some guarantee, place the accent on what seems to hold the
analyst's attention. Pausing at words, examining them, playing with them,
making an effort to inhabit the very thing that inhabits them, to bend to
their own game what they have begun to feel makes a plaything of them,
spelling out the discourse that they are learning spells them out. Thinking
maybe that they will, after so many detours, come back to some element,
some non-divisible utterance, some master-word whose capture would
guarantee a reconstruction of language, word by word?

They were playing with, making light of, the very law that presides over
their coming forth, their functioning, which is also in some ways that of
the analyst; they bewitch themselves, ensnare themselves as they listen.
Why start with such and such a word rather than some other? Where does
it get its power when removed from the context of the discourse, from a
network of differences? Does it not have it any more? So then why that
one? The supposed arbitrariness of the choice of word covers over some
encounter that, as fortuitous as it seems, is nonetheless signifying the
game, and the jouissance. What contexts are then summoned up? What
occurrences become possible? What does this word evoke, what does it
recall or call up? This word, is it *one*? It too deserves to be spelled out.
And the pleasure taken by the patient results perhaps from some collusion
of syllables, or phonemes, similar, different, associated with other chains,
calling up various emotions, that the player repeats, knowingly or unknowingly. It is up to the analyst to invite the patient to find the threads, mend
the fabric, because what the latter had intended as a whole piece of cloth,
gets frayed, and threatens to end up as a gaping hole.

And if the patient should get all the way back to the phoneme, the
element presumed ultimate, he or she could be shown that it is a bundle
of differential traits articulated on a field of absence, the empty space on
the game board necessary for their formation as network, permitting their
permutations and associations. No need for a course on phonology to
make the analysand understand that the phoneme itself is plural, not only
in that it refers to other phonemes, but in that it is itself the structuring of
differences. All that is needed is to ask the patient, the way the cat might

ask Alice: 'Did you say big or pig?' using, of course, and as many times as necessary, the terms of the patient's own utterance.

The phoneme is *one* only for someone who subverts it with the gaze, constitutes it as – acoustic – image, or for someone who transcribes it, represents it, which is also a way of submitting it to the formalization of the eye. For the one articulating it and the one receiving it, it is multiple from the beginning, the articulation of differences. Whatever is simple, identical to itself, always slips away, is from the beginning outlawed, unpronounceable, unreceivable, relegated to silence.

Thus are revealed the effects of the submission of humanity to the snares of language. We find no simple element, either at the origin of a construction, or at the end of a deconstruction; nor do we find the field of discourse, the totality of the text, inclusive, absorbing all differences. Our entry into discourse, and we have always been implicated in it, provokes our splitting. We will be the void, the blank, the place of exclusion permitting the functioning of combinations, articulations, and differences, as well as network, bundle, sedimentation of differences. If we come to analysis with the desire to find or recover some elementary or some totalizing discourse, a kind of summative theory or system, of which we ask the analyst to be the guarantor, the pedagogue, the hermeneut, or even the magician, it will be shown that there is no guarantor of discourse, that the analyst can be only the support, or the reminder, of the law of differences which presides over the functioning of language. As such, the analyst, unrepresentable, unspeakable, working the word from the inside, constitutes an outside-the-text, that does not encompass, that cannot be located, at work everywhere and nowhere.

One might, no doubt, understand castration in that way. Whereas what the patient expected from analysis, from the analyst, was the reconstitution or the constitution of a discourse-unit (either an element or a field), or of an indivisible or totalizing utterance, the covering over of lacunae, the resolution of splits, contradictions, divergences, what he or she ends up being confronted with is the status of the speaking subject, pure functioning, pure play of differences one can articulate, insofar as they articulate one. There is no finished text, either at the beginning, or at the end; the utterance is always arbitrarily closed off, and yet always polyvalent, and thus elliptical and ambiguous. Discourse, and therefore analysis as treatment dependent on its laws, is in-terminable.

But we resist explosion, fragmentation, nothingness, death. Animality, the body – inadequate names, notably because they are inscribed in dichotomous oppositions, delegating the neutral to whom? – loathe ex-centricity and spatial and temporal dispersion. They continue always to strive toward restoration at some center, which can happen only when an original, or a

supplemental, unity, whether it is called return, reappropriation, communion, narcissistic delegation, or jouissance, is projected as an end. Those
are some of the other names of the object of desire that will (a)rouse us as
speaking subjects, pulling us ever farther away from our origins, and
engaging us in some impossible communication with the other, for whom
we will be required to be all that we are not, to whom we will be required
to give all that we have not, and whose sole utterance will be heard only at
the price of a misunderstanding, an appropriation that is improper.

If one gives in to the temptation to stage our entry into language, one
might gain insight into the privileged place of the functioning of this
object of desire. The one who already speaks stands out as cause of evil;
she or he is the one who is the thief, at least the possible harborer of stolen
goods, the one from whom we have to take back our own. It is that which
is spoken about that we must find beyond the diffractions of language –
the safe, palpable, material object, the body perhaps, whose substance
compels, is resistant to the mischief of language. Or should we look to
discourse itself for explanations? Although it spirits us away from ourselves,
it does so in order to give us back our integrity. It is right we should take
it as the goal of our quest, take stock of it, invest in it, investigate it.

The privileged trajectories within enunciation and within transference
come together, deceptively transformed into entities – addressee, referent,
code, utterance – that function as causes of polarization, but also of
diffraction and distortion. These trajectories themselves form the network
whose dynamic underlies the programming of the utterance; they
punctuate it, mark it with retroactive effects, constrain it in what it says
and what it leaves out. This network does not lack logic, even if this logic
escapes the one who articulates it – the patient, for example. As effect of
the patient's story, of the manner of her or his integration into language,
this logic repeats itself, whatever twists and turns it may take, and has an
effect on transference and discourse. It implicates the patient, the analyst,
and the utterance, attributing to them certain variable, permutable
functions that always obey a certain law, and articulate themselves in a
certain field whose structuring can be detected in the avatars of transference, either the patient's or the analyst's.

It could be called putting the phantasm into play or into action. A
discourse that does not explicitly speak itself, but is rather an effect of
language: of the articulation, the split, the parceling up, a phantasmatic
residue or rejoinder that is always an attempt at subversion, at transgression
of the law of discourse, a stab at reinstating a continuum. However, it is a
continuum only for someone included, enclosed, on the inside, whatever
the illusion of a passage from inside to outside, metaphor where the
subject comes forth and then fades away. It is the analyst's job to detect,

and to question, still and always, the closures of the enclosure. . . .

Through work on the utterance itself, whose coherence is ceaselessly interrogated, disavowed, fractured, put into perspective, put back into a network of relations. These interventions show patients they cannot expect any guarantee of cohesion from the text, or any object to seal off their/its openings. There is no doubt that such a quest animates the project of discourse and its pursuit, but discourse shows itself to be the aim of a *matrix*, of a form, that always slips away, remains on the horizon, heterogeneous to discourse and yet the cause of its metonymic movement. Many objects try to get into it, to fit in there, but none conforms; hence the referral from object to object, from utterance to utterance. The formalization of language exposes, contra-dicts, the restitution of the phantasmatic shaping that tries to express itself therein. Such is the paradox of discourse: *saying contravenes meaning*. However, there is a *between-the-two* of enunciation where the aim of the object of desire is displaced, a movement resulting from the exclusion of the speaker from the utterance and from his or her ever renewed attempts to get back in, displacement whose process, or progress, is guaranteed by the analyst, who unleashes its suspensions and its stases.

The analyst – representing the function of addressee, among others – can be caught up in the domain of the phantasm on several accounts. He or she must rearticulate its limits in various ways, by functioning now on the inside, now on the outside of its closure.

Analysis, the analyst, will be, for example, the place of discourse, place where one can inscribe oneself, eventually as predicate. The analyst's silence can substantiate this phantasm; but her or his interpretation will say that discourse as such is a no-place. Putting differences into relation, it has the effect of circumscribing places as outside-the-text, as sedimentation of the functioning of language, articulated by it but irreducible to discourse. The analyst determines the 'place' of discourse in a process that inscribes, but into which it is impossible to inscribe oneself, notably because it inscribes the exclusion of the inscriber.

The analyst theoretically functions as master, guarantor of the discourse – analytic discourse, for example. The analyst is supposedly the one who knows, guarantees and legislates, and as such, is desirable; what the analyst supposedly possesses – knowledge, theory, law – becomes the object targeted by the patient. As gratifying as this postulate is, the analyst must expose it as a deception, or at least subvert the terms. No one knows better than the analyst that 'knowledge' and 'theory' are phantasmatic correlates where one is included, from whence one is excluded, and that they cannot function as attributes of any subject. As for the law, it is pure articulation of relations, references. Even though it is the condition of possibility of weavings, of networkings, indeed, of systems (although transgressed therein), it is itself neither matter nor form: never perceptible, never present, at work everywhere. And if the analyst can become its technician, and not its representative, it is because he or she has paid the price of submitting to its effects, to its manipulations, beforehand, during the course of his or her own treatment. On that condition, the analyst can in turn become reference.

The patient also brings phantasmatic desire of communication, communion and co-locution to the analysis. The patient and the other are supposedly speaking from the same place, from the same field, each understood by the other, accomplices, curbing misunderstandings, ambiguities, and breakdowns. When the other says nothing, how can the subject not be taken in? When the other speaks, how can the subject escape the evidence that the other speaks irreducibly from elsewhere, whatever the play of repetitions, intersections, and implications among her or his utterances may be? The subject can only act out the effects of his or her entry into the grid of language in transference, and in the aim and very structuring of discourse. Articulating, they are not strictly speaking articulatable. Speakable, however, is the result of the impact, the imprint, of the other's phantasm on one's own network. Hence, this ambiguous discourse where everyone is stuck, and where one's phantasm acts itself out, repeats itself, and where, in its own field, is uttered, or realized, the inscription of the other's phantasm, provoking the difference indispensable to collation of the two, and to speaking.

Thus the impasse and the well-spring of all communication becomes obvious: what one intends to say is unspeakable, and what one utters, against one's will, is unintelligible to the other. Discourse collides with this not spoken and this not heard, but takes off again. To each his or her own phantasm – to the patient, but also to the analyst.

Included in the field of the phantasm, the analyst will be able to intervene in the object position, targeted in and through the phantasm. It is the type of logical relation determining the functioning of the object that will have to be interrogated, and more specifically, the mode of its relation to the other's phantasmatic field. Can it be defined as a relation of equivalence, of implication, of disjunction, of deduction, etc.? Is intersection preferred there? In other words, what is the logical *copula* that articulates these phantasmatic fields, and what are their eventual points of intersection? It is up to the analyst to be vigilant and detect the functioning of her or his own transference as well as that of the patient. However, it is not the analyst's job to designate those transferences, or to make them explicit; that would lend credibility to the possibility of getting outside the phantasm – to the possibility of access to some meta-phantasmatic – and would favor only its displacement, if indeed it did not double-lock it down in closure. The phantasm is irreducible to the utterance, and it is through acting, non-verbalized as such, which is not to say non-symbolized, that the analyst can designate its horizon. Playing on silence and on his or her own word, the analyst suggests the word's limits, functioning now on the outside, now on the inside, of its field; complicit with the other's phantasm when saying nothing, contravening it when producing an utterance, where, no matter how aware she or he is, the analyst betrays her or his own phantasm. Unless the very adept analyst attempts to speak in turns of the other's phantasm and of her or his own, imitating their articulation and their demarcation. This endeavor may be able to induce a very pertinent question to take shape in the patient. However, it is a step that requires the highest prudence, even suspicion, because, beyond a certain limit, deceptions are not so easily detectable.

As for the relation to the function-object implicated in or by the phantasm, it can still be detected in the specificity of the constraints, in the violence and the distortions that it imposes on the structuring of the utterance, as it provokes systematizations, anomalies, slips of the tongue, etc.

The referent is also worth looking into as a pole that supports the phantasm. Its status as object, its so-called objectivity, presupposes a certain opacity or closing off that should be investigated, articulated. Defined by the functioning of language, it is erroneously credited, despite language, with identity to itself. It is itself determined by a network of differences whose game is ensured by the analyst. The anchoring, the fixed and safe guarantor the patient intended to find in the referent, would also constitute a closure from which he or she expects, even if at the price of a postponement, a kind of centering. … A sealing off, in the place of the referent, of the blanks and articulations of discourse, deferring its process and the efficiency of its laws.

This concept of the referent as counterpoint, counterweight to the always meta-stable articulation of enunciation, must be challenged, demobilized. 'Guaranteed' as outside-the-text by its belonging to a past, as well as by its pro-jection in the future, it must be retransformed into synchronic functioning by the underlining of its effects on the actual structuring of the utterance. 'Guaranteed' by the existence of some other, the referent must be unmasked as propping up the discourse of the patient onto the unpronounceable of the other's phantasm; which is to say, it must be unmasked as leftover from the profit the other derives from the interaction of the phantasmatic fields; unspeakable, of course, but whose action can be detected in the shaping and the realizations of the utterance. Founded on the materiality of some object, of some body, the stability, the recurrence, of the referent must be interpreted as an effort to check the processes of differentiation and elision of the speaking subject, at the price of fixing the schism, or of foreclosing the play of enunciation. Analysis will no doubt again be needed to solve the problem of too exact, too intimate, a complicity between the referent and the image, the referent and the concept.

*

'But what about sex?' you'll object.

'Yes. But what about the neutral? And why does the one need the other to be articulated?'

'And Oedipus?'

'The synchronic functioning of discourse puts into play what the myth stages.'

'And what about the unconscious?'

'A hypothesis concerning the process of discourse, its sense and its non-sense, and its failures, and concerning desire, as well as the deception of all communication?'

IX

Class Language, Unconscious Language

The Marr–Stalin debate concerning the existence, or the non-existence, of class language is undeniably marked by the theoretical and political imperatives of Marxism, but also by the state of linguistic methodology of the period. The position taken on this issue seems inadequate today; this should not be understood as a decision to intervene in the name of Marxist criteria, but rather to examine the linguistic approach to the problem.

The following are the essential points of Marr's theses.

(1) The search for a universal basis for language: Marr situates this search at the lexical level. He isolates four components that he defines as roots functioning as the basis for any lexicon: 'sal,' 'ber,' 'roch,' 'yon.' Using these elements, he elaborates a 'paleontology of language,' endeavoring to find these four syllables in the terms, roots and endings of all idioms. Marr's attempt to derive universals is coupled with a hypothesis concerning linguistic evolution. He posits a rigorous parallelism between economic development and the mutations of language. According to Marr's system, monosyllabic or 'synthetic' languages correspond to primitive economic formations or primitive communism; 'inflected' languages are found in class or caste societies, with the 'agglutinative' languages marking an intermediate phase, the beginning of the social division of labor. This study of linguistic evolution is based primarily on an analysis of the languages of the Caucasus.

(2) The language-economy parallel has as its corollary the existence of class language. Language is defined as a superstructure, and is produced by a class. One class can then impose its language on another, and a language can disappear when its corresponding class disappears. That is why there are 'revolutionary leaps' in linguistic evolution, languages being subject to rapid mutations, the consequences of social and economic revolutions. In fact, Marr made an attempt to elaborate a 'situational theory' of linguistic production; however, the lack of sufficiently sophisticated linguistic instruments, and, above all, of the language/speech distinction, caused significant confusion in his posing of the problem.

(3) The third essential element in Marr's theory is the attempt to carry out a synchronic study of the languages of the USSR Here also, the Soviet linguist shows himself to be relatively 'modern.' From his synchronic perspective, he writes a dictionary of the languages of the USSR: beginning with a description of their current state, he works back to ancient Slav, analyzing the successive strata that indicate the passage from one state of the language to another. This elaboration of what could be called an 'inside-out' dictionary came later to be seen as a kind of negation of history.

Marr's linguistic theory, which was the official linguistic theory of the Party, was criticized by Stalin in 1950. Stalin attempted to refute the notion of language as superstructure, and the concept of class language. The political exigencies of the moment, particularly the unification of the soviet countries, was probably the cause of this modification in the regime's position *vis-à-vis* the established linguists. Whatever the political imperatives of the time, and whatever the theoretical considerations invoked by one side and the other, it seems that both Marr and Stalin misconceived the terms of the problem, in the search for a universal or national base for language, as well as in the affirmation or negation of class language. These questions can be approached differently today, due to the development of structural, distributional, transformational, and generative linguistic theories and methods. The opposition between language and its realization in speech acts is ill conceived in the Marr–Stalin debate. In other words, what is missing is the articulation of the Chomskian distinction between competence and performance – based on Saussure's classic model of the difference between language and speech – permitting the differentiation of 'the grammatical system existing virtually in each brain' (Saussure, *Cours de linguistique générale*, 1916, p. 30)[1] from its various modes of realization in discourse, which are functions of the linguistic knowledge of the speaking subject, as well as of a certain number of individual factors like memory, attention, emotivity, etc., and of the linguistic and situational contexts in which utterances are expressed. It is only through this distinction that we can begin to conceive the existence of a universal basis of language, and the existence of a language of class.

Thus the problem of universals must be analyzed in terms of the opposition between deep and surface structures (cf. Chomsky), and not in terms of common lexical stock, as Marr claimed. Defined by the grammarians of Port-Royal as a function of logical/psychological steps, the question of universals inferred from *a priori* mental processes is scientifically framed by Chomsky. Using the distributional methods of Harris, he studies the surface structures of different languages, and derives, from realizations that are extremely variable, simple, regular structures. These 'deep' structures are not lexical morphemes, but rather grammatical categories, functions, and relations. Divergences between one language and another result from variations in application of morphological/phonological rules functioning between the underlying level of deep structure, and the level of the realization of utterances, or the surface structures. In other words, in order to consider the problem of universals, linguistics had to evolve away from an atomistic, lexical, semantic concept, into a structural or, better yet, generative concept, where the syntax/lexicon dissociation, such as it had been envisaged in the Marr–Stalin dispute, no longer makes sense, since the semantic information in utterances results above all from 'underlying syntagmatic indicators' (Chomsky). It is no longer appropriate to oppose syntax to semantics; what must be taken into consideration are two levels of syntactic information: the level of deep structures pertinent to semantic interpretation, and the level of surface structures pertinent to phonetic interpretation.

Debate about the existence or non-existence of a class language centers around an exaggerated dissociation of syntax and lexicon. Stalin concedes that there are 'class dialects and jargons' distinguished by lexical variants, but refuses to qualify them as 'noble language,' 'bourgeois language,' 'proletarian language,' or 'peasant language.' Indeed, 'these dialects and jargons have neither a specific grammatical system nor their own lexical stock; they borrow them from the national language.' Marr, on the contrary, affirms the existence of class grammars, either bourgeois or proletarian, which employ the universal lexical stock in variable combinations essentially determined by the socio-economic infrastructure.

The problem of universals can be analyzed differently thanks to new linguistic tools that permit us inductively to establish models of utterances, and can now be conceived in the following terms: using corpora collected in different classes, will linguistic analysis allow us to derive different structures from the utterances, or will we have to conclude that the models of discourse are similar, despite superficial variations in realization? This type of research has not been envisaged up until now, and I will put forth only a sketch.

Hypothesizing that the production of discourse is a function of the language, and of a sender, a referent and a context – of which the addressee represents an extremely important functional pole – in other words, of a code or rules of production, of a speaking subject and an object of communication conditioned by the situation – it is possible to assume that variations in the situation, and in the context in which the discourse is produced, imply variations in the structuring of the utterance. I analyzed, from this perspective, corpora of recordings of spontaneous and semi-induced discourse (sentence production exercise: integration of proposed lexemes into a minimal sentence pattern), produced on the one hand by working-class respondents, and on the other hand by middle-class respondents. Quickly noticeable in the corpora are certain divergences between the two groups: for example, variations in lexical specificity and availability, and a noticeably different vocabulary. One can also isolate, in the various structures of the utterance, other differences that are more useful in defining the specificity of a class language than the lexical variations, which can be explained just as well by different criteria: for example, rural as opposed to urban. Definition of these lexical criteria also requires syntactic and semantic analysis.

Examination of the working-class corpus shows that the subject noun phrases are preferentially 'I,' 'we,' or 'one,' that is, shifters manifesting minimal distance between the subject producing the message and the utterance produced. Other subject noun phrases are human animates or specific inanimates whose determinants emphasize references to a pragmatic or idiolectic context: 'my,' 'this,' 'a/an.' Verb phrases are mostly process, or action, verbs of the generic type 'to do.' The morphological procedures and the types of verb preferred show the prevalence of narrative, either in the present or the past. Human animates and specified concrete inanimates predominate in the object noun phrases. Expansions of the noun or verb phrases serve to clarify the spatio-temporal context and the modes of action. Certain types of transformation, in particular those that require distance from the syntactic schemata – pronominal or negative transformations, etc. – are rarely found; this would indicate that the problems posed by the integration of the lexemes into a minimal sentence had to be solved using specific strategies. For example, for the cue *rouge–voir–cheval* [red–see–horse], the solution *'Ce cheval tire une charrette rouge'* ['This horse pulls a red wagon'] or *'J'ai vu un cheval avec des pompons rouges'* ['I saw a horse with red pompoms'] is more common than *'Il n'y a pas de cheval rouge'* ['There are no red horses']. Also for *père–enfant–absent* [father–child–absent], performances are of the type: *'Le père est absent, l'enfant pleure'* ['The father is absent; the child is crying'], or *'Le père et l'enfant sont absents'* ['The father and the child are absent'], rather than *'Le père de l'enfant est absent'* ['The child's father is absent'], or *'L'enfant souffre de l'absence de son père'* ['The child suffers from its father's absence']. Several clauses – either juxtaposed or co-ordinated – had to be composed in order to comply with the instructions. This could have been avoided, at least at the performance level, through use of a nominal transformation. In addition, analysis of spontaneous discourse shows that the articulation of minimal utterances is most often effected through juxtaposition or co-ordination, the coherence of the utterance resulting from the temporal unfolding of the action, or of events related to it, rather than solely from the employment of linguistic means. The cohesion of the discourse is also ensured by redundancies within the utterance itself. This type of discourse is predominantly metonymic, with an action verb determining the structuring; the utterance is contiguous with the situation in which it is produced. Finally, from the lexical standpoint, one might point out the frequency of terms that are both 'concrete' and 'ambiguous,' in the sense that they are defined only in relation to a particular extra-linguistic context.

The subject noun phrases in the middle-class corpus consist mainly of the generic 'she/he/it,' referring to an ensemble of human animates or abstract inanimates. If the subject noun phrase is a specific term, it is an abstract inanimate noun modified by 'the.' This type of subject phrase requires distancing of the subject of enunciation from the subject of utterance. In addition, the shifter 'I' itself most often functions as a generic of the speaking subject, and not as articulation of the utterance into an idiosemiological context. Verb phrases, for the most part, consist of verbs of condition or attribution. Temporal modes of the past or present narrative type can be found, but one more often finds verbs in the so-called durative present, correlated with definitions of conditions or attributions. The distance from the enunciation also leaves space for the future, and, more specifically, for eventuality or potentiality. Due to the preferred types of verbs of the generic type 'to be,' the predicate, although it does express determinations relative to the subject phrase, contains few object phrases. In the cases where they do appear in the utterance, they are of the abstract inanimate class. Expansions of the noun and verb phrases serve to specify the condition or the attribution when it is not made explicit in the verb phrase, or else they consist of modalizations clarifying the relation of the speaking subject to the utterance – 'perhaps,' 'no doubt.' The types of transformation carried out show that the utterance functions as object to be manipulated. Pronominal, nominal and negative transformations are used to resolve the problems posed by the articulation of the lexemes into a minimal utterance: *'Il n'y a pas de cheval rouge'* ['There are no red horses'] for (red–see–horse); *'Le tiroir du bureau ne s'ouvre pas bien'* ['The drawer of the desk doesn't open easily'] for (*tiroir–ouvrir–bureau* [drawer–open–desk]); *'Le père de l'enfant est absent'* ['The child's father is absent'] or *'L'enfant souffre de l'absence de son père'* ['The child suffers from its father's absence'] for (father–child–absent). This constitutes a statement at the performance level alone, the only level at which there can be a response to the cue. The articulation of the statement into discourse takes place through the play of transformations or through processes of subordination. Furthermore, the coherence of the utterance is established through the structure itself, rather than through representation of, or reference to, an extra-linguistic context. Manipulation of and play with language elaborate new connections, produce new 'objects,' in which the verbs, mostly copula, articulate the functioning of a linguistic logic. Underlying the cohesion of the discourse, this logic guarantees its *metonymic progress*, as well as explicit or implicit references to other texts. However, at the time of its production, the utterance aims above all at constituting *metaphors* whose effectiveness is dependent upon their *particularity*. From the lexical standpoint, specific abstract terms predominate, disambiguated through reference to the language function rather than to an extralinguistic context. The utterances seem elliptical, even ambiguous, in relation to the situation, unless they are defined as a set of linguistic productions.

In conclusion, one might distinguish between two models of utterances: (1) a minimal sentence of the type (I, we, one, human animate, or concrete inanimate contiguous with $[I]^2$) + (action verb) + (human animate or concrete inanimate contiguous with [I]); and (2) a minimal sentence of the type (he/she/it or abstract inanimate) + (verb of condition or attribution) + (expansion of noun phrase 1, or abstract inanimate).

These different ways of structuring the utterance show a variable distance from the enunciation correlative to the actual purpose of the discourse. Action, or narrative of action, carried out on the 'world' in the one case; manipulation of language with the purpose of defining linguistic 'objects' in the other. These divergent functions for the utterance seem to be determined by the work status of the respondent. For the working class, work remains foreign to language itself, and, at best, *contiguous* with the speaking subject who can never be metaphorized in it, since he or she does not possess it; whereas, for the middle class, language itself is a production tool, in that its manipulation can produce grammars and theoretical concepts, as well as ideologies, ideologies that are mediations required for mastery over the network of economic production. The existence of different types of discourse could then be interpreted not only as an effect of the situation in which they are carried out and alienated, but also as a possible cause for the creation of the situation. The question then is: what connection can be established between a discourse linked to immediate experience and a discourse creating socio-cultural mediations?

*

Class membership determines the structure of the utterance through the impact it has on the situation and the object of communication. But to what extent? Is it the only constraining factor? From a psycholinguistic, or more precisely a psychoanalytic–linguistic, perspective, one might hazard the guess that class determinations occur at the preconscious–conscious level. However, locutors do not articulate 'class utterances' in a fully deliberate way, even if they are consciously aware of their explicit content. It would also seem that unconscious constraints exist. In other words, there are psychotic and neurotic levels of discourse that underlie class determinations and interfere with them. This hypothesis obviously implies a synchronic perspective.

Models of psychotic or neurotic utterance – we will here consider only the discourse of schizophrenics, hysterics and obsessives – were established using corpora recorded in a hospital setting or in the psychoanalytic context. In psychoanalysis, the situational impact is invariable: one identical situation, one addressee, always the same – silent – and no defined object for discourse. This is the same for all subjects, whatever their socio-economic status.

The effect of dissociation from the idiosemiological context shows up in an almost exaggerated fashion in schizophrenic language. Whatever her or his socio-economic background, the schizophrenic creates the same type of utterance: an utterance which, when first heard, appears to be a predominantly metaphoric *linguistic object*, manifesting a concern for lexical specificity and implying a complex play of transformations. For example: '*Tout en parlant, on constate une espèce d'annulation, si je puis dire d'effacement, ... une annulation des faits et gestes qui guident une personne*' ['While speaking, one takes note of a kind of annulment, or if you will effacement ... an annulment of facts and gestures that guide a person'] (engineer); '*Ce que tout le monde recherche, c'est le zéro ... Lorsqu'on fait une addition proprement à l'école, qu'on a fait la preuve par neuf ... on est satisfait, mais enfin pas tout à fait; il y a ... quelque chose qui taquine. Alors, il s'agit bien de trouver tout de même une issue ... c'est peut-être comme la mort ... il s'agit de rechercher l'issue fatale et de pouvoir poser son ultimatum*' ['What everyone seeks, is zero ... Doing addition at school, when one proved it by nine ... one is satisfied, but still not completely; there is ... something that is still bothersome. Then, it's all about finding a way out ... maybe it's like death ... it's all about seeking your fate and being able to deliver an ultimatum'] (metallurgical worker); '*Lorsque vous rêvez ... vous cherchez toujours à boucler, à fermer ... vous cherchez toujours la continuité; vous cherchez à ... une espèce d'ordre logique, qui, dans le fond, euh ... vous empêche de rencontrer toutes les personnes du monde entier*' ['When you dream ... you are always trying to finish off, close up ... you are always looking for continuity; you are looking for ... a kind of logical order, that, ultimately, uh ... prevents you from meeting all the people in the whole world'] (laborer); '*Quand je vais me promener ou n'importe quoi, les ... l'état des signes, c'est-à-dire leur considération, fait que je suis fatalement porté à voir quelque chose se rapportant à mon moi personnel ... laisser des marques ou des signes pour que leurs semblables les reçoivent et ... qu'ils soient persuadés de la relativité du temps ou de sa novicité [sic.]*' ['When I go out for a walk or whatever, the ... the state of the signs, that is as I contemplate them, makes me inevitably see something related to me personally in them ... leave marks or signs so their peers receive them and ... are persuaded of the relativity of time or of its novicity [*sic*]') (railroad worker); *Je ne le connais pas habituellement mais de technique et de fonction. Exactement ce qu'on appelle les ... terminaisons des ... phrases. C'est-à-dire les spécialistes des signatures et des cachets. Exactement ce n'est pas un cachet qu'il fallait, c'est l'effacer, soit effacer le cachet, ou soit ... déterminer la cause qui gênerait la présence des choses ... les unes devant les autres et c'est tout'* ['I don't know him habitually; only technically and by function. Exactly what they call the ... endings ... of sentences. That is specialists of signatures and seals. It is not exactly a seal that was needed, it's to erase it, or to erase the seal, or ... to determine the cause that would get in the way of the presence of things ... . Some things in front of others and that's all'] (clerk).

Analysis of such utterances points up the superficiality of the analogy that could be made with the discourse of the middle class. The schizophrenic is spoken much more than he or she speaks, spoken notably by language transformed into a free activity of generations and transformations, language that is no longer a set of rules or laws guaranteeing the elaboration of a message. There might not be any message in the utterance of the schizophrenic other than the formalistic play of language, or other than what the addressee wants to hear. Linguistic forms function solely as 'objects,' and it would be inaccurate to qualify them as metaphors, since the schizophrenic never really articulates enunciation to utterance. It is interesting to note that, without any higher education, or apprenticeship in language, the schizophrenic produces an 'abstract' and apparently scientific discourse, at times in the third person, where complex transformations are carried out. It must therefore be concluded that this linguistic creativity, dissociated from the creativity of the locutor, exists in virtually every speaking subject, and that it is either mobilized or inhibited by the situation, and by the object of communication. The unforeseen liberation – outside a normative context – of this creativity, in the case of schizophrenia, for example, is often interpreted by society, or by the family, as a symptom.

The analysis of neurotic discourses results in a different model. In addition to the messages neurotic subjects explicitly want to transmit, one can detect, through examination of the forms of the discourse itself, specific types of neurotic utterances. This requires going back through the play of transformations masking the minimal sentence underlying the discourse. The model of the minimal utterance can be symbolized as follows: (locutor) ← (NP1 + V + NP2) → (addressee).[3] These symbols are given different content according to whether the locutor is, for example, hysteric or obsessive.

The hysteric's utterance can consistently be represented as (you, human animate or concrete inanimate mediated by [you]) + (transitive action verb, indicating incompletion) + (me, concrete animate or inanimate related to [I]). It expresses an action the addressee executes with respect to the locutor, an incomplete, ongoing action, of which the locutor is the object. This utterance can often be reduced to an interrogative transformation. For example: (I) ← do you love me? → (you). The message is presented as incomplete; (you)'s 'yes' or 'no' must eliminate the ambiguity. The addressee not only appears to be the one who carries out the action expressed in the utterance, but is also the only real subject of enunciation in the discourse. As for the speaking subject, she or he is no more than a possible object of the addressee. This calls into question the very existence of an object of communication, since the unique subject is (you). The utterance, or its object, cannot therefore constitute a point of convergence for the partners of enunciation. Even if 'it' is represented in the utterance, it is still only (you)'s object, whether the speaking subject explicitly refers to it as the addressee's, or whether the utterance can be shown to be a copy, or a duplication, of a real or implicit discourse of (you): I love what you love; I love that (what you love).

The obsessive's utterance can be represented as follows: (I, abstract inanimate mediated by [I]) + (intransitive verb of condition or attribution conveying completion) + (attribute or abstract inanimate related to I). This utterance often includes a completive where the object of the discourse appears, a completive introduced by (I) + (verb expressing the process of enunciation itself): I tell myself that I am intelligent; I ask myself if I am loved. The message, most often actually conveyed in a completive, consists of an elaboration of an image of the self, or of the world, proposed as object for the subject of enunciation. The message appears to be assumed by the locutor. It is the speaker who determines its meaning with modalizations guaranteeing the meta-stable character of its signification, and allowing the speaking subject to take it back eventually, or to disambiguate it. *Doubt* functions as guarantor of the incompletion of the discourse: I tell myself that I am perhaps loved; I do not tell myself that I am not loved; etc. The utterance is also incomplete due to the elimination of the addressee from the message, as well as from the process of enunciation itself. 'You' is not detectable in the utterance, either as subject, or as agent, or as object. Furthermore, (you)s' function as co-locutor is questionable due to the reflexive character of the enunciation, and due to the fact that the object of communication is so extensively elaborated by (I)'s imagery that it becomes a quasi-unacceptable message for the receiver.

Analysis of hysterics' and obsessives' utterances raises the question of the functioning of the poles of enunciation; it leads to a grammar of enunciation.[4] Lack of differentiation between (I) and (you) cannot serve as explanatory principle for the structuring of neurotic discourse, although it is a defensible hypothesis, at least analogically, in the case of psychotic languages. We see instead a kind of differentiation within (you) and (I) themselves – (you') → (you); (I) → (I') – which guarantees the production of discourse by maintaining contact between the partners of enunciation, whatever their masks and deceptions may be. A space for the functioning of (I) and (you) is marked out, laid out, for an eventual emergence or resurgence. Traces of differentiation can be detected in the definitions of the co-locutors and in the mediations of the proposed object of communication.

Creating a model for enunciation using an analysis of utterances requires postponing interpretation. Enunciation constrains the structuring of the text, but cannot be unequivocally inferred from the examination of the structure produced. Thus, the hypothesis cannot yet be eliminated that the hysteric may exclude the addressee, while the obsessive may be constituted as pure object, and may not be able to function as subject of discourse. What the formalization of their utterances leads us to conclude could, in fact, be the inversion of the appropriate model of enunciation. Extreme example, and improbable, but it cannot be eliminated from consideration too quickly ...

Whatever the case may be, it seems that the structuring of the utterance should be attributed, at the very least, to two causes. One of them, resulting from an unconscious agency, and conveyed by the articulation of the structures of subject, code, world, and co-locutor, determines the dynamics of enunciation itself. In that case, the status of the object must be examined, not as object or referent of the utterance, but as what is at stake in the functioning of discourse itself. This structuring agency is caused by the phantasmatic dynamic in which the speaking subject is at one and the same time scene and actor, acted and acting.

The system of interrelations and interdependencies governing the process of enunciation is itself constrained by another determinant that partially masks, inhibits or represses it. Interfering with unconscious processes, it is situational, and may be designated either as the 'object' of the discourse, or as the context where it is produced, or as the addressee. Pertinent to the explanation of the articulation of enunciation with utterance, of the measure of their distance from each other, it also regulates the structuring of the utterance, whether it functions as goal of the discourse, or marks it with retroactive effects. The situational determinant is more easily detected in the analysis of the utterance than the unconscious deter-

minant, which is obscured by the play of transformations, and by the realizations of discourse itself. If it does happen that the unconscious determinant manifests itself in the sentence and in its immediate components – in
psychoanalytic treatment, for example – it is oftentimes conveyed only in
the totality of the discourse, the metaphor of the unconscious model. Its
effects appear to be subjacent to those related to the situation.

Resulting from at least two factors, the unconscious factor, f(UCS), and
the situational factor, f(SIT), the structuring of the utterance owes to their
interaction the maintenance of its metaphoric–metonymic movement, and
the always meta-stable character of its signification. Psychoanalytic treatment – in its attempts to constitute the situational factor as invariable –
would seem to be a privileged site for the analysis of the unconscious
determinant, its parameters currently granting us the only possible experience of the process of enunciation itself. It is the task of socio-linguistics to
isolate and analyze the effects of the situational factor, notably the class
determinant, on discourse.

Such a dissociation of the factors determining the articulation of
discourse may seem shocking, especially from an historical perspective.
History itself should be investigated as cause of the production and of the
definition of these factors. This analysis can have only synchronic import.
Interpretation of the functioning of discourse currently requires a model
making use of the operational agencies analyzed above. However, the
possibility of another explanation cannot be excluded, and to affirm the
contrary would represent an ideological position.

X

The Rape of the Letter

To read a text[1] is to fold it into a foreign network, to expatriate, dispossess, and disappropriate it. Even if the reader were nothing more than a blank page exposed to the text's writing, as medium, she or he would already be defined topologically, already inscribed, if not in black and white, then at least in relief. The medium or the matrix transforms the text as much as it is transformed by it. There is no reading or writing that is not subversion. Furthermore, the text's imprint or writing, even unaware and even unwilling, can operate indiscriminately because it does not convey, but rather *produces*. By the same token, any resistance to the imprint will provoke torsions and distortions in its program.[2] Close attention cannot flush out the silent efficiency of the phantasm.[3] Reading, speaking and writing are always effects, at times attempts at effacement, or 'replacement,'[4] or impossible appropriation – through mimeticism? repetition? – of the *impact* of phantasmatic fields, creating the difference necessary for representation and its articulation into utterance.

THE LETTER: UNKNOWN WITHOUT ROOTS

The letter/phoneme opposition is perhaps nothing more than a detour, a game, a gesture made in order to take up an issue that disconcerts theory.

The elements of the non-figurative occidental graphic code can be defined as distinct, distanced, spaced units. Each one identical to itself, non-identical to all the others – homogeneous, simple, and heterogeneous to all the others. Each letter of the alphabet constitutes, if you will, *one* set, or sub-set, comprised of *one* and *only one* element. The intersections among these sub-sets are, in the proper functioning of (alphabetic) writing and reading, null or void. At the literal level, there is no possible give and take of same and other. Any dissociations of letters, any hesitations caused by their possible common elements, any constitution of intersections among the graphemes, are assessed as pathological. For example: the difficulty dysgraphics and dyslexics have in recognizing 'p,' 'q,' ' d,' and ' b' as heterogeneous; or the play of permutations they go so far as to institute among these letters. Graphism does, however, justify the pertinence of such questions, hesitations and waverings. Some norm requires that we never stop to examine graphism itself: it is only a support, a medium, if you will. A letter cannot be taken literally under pain of anomaly or sanction. It is supposed to be *one*, identical to itself, non-identical to others. Training the hand, and assistance from the gaze, or submission to the gaze, are required in order to close off a graphic form, in order to isolate or recognize it.

Our alphabet is thus a set – or a field – of distinct forms. These forms are actually indifferent to each other. No law proper to graphism either regulates their order (unlike numbers), series, groupings, or operation, or justifies why the presence of one letter either implies or excludes some other letter. The intersection where two letters come together must be null and void – the void – inscriptable and virgin space-medium, containing no literal elements. The only imperatives are convenience and non-ambiguity in inscription. This code, close to nature, art, and religion when written long ago, has become a useful instrument, founded on convention.

Letters must be distanced, spaced out, as well as distinct, conditions of the directly legible cohesion of their form. However, this spacing out is not regulated by graphism itself. The inscriptable medium, which can consist of any imprintable matter – one can always discover new media, new styluses, or new substitutes – is indeterminate. Nor is there an *a priori* definition of the gap between the letters. It will be imposed only *after the fact* and by appeal to some Other, or to some other system(s) or functioning(s) of spacings, intervals, and gaps. Graphism can be a function of the limits or the liberty of gesture, of the mobility of the body, of the submission of the inscriber to certain rhythms, of the gaze, of the size or nature of the available medium, of the sharpness of the stylus, of the fluidity of the inscripting medium, etc. When structuring a space, organizing it, constructing it, as superimposed on the virgin or inert space of the medium, graphism is no longer literal.

Tracing letters requires a tool, at least in some cases. A finger and some sand suffice. However, media malleable to the finger, transformed into instrument, are rare, not always at hand. And the finger's traces get erased, unless the finger becomes stylus dipped in ink, paint or mud ... Impression requires the appropriateness of the tracer to the medium, and of the medium to the tracer, and, eventually, a supplemental substance ensuring the permanence of the trace. In order to be memorable, the inscription must either be violent or supported by an adequate substance; the furrow must be either deep, or supplemented with excess surface material. There is, however, no contiguity, no functional necessity, no formal analogy, between the tool and the product.

The letters of our alphabet make no sense, have no meaning, no direction, unless they are traced horizontally, from left to right. This graphic concession is the only strictly literal sense or direction, unless one reads into it, as non-sense if you like, the enslavement of the hand, its acculturation. The letter corresponds to no gesture. It constrains with complex, meticulous contours, the hand that stops or gets off the track; it bends it to the loop, or the closure, to centripetal or centrifugal motion; it submits it to the dictatorship of the eye, itself obedient to arbitrariness. Apart from this servitude, the letter says nothing. Representable, represented, appropriate for representation, it represents, it figures, nothing. Simple frame, skeleton. Trace without dignity, without truth (either logical, or material, or formal ...).

But the trick, the deception, is that this variable – precisely because of its arbitrary nature? – ends up imposing itself as the place-holder for a constant that is defined elsewhere. Sustaining the illusion – through duplication of arbitrariness – of a background of truth, or of a simple background, needing these strange little associates in order to appear. The without-origin of the letter, its non-genealogy, its rupture with all contiguity – with 'replacement' or with deferral[5] – substantiates the myth of the origin, of the original, delegated to NATURE or to the LOGOS, first Principle, engendering and encompassing.

Without doubt, the letter informs whomever gives it form; it is formed by that upon which it confers form. So-called, in *quid pro quo*. Indefinite alternation never switched on, never switched off, it neither produces, nor reproduces, but is the condition of production or of reproduction, necessary to the transformation of so-called raw materials into useful goods and services. This mechanism or apparatus would remain ineffective without earth, without productive source, both also useless without technique and labor. The problem is in the rupture between these two resources; the code has become arbitrary and no longer signifies its object; it creates an uprooted subject and social body, and a nature both exploited and uncultivated.

The letter is thus form, one, distinct, distanced, inscribed in a medium through a technique, and represents nothing *a priori*, if not the reduction of the scribe to the training and the stereotyping of the movement, to attention to the gaze, and to non-sense.
Unless the scribe finds in its unity, its difference, its distance, some technique for the production of her or his unity, difference, and distance? Tracing the letter, do I inaugurate myself as one, unique, distinct, distant? Is this the effect, or even the goal of alphabetic graphism? At the price of

how much of a detour into arbitrariness? Does it cause us to become signs without signification?

Is there any way to avoid relating the already traced letter to the image in the mirror? Even if it is only to distinguish them from each other. The specular image constitutes me as one and distinct, even if not always distanced. It is formed at the same time as it informs me. It stamps the body whose stamp it is. Dissociation between production and reproduction is impossible for the mirror image. It requires the contours of the eye, the submission to the gaze, and needs a surface-medium. However, the technique is a function of the medium; it is not manipulated by a scribe, or at the service of a scribe. If the scribe takes advantage of it, he or she does so entirely without tools or work. Apart from the play of the eyelids? Gesture, enslaved in writing, is excluded from specularization; constrained in writing, in specularization it is totally frozen, immobilized, at least for the time of *one* image.[6] Each movement corresponds to another image, irreducible to the previous one. The unity of the image in the mirror is the sole jurisdiction of the gaze, and of a technically adequate medium.

On the other hand, it *represents*, requiring presence for a representation that is erased as soon as the presence pulls away, without permanence or temporality other than the moment, anxiety-producing in its very evanescence. The specular representation has only illusory fidelity to presence, which it steals away in incredible symmetry; it truncates it, flattens it out, is unreadable, unacceptable in its impropriety and its strangeness. It disappropriates, without the pretext of arbitrariness, instantaneously subtracting presence from itself, digging out a gaping hole in it, opening it up into space for another eye. In this place, other eyes will come to function, but first it belongs to a magician's eye, a magic eye, an extra eye or one eye too many: eye open henceforth in and onto the center of self-presence. Eye of God or of conscience? Of the other? Of the self as other? That no vigilance can deceive?

Consequently – a plan to exorcize the spell, to evict the intruder, to get rid of the occupier, conferring unity on the self.

By outlining it as object, closing it off. It is still gaping open, by necessity.

By confronting another body? But even in darkness, or even in blindness, the inverted symmetry dispossesses, ex-centers for the benefit of some virtual, elusive, implicit axis of symmetry.

And the *a tergo* embrace will be even more resolvent of unity, reimposing what was always excluded from postulated unity, reintroducing what is foreclosed, foreign and strange, through splitting and transferring, the back preceding the front.

Deliberately inscribing a medium, with the help of a technique, of a gesture, gestures, giving oneself form by informing space to one's measure, to one's rhythm, to one's color; creating space from a multiplicity of single gestures; reproducing or rather producing a unity ... So-called abstract painting may elude, or at least try to elude, problems of symmetry, but it is not clear that it settles the score with that one eye too many; it might even grant it the starring role as inspiration for the tracings of the brush. Thus the eye actually functions, and is not delegated to some transcendence, divinity or conscience. But the painter knows very well that there is no unity to be found there, whatever the illusion he or she may inspire in the viewer. Or maybe the unity of the canvas lasts for just a heartbeat, a momentary conclusion to, or suspension of, the battle he or she wages, the wager he or she lays, against fragmentation, splitting up, dispersion. If the painter were satisfied with repeating this unity, with a technique for producing this unity, her or his canvasses would literally be of no interest – dead letters.

Back to literal graphism ... Submissive to the attentive gaze, that of the scribe, the hand traces, from left to right, finished, definite, single, unique forms. The trained gesture inscribes the form of the *unit*. This behavior can no doubt produce the unit as medium-form, empty form, arbitrary graphism, suspension of meaning. Thus deprived of all signifying aim, of all intent to convey a meaningful message, the scribe notices after the fact the effect of sense and non-sense of the inscription, or rather the effect that precedes that dichotomy. It is constituted as form, as matrix, where meaning can inscribe itself or be inscribed. Interrupting the articulation of the gesture, the indication of the referent, the specular game, the need, or the desire, the letter outlines the writer as an arbitrary, distinct, discontinuous form, the space of suspension, space deferring time, the becoming-space of time. This implies in-finite, unfinished repetition – the effect of the trace is never conclusive, always to be started over – and opens up a *topos* for the functioning of images, representation, and concepts. Revenge taken on specularization, graphism has the power to produce the scribe as form, conferring on herself or himself absence from presence, playing at dispossessing the scribe, at engendering her or his own eclipse, at provoking her or his own downfall, her or his own dehiscence. But only at the price of, only on condition of, letting arbitrariness control the game, letting it be the very play of arbitrariness itself. This freedom is all the cleverer, and all the more resourceful, for being arbitrary; however, it is a freedom that may run out of steam due to its own gratuitousness, that may get bored or obsessed with reiteration, that may anguish over its own dismemberment, or over the expanse, or the virginity, or the excess of the medium?

THE PHONETIC PRO-LOGUE

The phoneme is not *one*.[7] It is a bundle of differential traits. The most elementary, the simplest, the most distinctive trait is unpronounceable, inaudible. It can be isolated only through analysis and artifice, suspension of articulation, of the articulator.[8] In pronunciation, the phoneme is plural from the very beginning, a combination of differences imperceptible to the one pronouncing them, articulated thanks to an unoccupied space, a blank, an absence, a zero, that authorizes permutations and associations, and provides the give and take required for their insertion into a network. This unoccupied space is ambiguous; it can be understood either as the absence of all phonemes, silence, a non-field of phonemes; or as absence, neutralization of distinctive traits, empty set regulating the structuring of the phoneme-field; or even as empty sub-set, neutralization of one or of several pertinent traits, defining the relation between two phonemes. Absence is from then on defined and regulated, functioning within a play of relations, even though it is the very possibility of their articulation. However, the ambiguity of this zero is that it is played out both in turns, and simultaneously, at the edge of a *natural* limit and of an *arbitrary* limitation: all pronounceable phonemes are not necessarily pronounceable in any given language. The articulation of certain phonemes can be impossible or prohibited. Their silence is prescribed by *nature* or prescribed by *law*; as is their pronunciation. Phonetics and phonology are irreducible to each other on several accounts, but the latter comes up against the stumbling block of the distinctive trait, and is unable to conclude if it is natural or arbitrary. Both nature and arbitrariness contribute to it.

As set, the phoneme is defined by a network of relations with respect to a set or to a field of differential traits, just as it circumscribes, in a play of relations to other phonemes, other sub-sets of pertinent traits or empty sub-sets. Bundle of differences, the phoneme is itself the knot in a network of differences that articulate it, as a site of references, into the set of distinctive traits, and with the other phonemes. Not one, the phoneme is also not unique. Or at least its singularity is criss-crossed with relations of identity and non-identity to other phonemes, with inclusion or exclusion of differences, with their neutralization. Only erroneously could it be defined as distinct like the letter. The intersection functions differently in the set of letters from the set of phonemes; prohibited or prescribed, its interventions leave nothing of its own to the phoneme, except the concurrence of a certain number of relations.

Nor is the phoneme distanced, spaced, or capable of spacing. It is more like a system of switches, not pronounceable without supplementary traits, articulatable through the implication or exclusion of certain differential traits, which, in turn, require the activation of defined relations. No doubt there is still give and take in articulation, where impossible differentiations or gaps in natural requirements and arbitrary imperatives are reintroduced, where nature slips away from the very place where the articulator thought she or he was just submitting to nature; the articulator is already absent from the very place where he or she thought to be most irreducibly present – in their physiological equipment.

The phoneme is nonetheless institution of relations, actualization of relations, much more than it is a phenomenon of rupture or of closure. Spacing out is difficult to regulate in the phoneme. Or rather, it functions differently. It is at work in what is defined as elementary; it operates within what is elementary and its articulation. It is the condition of the realization of the play of difference, of differences. It cannot be manipulated as a technique for differing, but rather contributes to the process of difference, escaping the alternation of passivity and activity, of cause and effect (at least the way these are conceived from a certain philosophical viewpoint), of inside and outside. The phoneme is always produced in an almost tear-proof weaving of differences, whose origin or ending it would be useless to question. One is always already implicated in a network whose functioning one can try to describe through a suspension of pronunciation, or through the counterpoint, the point of view, of another language, or of another game, or of another supposed deferral. Competition or repetition inappropriately open up space for the gaze, for graphism, for figuration, for representation, for theory. However, this methodological opening does not check the process in which the articulator is caught up. For him or for her, there is no outside the play of deferral. She or he is located within and throughout the process, caught in the network of relations where, even if there are crossings, intersections, and marked paths, there is no progress, no beginning and no end – for habitual language. The order is not at all teleological. For whoever has entered into articulation, there are no landmarks or road signs indicating a straight pathway, no rest stops along the way that would allow him or her to assume that the development could one day be surveyed, recapitulated, summed up in some unity. Unity always slips away, relegated to some mythic silence, or to some primeval humming sound or some original chant, before God or before death. But for the moment – and there is only the actual moment (which is not to say the present), there is only actualization in this process that resists temporal unfolding, that temporizes without temporalizing – deferral is always at work. Each phoneme comes into existence as part of a bundle of relations articulating it with the one that precedes it and the one that follows, but also with all other possible and impossible ones, in a strange procession evoking neither circularity nor reiteration – even though recursivity has a role to play in it – nor linearity, nor some dance where two steps forward mean one step back. In this choreography each figure participates with all the others, intersects with them, evokes them, calls them up, and implicates them, and once the dance begins, it goes on indefinitely with no horizon. Untamed yet regulated dance that children, in their litanies of nonsensical syllables, are wild about, trying perhaps to make a game of the uncontrollable drift.

Such are the first effects, if not the first laws, of pronunciation: positioning, once and for all, as part of a network; logical functioning, where the definition of constants and of variables develops under natural and arbitrary, but non-teleological, constraints; the impossible unit, the zero, the unoccupied space, taking the place of what is always already lost, eclipsed into a network of differences; non-temporal differing or temporizing without measure, and without history, based on no countable unit; imperceptible articulation of the proper with the improper; in-finite, unfinished dispersion; system of referrals with no assigned goal or representable objective; law with no legislator, no instructions and no commands, which does not mean without order or organization; structuring outside of all dichotomies:[9] time/space, continuous/discontinuous, before/after, inside/outside, nature/culture, etc., which should be interpreted as secondary structures elaborated in order to master or to defend against the process of deferral. Deferral unfolds between impossible identity to self and not yet (possible) imaginable identification, between the two grounds, the two bases, of nature and representation. Wanting to insert it, to integrate it, even if only into a supposedly definable between two, into neither the one nor the other, into neither this nor that, is already to betray its efficacy, which cannot be conveyed.

Perhaps it should be added that pronunciation is the most irreducible, and the closest (if degree has any pertinence here ...) expatriation – a regulating function that imperceptibly produces the producer, unbeknownst to himself or herself, as outside and as other to himself or herself, without detectable production, without localizable displacement, without designatable exile. However, the excess left over after insertion into the network evokes an impossible quest, a claim, for a center.

Not counting the fact that the pronounced sound projects, diffuses, or diffracts the one who pronounces it into an undelimited *outside*. That she or he is heard does not really help matters. It is always already too late. It is an other – x others – the pronouncer is listening to; she or he is already not even there any more, and in truth, never was there as one or as unique. Like the thing or the one she or he is waiting for?

Phonetic articulation also marks the 'replacement' – or better yet, fictive deferral, the difference is not negligible – for kinetic articulation and kinesthetics. Gesture is relegated to it, transported into it, and abandons its games or its communications to one specific, localized type of motor activity. Its mask as place-holder is all the more convincing in that it is neither totally active nor totally passive. The body movements hold still in order to let the voice speak, itself always already lost.

And the eyes go blind. There is nothing there to see: no centering object to know or to recognize, no horizon by which to position oneself, no world to circumscribe. Phonetic deferral works in shadow. It cannot be controlled or delimited by the gaze. Whoever would like to meet it face to face would find only phantoms rising up out of the rejection of this invisible process.

One resists this elusive – imperceptible, unimaginable – articulation, this diffraction, this explosion of polarization, with difficulty. At least that is what one might logically infer from what follows as structuring of discourse. One still and always tries to come back to the center: agent, subject, object; source or project; locutor–utterance–addressee; producer–product–consumer, etc. And if their determination, their identity, is shaky, if the artificiality of their unity is revealed or stands out, one invents other illusions: *the referent*. As if, itself the result of pronunciation (or of whatever concurrence of other determinants), the referent could escape its laws. Or the *concept*, for example, violently cut from the weave, effect – at least by definition – of a call to graphism (and to the mirror) for help. Their assistance will be required each time the dance or the chant is interrupted and articulated into separable, spaceable, identifiable figures.

But that's going too fast. So let us review.

DEFERRAL DEFERRED

The letter is a finite, definite, single, unique, distinct and distanced, spaceable form. It is undifferentiated, except with reference to phonetics, or to the other letters: not sequential, not numeric, not associatable, not groupable, not operable ... As individual member of a genus and species belonging to no family, it has no genealogy, no filiation or alliances, except through procuration, delegation, or artifice; it can only be combined in a game with so-called others, and then all of them must be taken together at the same time, *all of them* referring to nothing more than neutral parts and particles, and *all at the same time* meaning nothing more than a prescribed juxtaposition without polarization. Without generation?

It repeats its finite, definite, single, unique form ... as often as one likes, but without process, without history, without production or transformation, at least within itself.

Single and unique form ... it represents nothing. Needing the help of gesture and gaze, it somehow suspends both of them. It constrains the servile hand to arbitrary gesture, without direction (except from left to right, horizontally), without a plan. It works toward enslaving the gaze, whose assistance is called up in order to see – nothing: images, ideas, ideas as images, stories as idea-images, themes, subjects.

Thus logocentrism[10] could be understood as the result of the castration of the gaze, of the voice, and of gesture, by non-figurative graphism which results in the production, or the reproduction, the representation, of hallucinatory spectacles: oculocentrism by default. The eye focuses in on phantom objects or ideals that come to occupy reality, after the forced eviction of any real objects to look at. The gaze is overshadowed, occluded, blinded. But it creates, from then on, the invisible.

Form that represents nothing, the letter gives rise to the presence of its pre-scriber, the guarantor, the Other, it must function to re-present. In back? In front? Because facing us there is nothing. Or up above? Or down below? Head or tail? Evoking verticality, which, in literal graphism, is annulled, desperately flat, laid out, despite the *I's* (penis, violation, virgin, filiation ...), despite the cries, marching in step, in ranks, lined up, coded. Either all the way to the left, or all the way to the right, representations of the origin and of the end, horizon without a landscape. Either in the intimacy of the inside, on the periphery of the outside, at work in the hollow spaces, or as justification for the hollowness opened up by the arbitrariness of the graphemes, maintaining confusion between those neutral hollow spaces traced without polarity, and other hollow spaces, other spaces between, other antrums, other caverns (terms brought together by Jacques Derrida),[11] fictitiously taking their places, closing them off: the hollows of articulation, of the topology of the body, of the economy of specularization ...
...Well, in another setting, perhaps, because nothing more can happen in this one, created out of nothing by the alphabetic economy – without gaze, without gesture, without voice, without erection. This alphabetic economy, claiming to have regulated, through its arbitrariness, all economic problems, jammed up the works once and for all. Imposing, for economy's sake, cadavers or vampires (connected to so-called nature, or presence, or source), as pawns, mediums, masks, tools, representatives – it makes cadaver, vampire, pawn, tool, etc., out of the scribe, who plays the scene, in an artificially framed setting, surrounded by a visually meaningless decor, of his or her own foreclosure. Who plays a game with real, and not with plastic, knucklebones. Trying to resuscitate in this – fraudulent – setting, the other lost scene that has been cut off, foreclosed by the arbitrary cut of graphism.

Effective, no doubt: the schiz that you find everywhere, at least in western culture. It even shows up in the utterance. As plan for its own subversion? It might not be anything more than a sterilizing repetition of subversion, all too fertile parapraxis, closing subversion down. Everyone is invited to wear insignia signifying their mutilation. We are cut, cuttable, guilty, split, divisible, etc. That doesn't mean castrated, of course. Castration is something else. However, the cut at work in *these* graphemes,[12] that is to say, these letters, is supposed to be able to suspend castration's power. Steal it away, intercept it, cut off its articulation. We look forward to *that* castration as if were reviviscence! Nostalgic reminiscence, put in place where the cut took hold. The less it really works, the more it is imagined, represented, spoken, imitated?[13] That's the way it is. A question of economics! Displaced – -here to be understood as deported – into some artificial frame, framing, or enframing, all inter-dicted (or inter-graphed) tragedies, apologues, or fables come to be painted, projected, taken up. Opening an always false – falsified because constructed – framework, allowing them (only) to show themselves, provided there is an out-of-frame, an off-stage.

This framework of the letter, whose after-effects are capable of constituting me as single, unique, distinct, distanced, empty form, form—medium, projection screen for images, concepts, representations of all kinds, etc., contravenes my positioning in the discourse of others, my framing in or through others' discourse – or network of traces – that determines and over-determines my functioning as speaker, and even as actor, imitator, repeater, writer, *deferrer*. This deferral might occur, despite the graphematic mask, and its avatars, through appealing, or re-appealing, to *archi-writing*. It tries to force the barricade, the bars, of (alphabetic) writing, through a play of spacings, scansions, splits, lines, unwritings, overtakings or overthrowings, subversions of sur-faces or about-faces, through broken alignment, multiplication of angles and deconstruction of the architectonics of the (so-called) classical page of writing, through parentheses, apostrophes, narratives, grafts, recurrences, enumerations, etc., insemination, or rather dissemination. However, this re-appeal, or this appeal, to archi-writing stumbles against, breaks up on, the inert, arbitrary, despotic armor of the writing we are talking about here – alphabetic writing – instruments blocking archi-writing's process, its purpose. Turning it away, knocking it off course, even neutralizing it, despite everything, alphabetic writing prevents deferral, thenceforth deferred, in the future, threatened in turn with some kind of hypostatic suspension, from taking effect. Death, by these graphemes, comes too early, too quickly, all at once, with no economy. And this death has always already taken place. Even if you try to get the better of it, it has already produced asphyxiation, paralysis, blindness, castration … cadaverization. It is as ghost – or soul, or demon – that you will play it over, having already played it out in and through the deadly experience.

Furthermore: the cut-outs and delimited spaces, topographical demarcations, resulting from graphematic tracings, are competition for the frameworks, topologies, scenic devices articulated in the crossing of the gaze and the mirror. Or of gazes like mirrors, even blind or two-way mirrors. The letter proposes or imposes its empty, deserted, undifferentiated, dead support, skeleton, or framing, as aseptic substitute for all imaginable stories – making deferral impossible. This substitution is too irreducibly other, wholly other – with no possible play of same and other – to allow, favor, or provoke real displacement. A necessary condition, which is not to say sufficient, for the process of deferral. Calling for assistance, even therapeutic assistance, from *this* writing is teratogenic. Its conventional formation, arbitrary for everyone – one might as well say for no one – socializes you only through infirmity, deformity, and the resurgence of mistreated, unwelcome phantasms, shadows, monsters, devils.

Of course, there is fiction. This one, for example. But its articulation in these fictitious graphemes means that you've been taken in more subtly, more surreptitiously than you intended, wanted, or desired to take in or be taken in. Graphematic fiction is the screen for your projections, your programs. It covers your tracks, makes you forget (partly because it remains), perverts you, while guaranteeing the norm, the normalcy, of some 'symbolic castration.' It steers you into other imaginary circuits, into the snare of fiction. It thwarts all economy, drowning it in pseudo-mirrors, place-holders, representatives. Its trap is laid in the visibility of graphematic tracings, which require the help of the gaze, etc., even though they present nothing to see. The bait is tendered in their representation of your phantasms, spectacles, scenes, whereas what these tracings really do is eclipse them, no doubt calling up in the reader, phantasms, spectacles, and scenes, through the play of differences, through calculation and replacement of the dispossession, loss, and deviation resulting from the passage through (alphabetic) writing–reading.

Of course, screens, instruments, tools, media, and even resistance are necessary for any reinscription of traces or engrams. But you are always already caught up (I'm not telling you anything you don't already know) in mazes of mirrors, in veils, in appearances or in appearing. By the same token, you have at your disposal (sometimes you have to make a real effort to remember it) eyes, hands, mouths, genitals, as well as those of others, to use for tools, instruments, media, or even resistance. Furthermore: you have at your disposal your desire to serve as apparatus, machine, game board, goal, and others' desire to serve as resistance. You can use them for the work of archi-writing, for the play of deferral, recollection supposedly still to come, twisted around an axis of the present. The present is sometimes no more than the confrontation of your resistances and of mine, of all current resistances. Graphematic beyond-time banishes them. To gain what? Neither absent, nor present, nor representing, but presenting itself as all of the above, the letter suspends them, defers them. It grants you time, forgetfulness of time, theft of time, flight of time. Infinite, unfinished time? In the infinitive.

BETWEEN IN PLAY OR THE PLAY OF BETWEEN[14]

I fear we must come back to phonetic articulation. We are attempting the impossible, of course. For phonetic articulation has no end to grab onto, no handle to take hold of, no handholds – except the ones we ourselves will make – no entry that has not allowed access without return, no exit.

Such is articulation.[15] It cannot even be taken from an angle. Any joint is already closed in its flexing – where it is jointed/joined without joining or rejoining (together), where it bends, attaches, latches onto, or brings close, with no chance of rebinding, reattaching, relatching onto, bringing close again. It stays in gear, without shifting, in infinite process, neither active nor passive. Without voice, aspect, or time ... It is *neither the one, nor the other*; it is that which prevents what is jointed from splitting apart, and from locking together. It is the *between in play,* even imperceptible, unimaginable – or precisely because imperceptible, unimaginable – that can intervene as many times as you please; imperceptible attempts at reiteration, at appropriation through reproduction, give rise to between, call it, call it up, or recall it.

The between in play cannot be appropriated. It cannot be questioned. Like life or death. The cause of all reprises, all repetitions, it cannot be repeated, because it is not. Condition of all imprinting, it prints nothing that can be noted. Motive for the not-ation, it slips away from its product, is deducted from the expected profits. It incites an in-finity of not-ations, and therefore all kinds of between: space opened up (ripped open) between a so-called first time and its memory, between this time and the other times, between this notation and all others, between the supported and the supporting, between the noted and the notable, between the manifest and the manifesting, etc. As many kinds of *between* as you please, except the *between in play* in articulation. It forces all kinds of displacements, supplements, spacings, intervals ... and even the elaboration of metaphors, and the establishment of all equivalences. But it is outside of every transposition it makes possible, marked off from every result. It remains without representation, without substitute in or through representation, no matter how many repetitions or recurrences are carried out, or what process of recursivity is in operation.

The curious name of *castration* can be applied to maintaining, or to putting back into play, the un-re-pre-sent-able of between, functioning as *copula* for all articulation or rearticulation. Without present (or past, or future), without form, without figure, without being, without substance. *Without* – or better yet, *neither the one, nor the other,* or *between* – evokes pedagogy, methodology, nostalgia or mask of a discourse postulating negativity, only for those who would still want or need *to be* in *the cavern, the antrum,*[16] or still want or need an eternal present, an infinite form, an (if possible) absolute being, a preferentially immaterial substance. That which confiscates, extrapolates, annuls, in some origin or some ending, all contradiction, whose terms and motives one would do well to interrogate.

In the processes of language, and not only just in language, are affirmed the intention and the desire, to *master* between games, cause of all liaisons, copulations, associations, accords, combinations, groupings, etc. To get the better of them through manipulations, multiplications (and also divisions, and other calculations and operations), spacings, intervals, separations. The strange part is that blanks or silences can still appear as almost real or substantial, as beings in between, while, at the same time, they are split up (and eventually sewn up), divided up, parcelled up, cut out, cut up. The illusion, this time, is in interpreting them, reading them and writing them as forms, as good form, great form, forming or re-forming on the quasi-substantial white or silent background. Which suspends the game. At best, some other limited and delimited game will be substituted for it, with game pieces of different values, defined once and for all – king, queen, pawn, madman ... – with compartmentalized spaces, where the moves are specified, regulated (once and for all), and are founded on principles (laid down once ...) that cannot be ignored. The calculated and relatively predictable – because reiterated – character of the plays limits the expected stakes, the import of the game, and the pleasure. On occasion, this game could be used to teach us to play the between game, which is much more complex obviously, and never-ending. Because when we try our hand at that game we find that no element is ever determined in any definitive way. What is elementary or simple intervenes only as fiction that will have to be unmasked over and over again, deconstructed. The same goes for the always retraced frameworks, spaces, spacings, intervals, and also for the displacements. Their regularity, stereotypicality, coding and privileges are susceptible to innumerable remanipulations, deviations, detours, angles, biases, trangressions, subversions, stories. If one risks it. Because what happens afterwards – the 'afterplay' – cannot be foreseen, except if it is confused with some other limited, delimited game. Between cannot be taken through any kind of repetition or reiteration. One could even say that the harder one tries to appropriate it, through reproduction or repetition, for example, the more one is taken in by the game, is caught up in the game, puts into the game. The more one produces, the more efforts one makes, endlessly, never slowing down, unless one gets mixed up with some other game.

Unfortunately, we have been taught, from the very beginning of the game and under constraint, to cheat at between games. We have even been told that it is necessary, intrinsic, to their development and functioning. Out of fear of losing, of losing ourselves, of being lost? Out of desire for mastery, for definition, for representation? Or because we forget that not all economies come from echo-nomists?

In short, we have cheated. We have cut out some units (so-called) – cut up and not really cut out because between is not a cutting – fixed once and for all, with which, thanks to which, we construct an infinity of other units, and intervals, spacings, separations, etc., out of, and thanks to, the first ones. With these units, we envelop between in a network, a net, to get the better of it. Utopia sustained by *one* repetition (which is, strictly speaking, impossible) producing oneness, even uniqueness; this fiction is assisted by the obfuscation of that which is left over – that is, between and its displacements – and by the deceptions of repetition, simulating replies, responses, and redoublings. Mark (and not re-mark) drawn in black, cutting up white, destined to last.

You have no doubt recognized the phoneme, this network erroneously defined as *one*, even as *unique*, for the space of *one* repetition, network that catches articulation in its nets. This trickery or feint, always already learned by us, is assisted, made possible through the assistance, and not really the substitution, of the letter. Single, unique, distinct, distanced, undifferentiated form ..., it fictively represents the fiction it sustains of the fictive phoneme, or arbitrarily the arbitrariness of the arbitrary phoneme.

The privilege of this so-called – and so-called first – repetition, whose illusion cannot be durably sustained without the complicity of alphabetic, non-figurative writing, has jammed up the between game, cutting it off from the between in play there.[17] Fortunately, between slips out of all networks, mesh, nets, but only after the imposition of a privileged split or schiz that counters the efficacy of its displacements, productions of spacings, intervals and separations, as well as its liaisons, copulations, associations, accords, combinations, groupings, etc.

Actually, there is an analytic *being between* us, still susceptible to all kinds of analyses – and by psychoanalysts too. Strange story! Let us bet it is the unconscious that shows through; that's what happens every time we cheat – and is it really as unavoidable as we claim it is? – at the between game, substituting some other game for it.

XI

Sex as Sign

Speak. Say everything that comes to you. Just as it comes to you, right here, now. Don't omit or exclude anything. And don't worry about contradictions or conventions. Don't organize what you say. Etc.

That is what you undertake if you want to enter psychoanalysis. Which means that you never will enter it, and also that you will never leave it, as the joke goes. All the reiterated questions and inquiries about entering psychoanalysis are really about something else. Because psychoanalysis functions as a problematics of *between*, whether it is between two signifiers, or a signifying between-two. *Between* is related to the question of entering;[1] it intersects with entering from both the inside and the outside, making dichotomies – the simplicity of dichotomies and divisions – obsolete: to enter/to leave, inside/outside, interior/exterior, etc. The issue could provisionally be formulated as follows: 'you will never enter analysis, because it [the id],[2] was always already functioning, or it [the id] will have always still functioned.' What is impossible in the fundamental rule is *to say it, now*.

Impossible *to say* it now, because the permission to speak, the incitement to speak, and the perspective of speaking and saying everything – including the imperfect, the future perfect, and their relationship[3] – without interdiction, paradoxically ends up in *nothing to say*, due to the repeal of the laws structuring discourse (especially the law of non-contradiction). The rule about saying everything re-establishes the inter-diction, the unpronounceable articulation of speaking, *between* that crosses from the inside to the outside of discourse.

Impossible to say it *now*, because the inter-diction cannot be presented, expressed as present, or as presence, cannot be uttered in any remark proffered at present. The work – or play – of a machine, an instrument, is irreducible to its formation, to what it formalizes. Which should not be confused with one of its possible representations: the law (of functioning) belongs to no one. The relations between inter-diction and the operation of the law – the interdiction – evoke too much for us to evoke them only a little. Let us just say that analysis – after the repeal of the one, at least as far as discourse is concerned – brings us up against the stumbling-block of the other.

It. Or it *is* (not). If analysands are able to formulate their request as a wish or plan to enter analysis, it is by way of a metaphor whose terms they would be at a loss to designate or even point to, and the same for that *as/like* intervening *between* them, the process or procedure of substitution having taken place in the transfer/transference from the one to the other. The functioning of between-two, irreducible to *it,* or to it *is* (not), will actually come to pass in analysis. In other words, the patient will have to shuttle back and forth from *between* inter-vening, coming into, her or his desire to enter, to *between* at play in the functioning of language and of discourse, as well as in what is designated as object or project of desire. The goal his or her remarks lead up to by the back way. The metaphorical guarantee will, through the very impossibility of saying everything, and therefore of entering analysis, be deconstructed, unveiled as illusion masking the inter-diction, which then returns to its function of production.

The impossibility of saying it now, particularly foregrounded by the 'fundamental rule,' and by all kinds of so-called benevolent (?) neutrality (to be understood in its etymological sense) is the linchpin of the economy of enunciation. However, since enunciation itself does not consist of *it* or of it *is* (not), one can discover it only through its effects, its productions, transformations, displacements, representations. Or in the resistances and defenses elaborated to veil the undesignatable in speaking. These resistances or defenses show up not only in the discourse of the analysand, but also almost ineluctably in analytic theory. One finds in them the economic relation between what is named or affirmed, even unwillingly, as interdiction, and what must be seen as inter-diction, including negation or foreclosure.

ENUNCIATING MACHINERY

Nothing is authorized here but the order of the word. This is what marks off the analytic field. Nothing else happens there, at least nothing else is explicitly permitted. We have nothing to say to each other, to debate, to plan together, no defined work to carry out. We will not take each other as confidante, and will tell each other no stories. Nor will we exchange any remarks, conversation where the utterance of one of us might serve as pretext, as object to understand, close in, circumvent, reject ... for the other. In sum, we have nothing at all to do with each other. And yet ... So what are you, what are we, going to say? Nothing, in some ways, except produce the very modes of the economy of enunciation: of all enunciation, of yours, and in particular of ours, and the conditions of possibility of the structuring of all utterance. The merciless character of the analytic framework or scenario requires it, through suspension of, parentheses around, all that is usually given as the foundation of discourse: referent or communicable object, coherent utterance, presence of the locutor–addressee, specific situation, common language, etc. With all of this suspended, the functioning of the machine itself, the enunciating machinery, is uncovered. Curious, complex machine, always already programmed – and a multiple programming.

Programmed first of all by the irreducibility of its very production. Thus, the fact that it is sexed, and determined in its sex, constrains, in complex ways, the polarization of its circuits and its sign, opens up possibilities of copulation, conjunction, intersection, exclusion, etc., and their retroactive effects.

However, the fact that it has a sex does not exclude all sorts of other properties, and therefore capabilities. This machine also has noses, mouths, eyes, ears, and hands, for example. It comprises various possible entries or exits of interchangeable use, contiguous, concurrent, interfering with each other, implicating each other, excluding each other, etc.

Furthermore, a neuter code has been assigned to it: a language belonging to neither sex. We are supposedly programmed by a language foreign to sex, even though it includes masculine and feminine connotations, even though sex is reinscribed in it. This coding functions only as a play of differences, a system of references, with mechanisms of associations, conjunctions, substitutions, etc. Nonetheless, these differences are supposed to be neuter. One could get lost in it, or lose one's head.... Which has certainly happened. The functional confusion functions rather well, in theory and in practice. Not without effects, of course!

It must be added that language, neuter in dictionaries and in theories, has been attributed to the mother tongue, or the language of the mother, with its sexual and social determinants, with its multiple and overdetermined economies. That's obviously somewhat less neuter already. Especially since we are no longer in a network, or a net, of in-finite references, having no organizing center, but rather in an interlacing of threads whose weave follows a certain pattern. It is structured around supports and a center, despite its gaps, and has defined and delimited links. This language of the mother functions as first glossary and grammar, thesaurus (or dictionary of one tongue), 'treasure of signifiers' (Lacan), whose circulation will be finite, closed off, if it is not plugged into other circuits or networks relaying it and ensuring innumerable, determined, vectored references. Other languages, or rather other speech, must inter-vene, putting *neither the one nor the other*, the work of difference, back into play, through articulation of that mother tongue with another, with its other, both same and different. This process is always already vectored, and although permitting in-finite references from signifier to signifier, it is not the double of the 'neuter' language (dead language?) everybody supposedly speaks, codified in the dictionaries and encyclopedias used in schools. The latter comes to exist at the intersection of two or of several languages, or of types of speech; it is a question of life and death, depending on whether the code is imposed legally as deadly counterpoint to a confusion of languages, or types of speech, or on whether it takes hold as abuse of metalanguage, or on whether one of the languages seizes on neutrality in order to enact lawmaking syntax, or ... on whether it functions as horizon, as double background, providing the stakes for all language and speech.

Speech – at least the one explicitly prescribed in analysis – privileges the *voice*, whether it uses the voice as instrument of (re)production, or (re)inscription, as vehicle, or as object, or whether – even unbeknownst to its producer – it is subjugated to voice, since language, even consigned to writing in codes, dictionaries, or grammars, is dependent on the *phonè*, subservient to phonetics. Everything must be done through the voice, or at least recalculated with respect to its economy. However, the voice, although marked by the one who speaks, is already fabricated product, irreducible to the one producing it or to the vocal machinery. This can be seen in its specific characteristics: accent, amplitude, range, inflection, intensity, timbre, volume ... contiguity connecting discourse to producer, who is frustrated by the loss of the voice as voice, effected in its passage through the networks of language and speech. Even though linguistic articulation is dependent on the *phonè*, it cannot be appropriated to it; no language, in speech, takes up all phonic virtualities. They require an operation whose sedimentation is voice; rearticulating phonic articulation, this operation leaves the voice left over. The voice participates in the characteristics of *air*, matter whose properties should be recapitulated in an interpretation of its economy, of its relationship to its other implied functions (for example, its role as medium, as mediation, as intermediary), as well as the effects of vocal displacement, or of vocal substitution, in the analytic protocol.

METAPHORIZING PRESCRIBED

Speak. Say everything that comes to you, just as it comes ... What a wager! How to speak of the multiple stakes (here, of necessity, diminished), and, above all, of the play of their articulation: between sex and voice, and all their possible displacements or substitutions; between phonic articulation and phonetic, or linguistic, articulation; between 'neuter' code and mother tongue, not to mention the intervals between-two, neither one nor the other, that regulate their particular and shared syntaxes; between speech produced and speech imputed, assignation in and through speech and its rearticulations (articulation between history and repetition, history as repetition, and repetition as history); between emission and reception, emission between reception and reception; between the same and other (notably within the scene between emission and reception, eventually turned into drama or conflict between sender and receiver), the other as same and the same as other; between to mean and to say, the always inadequate realization of the program and its retroactive effects, the imperfect and the future perfect; etc. Many different types of *between* in play, plus the play of their articulation: that which is impossible to say, in analysis or anywhere else.

Or perhaps only through a metaphoric turn, or detour, or bypass? Through abuse of metaphors? Or through what is erroneously called metaphors. No question here of ideas re-presented by the sign of another idea, by virtue of a certain conformity or analogy, in order to produce an effect of language, to speak more correctly, more clearly, more nobly, etc. In analysis (or anywhere else, for that matter) metaphoric practice cannot be understood as a simple stylistic procedure, unless stylistic practice is subverted and reframed. In stylistics, metaphor translates, through an obligatory detour, the *aporia* of speaking with respect to the articulation, to the unrepresentable (inarticulatable) functioning of the copula, of sex (of style, on the condition that it write with a stylus, a plume, or a sex).[4] Which also means of copulation, or play (of) between. Metaphorizing translates, through a show of force prescribed in analysis, sexual play into discursive practice, thanks to a resemblance or an analogy that can only be syntactical, and not thematic or related to content. The latter refer, or are referred through interpretation, to some thematics, some sense or signification, that cannot be spoken or decreed.

But this transfer, or this transference, is not without risks. If the psychoanalyst listens too complacently or too attentively, or if she or he is too ignorant of, or deaf to, the turns of language, the jouissance of the analysand will be suspended in that listening, with no way out. If metaphor is heard as *metaphor*, as *terminus* and not as *passage* through the text of what cannot be spoken, of what is impossible to say (now), if it is ratified and interpreted only as linguistic process, simple mechanism within language or metalanguage, and not as what always subverts its non-contradiction, its coherence, its concordance, its identities, its accords, its differences (coded, neuter), etc., and questions them, then the syntax, as well as the syncope, of copulation are ossified into linguistic copula. They are immobilized in assertion, in its eventual suspension, sometimes in its negation or denial. '*Is*' that links analysand to his or her discourse or text, speaker to utterance, a subject to its attribute(s) unequivocally, even transitively, or indeed symmetrically. The play of *as/like*, or, better still, of *as if*, is a play of multiple mirrors, pseudo-mirrors – unless we rethink the structure of the mirror, because there is, of course, no question here of specular doubling through simple surface reflections in the face-to-face, but rather the illusion of a possible translation of one into the other through repetitions in mirrors of all kinds, *as if* obliquely, from an angle, in an almost circular way, etc., mirrors re-inter-vening where terms refer to each other; it is play *between*, the stakes in metaphor (or for the analyst, in all enunciating practice, all enunciation), being, through listening or interpretation, included/understood in the process of discourse, as a simple, supposedly analyzable relation between two signifiers. And not, for example: signifying between-two.

Then *trope* seizes upon *tropism*. The turns of language capture, in their obligatory detours and in their relations between terms, the termless operations, articulations of the sexes. The movement *toward* the (other) term found in style, with its character of (positive) finality, teleology, adequacy or inadequacy, correctness, truth, coherence, elevation, etc., inappropriately relays and even retroactively regulates (in this context one might examine the edicts of proper morality and their structurally perverting character) the tropism, the tension, the erection, and the scenario of sex. It also underlies in similar, but in even subtler, ways – that phallocentrism in its complicity with logocentrism, and a certain structure of mirroring that privileges the surface and the face-to-face, and at the same time, a certain problematics of form, of phallomorphism, of castration, have kept hidden, even foreclosed – the illusion of all substitutions for any, or for the, hymen:[5] stopper, line, between, antrum, cavern, all at once.[6] The final term including all the rest of them in its antrum, cave or womb.

That is not to say that linguistic metaphor does not represent a displacement of the hymen. It even presupposes that displacement can become its unique placement.[7] If one, as, or as if, obligated, forgets its detours and contours. Metaphor, sanctioned *as such*, understood as term, or as discursive process, traps it (in a 'this is that' where subject, predicate and copula must be erased in order to resuscitate *as/like* or *as if* – process without a name), extrapolates it, per-verts it, fragments it, disintegrates it, fractures it into associations of signifiers: pieces of mirrors, of reflections, broken and glued back together. Or else, it is dissected by the metaphoric practice of the analyst or of analytic theory, inter-sected by the conscious or unconscious conception of the practitioner, fragmented into nosological classifications, caught up in synchronic taxonomies, normative genetic systematizations. Metaphoric doublings unquestioned as to their procedure, economy or effects.

Without doubt, the analytic scene is complex. Metaphor is never produced there – or anywhere for that matter – as one, simple and unique.

Analytic practice is fortunate in that way. Metaphorizing is to be understood there as the play of sex in language, as well as, though not in simple reciprocity, the play of language in sex, but its evolutions are multiply overdetermined, intertwined, entangled. Sex is always inter-sexuality whose synchronic functioning marks its sedimentations, just as language is always inter-textuality with diversified plots, formations and stories.

The intervention of sex in language, and the displacement of sex within and through language, has always already taken place. Metaphoric operation thus composes, thus reassembles, a plurality of relations and a plurality of types of *between* from across time, in addition to the play of their articulation within a transfer, or a transference, toward another place, or term, presumed able to take them in.

METAPHOR INTERPRETED

It is into this scene, or this score, of metaphor, that interpretation worms its way. It loosens, without breaking into, without cutting into, the tightness of its knots, the way they come together or close up into one single point, supposedly final, of multiple relations. Operating through connections linked back to other, same and other, chains, through transfers to different circuits branching off, joined, to various networks, and their respective syntaxes, interpretation emphasizes, through allusion, the artifice of their confusion, convergence and assimilation. The latter are made possible by an affinity, by some economy of kinship, not excluding differences, gaps, intervals, differences in gaps and intervals, differences between so-called terms, as well as between always already plural combinations, groupings and operations in always already metaphorical chains, related to each other through metaphor. Resemblance, or analogy – if it is taken as such (and such a term) – tends to cover over, to recover (?), in its loops, rings and envelopings, all types of play *between*, and their ordering, since resemblance's aim is the limit of the series: the biggest, the strongest, the highest, the truest, the most natural, etc., but also their variations and determinations, through the anticipation, or foresight, of their recurrence, and also through mastery of the gap between the plan and its possible repercussions, between the aim and its deferred action, its retroactive effects, between the imperfect and the future perfect. Etc. Sex represents its operations, as well as their suspension, summary, resorption, into a 'correct' (just, true, natural, strong, elevated …) term, a term as right as anything, the best, the most sublime, with no possible response. The last word! Without approximate repetitions, reproductions. Play of the same and other. Positing the other out of inability to repeat the same, which, here, is the simple reiteration or the return of the end reabsorbing the origin, encompassing it, enveloping it, as well as their gaps, and their tropisms, and the history of their relations, under the pretext of the same.

Which could be translated, out of facility for and indulgence in final metaphors, as life *is* death – and not life and death are linked through comparison. We can thus extrapolate the function of *as/like*, of between-two, of the waiting, the uncertainty, the doubt and the unforeseen of the relation between necessity and chance, between tropism and *aphanisis*, between illusion and unveiling, unveiling *as* illusion, the hymen *as* illusion of unveiling, *as* unveiling of illusion, etc. It is relegated to an eternity neither fortunate nor unfortunate, removed from contingencies, from the interminable games of sex and their polarity. The latter are transferred, in an (acceptable) metaphor, an (acceptable) metaphoric practice, deviated and merged, into sublime terms. Into sublimation? Who knows? Read for yourselves, right here, the risks of letting oneself get carried away by metaphor, even, or especially, for an analyst.

Because the analyst has no other business but that. All enunciating practice, all enunciation, is already metaphorical for her or for him; all utterances are referred to a network of *as/like, as if,* which wind up and unwind its threads, which detach it from 'the' 'present' 'good' 'sense,' or good sense. It is not about substituting *an* other for it – we have to remember – but about articulating that fragment to the text, to texts, and inter-texts. Which calls into question, by the very same act, the simple character of the present, or of simple presence. Metaphoric process has already divided them, even when, verbal, it affects the present. Equivocal time, in any case, that marks division, distinction and the instant, or development and duration. It plays on continuous and discontinuous. Ambiguous time of enunciation, privileged time of fiction, it takes up and displaces fission? It eludes interference from precise temporal landmarks, supposedly exact reporting, supposedly true narrative, the simple future or the past definite, while resorting to the imperfect, the future perfect, and, of course, to the infinitive, to participles: tenses where we note the intervention – to have taken, or will have taken, place – of *as/like* or *as if* in order to re-suscitate. Which at one and the same time interprets the figurative, fictive – by process – character of the relation; suspends assertion and simple opposition between affirmation and negation, and all of their dichotomous re-presentations; defers judgment and the unequivocal attribution of qualities. Which calls into question the very existence of a determined, determinable relation between terms, the simple and innocent functioning (except in fiction, the covering over fission) of the copula, of copulation, and of their displacements, and therefore of metaphor. Never simply good or bad, true or false, correct or incorrect, right or wrong, high or low, natural or artificial, light or dark, it remains as neither one nor the other, unavoidable obstacle of any relation, whatever the illusion of a consciousness that claims to be good and true and just and noble and clear and coherent ... the guardian of good sense, proper meaning. As if sense or meaning could be looked after, or looked at! Tropism carries on dissimulated, under wraps, in veiled terms, through turns, turning back and turning round, perhaps – tropes, as they say. But it fades away as soon as anyone tries to zero in on it, give it a face, assign it a term (either final or original), implicate it in a statement, make a judgment about it. It exceeds or escapes from any predicate. All formulas or formulations are inadequate to it, because adequacy results from a logic, a *logos*, to which it cannot be reduced, and in which it moves about only with difficulty, and wanders without end but not without loss, if one tries to seduce it there, wait for or hear it there, grab onto it there, envelop or shut it in there. That would violate it or steal its play of *as/like, as if,* play *between,* over-determining the space *between* two signifiers, and concealing the sham of all terms or endings. Which can happen due to an alleged knowledge and practice of unveiling, notably of the ending, by whomever reserved to himself or herself what is undoubtedly the most interesting attribute of what is designated 'as' God, whose veils, we must acknowledge, have not yet all been lifted. True, the trap is laid, seizing on fiction, its process, and its final metaphors, in order to analyze them.

Curious word – analysis – for qualifying a practice whose elemental nature is questionable, always already fictive reprise of fission. It can only reckon with this unnameable sham: through (re-)exhibiting its economy, its turns, turnings back, turnings round, its retroactive effects, its games irreducible to the logic of non-contradiction. Such is the syntax of tropes, the economy of tropism, of its operations, never to be taken simply as is, as terms to accept or to judge as good terms, true, right, etc. That would risk cutting them off short, by eliminating their after-effects, whose traces must be recorded, reread and re-marked by interpretation.

METAPHORIC PRACTICE, WORD PLAY

Sometimes it resorts to plays on words, reminders of relations, relations *between* included in the metaphoric term, revealing its own workings, 'as if' in reverse. Metaphoric practice re-suscitates comparison, and emphasizes the particularity and singularity of distinctive witticisms within transference – always complex and working toward some putting together, some bringing together, in a package that can take in, harbor, and enclose it. It dissimulates under cover of this vestment, investment, its differences and articulations, and all of those maintained with other witticisms. The play on words makes us burst into laughter as it bursts open the simplicity, the exhaustiveness, the coherence of the form, formula or formulation, taking

off its mask of good term(s), elevated, true, correct, clear, noble ...
sublime term(s). Sublimation(?) disguising and concealing the compromise.
This burst of laughter is not without economic effects, without repercussions on value and sense, suddenly devalued. Not without resistance,
sometimes! The placement and displacement of investments are revealed,
at least apparently, as precarious and without decidable plan or realization;
half returns can often be preferred to full returns. But what difference does
it make if in the meantime we enjoyed it? Flash of wit, or discharge, it
comes as an additional bonus, authorizing new placements and displacements.

That economics is disorienting. It is difficult to conceive. That type of
expenditure outwits thought, or at least a certain form of thought. Its
present form? Word play confounds the confusion of plans, programs,
projects, times, aspects, and voices, or rather re-marks them with its
syntax. It emphasizes the equivocal, but reveals it as inevitable, constitutive
of the very process of thought: always already a rearticulation of intersexu-
ality and intertextuality, of their fictive composition, even in its most
elemental forms and formations – words, syllables, and phonemes, for
example. Word play reveals their complexity and ambiguity, the artificiality
of their intervention in a linear chain. It exposes, insofar as it is presented
as utterance, or text, actually taking place, right then, as place-holder in
the process of enunciation, the traits or the hidden faces of all figures,
figuration, the mandate of all representation, the *as/like* or *as if* of all utterance, of all the articulations or the junctions of its development. It unveils
the enactment of metaphor, of transfer, of transference and of displacement through and by the copula, the copulation, in a sign that represents,
recalls, certain of its traits, so that it can work like a sign. Word play
emphasizes that semaphoric function, replays it, as if in reverse, preventing
it from freezing up into in-signia, final term, ending, last word.

THE ECONOMY OF THE STAKES ...

Maybe that is the source of the interest in metaphor in the history of style,
and in psychoanalysis, and also perhaps the ambiguity of the subordination
of the one to the other, that repeats like an edict the subordination within
metaphor. It is not the most eminent, the noblest, the bravest, etc., under
which all the other tropes would have to be classified, or filed; nor is it the
most natural one on which all the others would have to be based. Its
demonstrated, codified importance runs the risk of compromising what is
important in it. The distances between the lowest and the highest, the
deepest and the most elevated, the first and the last, the weakest and the
strongest, the most natural and the most artificial ... function as that

which is in play or at stake – if they are read as already being metaphors, as being that which activates the transfer, the transference and the passage. As being that for which, through which, and between which, the id, or the metaphor, passes, or comes to pass. Metaphor must remain a passageway, without resolution or resorption of the difference between the terms of its recurrence.

Even their direction cannot be foreseen; the series does not move toward a simple reduction of or a simple increase in the gap. The variables implicated are complex in number and quantity, and linked according to a function whose form is complex. Complex operation of metaphorizing that, while attempting to represent certain vector(s), and to give form to their size, direction, and sense, principally reveals their degree of liberty. It posits new relations, notably between dependence and independence, and re-suscitates those that are bound or rebound to that function or functioning. It calls up or recalls further operations, comparisons, transfers, and transferences, both the same and different.

The elaboration of the stakes is never-ending. Except for whomever would imagine he or she could resolve it with indices, assign it terms, circumscribe or circumvent its economy, assimilate it in some way to a constant: complex x, symptom y, structure a ... forgetting the wager, the historical wager, for example, that permits its utterance, its formation(s), and the effects of its placements and displacements, always in progress. No one stops or regulates its economy. The most effective metaphors take or make their own time, even if one tries to fix them in time, use them to subjugate time, getting caught up in the process of metaphor that gets over on time.

But the fact that we take it, take it on, or get taken, does not prevent the game from going on somewhere else, where there is still play. Where, not taking any metaphor seriously, which means not taking ourselves seriously, we can still play with it, play *between,* play with, or dupe, each other. All types of *between*, that no element and no relation between elements can determine, except by way of fiction sustained. That capture would check the play of the copula; the grip, the connection *between*, would interrupt its work of articulation, always to be restarted.

Which is to say, referring only to a certain functioning of the copula and certain turns of metaphor, that no utterance can reabsorb all that is at stake in enunciation, no text all that is at stake for the scribe, no figure all that is at stake in figuration, and no representation can entirely account for its mandate, etc.

No substantive can fulfill the function of a verb. It is always already a sign – made into a sign – an attribute, dependent. However many transformations come together to give it its form, its definition, or perhaps because of this series, this multiplicity of operations, it evokes more than a verb, several relations and their articulation, whose repetition it will prescribe in the unfolding of discourse. This reverses the roles for whomever does nothing more than read the distribution present in the utterance, the actual statement. What must be questioned is the complex and sedimented elaboration of the subject, its relation to the predicate, their retroactive effects. Furthermore, the present (tense) of the utterance itself, its intent, its direct meaning or direct address, must be questioned, for what it really does is transpose, transfer, and displace, and this transposition, transfer/transference, and displacement have always already taken place through the intermediary, furtive no doubt, of *as/like* or *as if*, of metaphorizing. This present is only *like* a present. And its metaphor has no import except insofar as it conceals the process. It consists, precisely, of feigning, of behaving as if sex, the sign, or the sign of sex, could become or simply be a sign. And it never appears except *as sign, made into sign, making like a sign*, through various materials, techniques, and machineries. Metaphor claims to transgress the intervention of the sign, to cut through its materiality, as well as to transmute the materiality of sex into a sign whose comparison recalls the irreducible difference of materials supposedly in presence, of their properties, resistances, treatments . . .

. . . HAVING TO RECKON WITH THE INCALCULABLE OPERATIONS OF THE MIRROR

As/like maintains the gap, emphasizes it even as it tries to reduce or reabsorb it. It is a reminder of the play of mirrors permitting analogy, relation, congruence, interference, and even assimilation, through relays, reflections, derivations, deviations, refractions, diffractions, etc., that have already transformed, treated, and replaced them, notably as forms, both the same and different, and appearances, or appearing.

Metaphorizing has to reckon with this quasi-morphology, these quasi-morphemes (not necessarily linguistic), has to compromise with them, even as it contravenes them. Its operation is not so simple. It transgresses, as in transfixing and outlining the form, or rather its formation, while it represents another form as present. It simulates crossing through mirrors – or rather recrossing – and their total transparency, their transitivity, the possibility of transpiercing. In fact, it displaces the mirrors' intervention, re-marks it, plays with their properties, particularly their reflective properties, with their brilliance, with the opacity of their backing, with the disposition of their multiple, multiplied surfaces, placed now at an angle to allow the ricochet, now face to face to measure the angles of divergence, inscribed or circumscribed at a distance in order to fix the facets, and especially to concentrate their energy, and now introduced, in volume, into the other term – supposedly big, strong, voluminous and powerful enough ... to take everything in. This concrete, natural, sensible term ... will from now on include the mirror, its powers of abstraction, but also, in a more complex way, of idealization.

And the game is over. Here, they say, is matter that is animated, elevated above its origin, that becomes transparent, coherent, sublime reflection ... sublimated? While remaining natural, of course. Or else, the harmonious transformation or assumption of matter by the spirit, the idea, thanks to the specifically human tool that is language, etc. Or rather, tropism that tries to locate, relocate, its sense, sometimes its good sense, in re-presenting (itself), in doubling (itself), (as) its own cause, origin, agent, marks and insignia, in a figure where it makes (itself) a sign. Trying to outplay, or at least to play, the intervention of the mirror, of mirrors, whose economy is too complex for it to reckon with, or foresee its effects, repercussions, ricochets, or pick up on those that have already taken place.

Thus, one cannot decide the term(s), no matter how appropriate it appears or feels, or they appear or feel, of his or her own transference, nor decide that it will not take place or has not already taken place – had not or will not have taken place – within that term precisely, or in some other, perhaps judged inappropriate. These terms themselves are caught up in a play of repeated reflections, refractions, etc. It is not possible to anticipate the turn its displacement, always in progress, will have taken. Transporting even a shard of mirror – metaphorizing plays with the fragments of the mirror, but also with the relation of the fragments to the whole of the mirror – into a figure makes it begin to shimmer. It shines and dazzles. One sees nothing else; one sees nothing. One feels (oneself) no more. Tropism, seduced, will depend on that ideal, if one does not remind it of *as/like, as if*: like present, like presence, like in presence, like being, or to be, in the presence of, etc., developing, deploying, unveiling (interminable operation), the complexity of the *go-between* of *as/like or as if* that gets over on the sign.

Other multiple, contradictory effects, never simple or unique, will have also been produced. Even a little piece of mirror inserted into a so-called natural environment recalls its fissionable character, and fission, and therefore the risk of explosion, of shattering, but also its precariousness, the provisional nature of its volume and its suture, the possibility of throwing it out or throwing it back – or up. Especially since mirrors are rather indigestible.

Furthermore, the nature of this contribution, or relation, is postponed, along with all the comparisons and substitutions it undertakes to resuscitate. Not to mention that the introduction of a reflector denatures in unforeseeable ways. You have at least to reckon with reflexivity and reflection that absorb and deflect the rays, and since this is an already much used reflector, with the relation of its reflections to new incidences. So there are all kinds of relations of angles, of intensities, of meanings ... that are not easy to guess. The transference in the mirror implies many calculations. And we have not finished, perhaps never will have finished, either enumerating and elaborating the multiplicity of the operations in play, or defining the singularity of their science. Analytic practice has not fixed its mathematics. No more than those of writing, of enunciation or of metaphorizing.

TO FUNCTION/TO FEIGN

We already know that it must have something to do with fiction – and therefore fission – with *du*plicity, *du*plication, *re*petition, *re*presentation, and *re*currence, but also with *dis*placement, *de*formation, *de*tour, *de*velopment, and with *trans*ference, *trans*position, *trans*formation, etc. We get only a glimpse of the complexity, number, power and indices ... of these operations, but we cannot ignore that they are all about numbers, a relation of numbers; in representation at least two. Which is not to say a return to simple dichotomy. Division – scission – is only one type of relation among others, and division into two a type of division requiring only one difference. Furthermore, dividing up a relation, or more precisely a function, results only in another function, in the modification of relations between variables, and not in their disjunction. As for the variables, in any case for our purposes, they represent and refer to a plurality of irreducible functions. Beside the fact that a variable never has definite, definitive or unique ... value, form, gender, number, aspect. Just go ahead and try to resolve this issue.

For example: 'say it (is or is not) now'. All you can do is simulate. Which is the same thing as starting to count, to take into account, the difference between what you can say, or rather feign to say, and what you will not say. In fact, it is impossible to say everything at once, because everything cannot be said; the calculation of what is at stake and in play is too complex to solve at present; it is impossible to determine its form or formulation in definitive terms, especially not here and now; the formula is (undoubtedly) not representable, particularly not in these signs, nor in linear fashion, etc. All you can do is play, represent, figure, interpret, a difference whose sum, nature, gender/genre, species and meaning (more? or less?) you do not exactly know, any more than you know the divisions, separations, or transformations, your moves, or the interventions of others, or their interpretations, will bring about in it ...

High stakes of enunciation, of the analytic match, from which no category can escape,[8] that plays out between them all, without its being possible to analyze or break it down into components, or place a cash value on it. Metaphoric operation applies to all forms of speech and to all elements of language, unlike other tropes. It includes and confounds their division, their differences, but cannot itself be reduced to different terms. It always operates between them. It elaborates the *copula*, working *as* a verb, and all the verbs of the utterance can do is re-mark its modes or aspects, *like* a verb that would mean, count, enumerate, measure, link, move from one number to another (a number from which one can deduct the previous one), or connect; or they can estimate and (re-)establish relations between numbers; or make connections and correlations through identities, differences, divisions; or attribute values, quantities, properties ... to numbers, or rather to relations between numbers. (These numbers being already functions, relations between functions.) Metaphorizing acts *like* a verb that means *to function*. This function, this functioning, of the copula is unrepresentable given the number of variables. What can be done is to specify, through fiction, a possible or probable relation, in order to estimate the values in play, the direction of their progression, their separation from the excessiveness of the infinite. Because these different unrepresentable variables run the risk of merging together.

F (METAPHOR): F (METONYMY). F (SYNECDOCHE) → ∞

Barely conceivable scene of metaphor – of enunciation, of analysis, of writing – where one would appreciate some landmarks: designation of the author, the agent, the object; sharing out of roles, acts; naming of actors, knowing how many of them there are; indications of place and time; (re)discovery of the setting and the decor; study of the materials, the way they will be treated; an account of the instrument, means, execution, and effects; in sum, a staging and a representation. That will require resorting to other figures and figurations, other functions, relations, and connections that will indicate, index, the ones in play in the metaphoric process, in the copula. They will take the place of indices, signs, traces, marks, and ciphers, and decompose the function of the copula, reduce the number of variables (functions, actually) it requires, for an – impossible – representation. They respond to the '(it is) *like* that' *like* a sign, of metaphor, with a series of questions asking for an accounting. First of all: *what (is it)*?; a question whose insistence continues to constrain the programming of utterance; and also: *who? what? why? for whom? in what? by what? how? how many? when? where?* etc. These questions are correlated with the position of the terms of the utterance, with their determinations, defini-tions, materializations, and modes, with the particularity of their interde-pendencies and associations.

Through the same process, they are associated with all representations of transference, of its protagonists, of their assessment of their respective attributes, of the itemization of their interventions, and their causes, effects, and stories; and with all representations and representatives of its economy. The latter are produced as efforts to escape from what is played out on the psychoanalytic scene, or as attempts to attend (to) its functioning, if need be through imitations of displacements of time, place, and actors, supposedly *other*, since carried over from contexts where it would have all already taken place. Analytic <subjects> leave the scene in order to be present at their own spectacle, or in order to comment on it from the wings; which eclipses them. They try to make the process explicit, through explanations and analyses, through (re)division of their acts into fictively elementary, separable operations, and through the figuration of their terms and stakes.

Which implies – to use a certain terminology, which is not to say a certain interpretation – resorting to the functions of metonymy and synecdoche, to the products of their processes. Designating the supposed causes, effects, origins, instruments, places, signs ... of the operation of the copula; which would determine, situate, activate, execute its tropism, projection, play between, but also what they are applied to, what they aim at, point at and eventually transform: matter(s), genre(s)/gender(s), species, individual(s), number(s), and relation(s) of the part with the whole.

These figures distinguish the so-called terms, disjoin the relations between them to re-articulate them in a representable, sayable, enactable way. That does not happen without effects, without loss. There is no doubt that loss can become a function of production. The fact remains that its economy can be calculated only with difficulty. Because it tends, for all operations, toward infinity.

XII
Idiolect or Other Logic

THE CORPUS

Fifty respondents were recorded at the Hôpital Sainte-Anne, and the recordings were transcribed. The corpus consists of 600 typewritten pages, and includes spontaneous and semi-induced (questions about reasons for hospitalization, professional and family life, etc.) language, and responses to various exercises that can be analyzed to show how schizophrenics use language and linguistic forms: exercises calling for morphological or lexical negative transformations, for synonyms, for word definitions, for sentence production, etc. Certain of the exercises were also given to senile dementia patients and to different types of aphasics (cf. the work of H. Hécaen, J. Dubois, P. Marcie, etc.), permitting comparative studies among the different populations.

The corpora of schizophrenic language were classified in three ways.

(1) By respondent: for each respondent, I grouped together the transcriptions of the spontaneous and semi-induced language, the results of the linguistic exercises, and any recordings that had taken place. This allowed a certain number of comparative analyses among different types of language production, different types of interlocutory situations, and different stages of the illness, and its chemotherapeutic and psychotherapeutic treatment, etc.

(2) By type of exercise: the results of the linguistic exercises were grouped together, as were the spontaneous and semi-induced utterances, in order to carry out comparative statistical studies, either within the schizophrenic group, or between the schizophrenics and the other groups of respondents (normal or pathological).

(3) In tables: the corpora were organized into tables for clearer reading of the results. The tables constitute an initial interpretation.

ANALYSIS OF RESULTS

CHAPTERS ON THE LINGUISTIC EXERCISES

In the study of schizophrenic language, each chapter, of which I will give only a résumé, includes the corpus and the analysis of results for each exercise.

The chapters are organized as follows:

- rationale for the exercise
- ways of presenting the instructions
- corpora collected
- tables
- analysis of results
- interpretation of types of errors.

The chapter headings:
1 negative transformation exercise: morphological and lexical (polite/ impolite; true/false)
2 lexical micro-system exercise: kinship terms
3 paraphrasing of proverbs exercise
4 synonyms exercise
5 word definition exercise (substantives, verbs, adjectives)
6 shifters exercise
7 sentence production exercise.

Analysis of results from these different exercises confirms certain hypotheses, and allows formulation of several others, concerning spontaneous language. The goal is principally to show that schizophrenics, who have the linguistic code at their disposal, do not convert it into discourse. In other words, in the case of schizophrenia, there is no appropriation of the linguistic code in a speech act by an <I> who wants to send a message to a <you>, a message concerning the world – <he/she/it> – constituted as referent.

Negative transformation exercise

The negative transformation exercise – the results of which are analyzed at length in Chapter III, 'Negation and Negative Transformations in the Language of Schizophrenics' – was administered in two ways.

- The respondent is given a predicative sentence – *he closes the door* – and is asked, after being shown the morphological procedure he or she will have to use – ... *does not* ... – to apply a negative transformation to it.

- The respondent is asked to supply the opposite of a given word. The opposites requested belong to two different grammatical classes: adjectives (*grand, chaud, doux, profond* [big, hot, sweet/soft, deep], etc.), and verbs (*naître, aimer, mourir* [to be born, to love, to die], etc.). These words present various types of ambiguities: between several possible grammatical classes, between a word and a phrase, between homonyms, etc. The ambiguities must be resolved by the respondent before making a negative transformation.

The exercise was given to:

- a schizophenic group (45 respondents);
- a control group (15 respondents) from the same socio-cultural background as the schizophrenics;
- a group of students in the humanities (49 respondents);
- pathological groups: senile dementia patients and aphasics.

The principal characteristics of the responses of the schizophrenics can be grouped under the following rubrics:

(a) much greater diversity of responses than among 'normal' respondents or among the other pathological groups

(b) systematic quantification through negative hypertransformation: neutral terms are set aside in favor of terms marked '+': *grand* → *nain, minus, minuscule* [big → dwarf, minus, minuscule]; *doux* → *brutal, violent, cruel, coléreux* [sweet/soft → brutal, violent, cruel, irascible], etc.

(c) tendency to prefer animates: when one term can have two distributions – one animate, the other inanimate – the term selected is usually the metaphorical or figurative term, the one that applies to animates. For example, the opposites of *doux* [sweet/soft] among the 'normal' group are *dur, rugueux, rêche, amer, aigre* [hard, coarse, rough, bitter, sour]. Schizophrenics prefer: *rigide, coléreux, cruel, austère, intransigeant* [rigid, irascible, cruel, austere, intransigent], etc.

(d) predominance of stylistically marked terms over 'neutral' terms: the stylistic mark, modalization of the response, sets a tone, either colloquial – *moche* [tacky] for 'ugly,' *crever* [to croak] for 'to die' – or elevated, literary, administrative – *décéder, disparaître* [to be deceased, to disappear] for 'to die.'

(e) tendency to privilege the signifier: chosen terms show a certain phonic homology with the cue word: *naître* [to be born] → *renaître, disparaître, ne pas être* [to be reborn, to disappear, not to be], etc.[1]

(f) tendency to operate across different lexical classes, preferring adjectives and substantives: for example: *naître* → *le décès, le néant, absent, mort, stérile* [to be born → decease, nothingness, absent, death, sterile]; *aimer* → *insociable, froid, stylé, indifférence* [to love → unsociable, cold, trained, indifference], etc.

(g) schizophasic responses: there are few neoforms, but numerous examples of deviant usage, and neologisms in the distribution of terms.

These types of error can be interpreted as showing that what fundamentally differentiates schizophrenic responses from those of so-called normal respondents, and even from those of other pathological group is the relationship between the subject of enunciation and the utterance produced. Exercises performed on the code, particularly the negative transformation exercise, require that the schizophrenic experience the researcher's utterance as well as her or his own as proposed objects of communication or of dialogue, or as objects to be transformed. One consistent feature of schizophrenic responses seems to be difficulty in assuming the produced utterance, in dissociating the subject of enunciation from the subject of the utterance. This can also be detected in the way that disambiguation of the messages of both reseacher and respondent is left to the researcher, in the way that responses, and indeed any message at all, are transformed into a *play of signifiers*, as well as in the way that utterances are modalized.

The analyses call into question the very aptitude of the schizophrenic to carry out a negative transformation, whatever his or her skill in manipulating the appropriate morphological procedures. The transformation exercise on a predicative sentence readily demonstrates that what is obtained from the schizophrenic is not really a negative transformation. The respondent most often answers this exercise with a new sentence that simply excludes the example given by the researcher. For example: 'He ate oranges' provokes the response: 'He ate bananas' rather than 'He did not eat oranges.' This procedure can be said to constitute negation only in that it consists of the exclusion of the utterance of the researcher (perhaps the researcher as well); it is not the negative transformation of a referential utterance.

Use of negation can also be found in the spontaneous and semi-induced discourse. The morphological procedures are both operative and deviant, insofar as they do not actually carry out negative transformations.

These results indicate the need to examine the relationship between the manipulation of linguistic forms and their conversion into discourse. They also raise the issues of the linguistic formalization of negation, and of the moment of its intervention in the utterance, etc.

Kinship structures exercise

This exercise (cf. Chapter VI, entitled 'Linguistic Structures of Kinship and Their Perturbations in Schizophrenia') was also given to respondents in two ways, the second exercise having been developed to verify hypotheses formulated as a result of the first.

The goals were to analyze the ways schizophrenics manipulate the micro-structure of the lexical code constituted by kinship relations, in order to determine if the sub-code is intact for schizophrenics, and if they can make use of it on demand, as well as to determine how they deal with the fact that *ego* is the privileged referent of this lexical micro-system, and that the subject, as *ego*, must express, in the immediate linguistic context, how she or he is situated in the kinship structure. In other words, in addition to the integrity of the lexical micro-system, the exercise examines the relation of the subject actually producing the utterance (the subject of enunciation) to the subject of the utterance (who here is always *ego*).

The identity between the subject producing the message and *ego*, privileged referent of the lexical micro-system of kinship, leads to reactions of reticence, and to interference from delusional themes, rare on the part of the schizophrenics in response to the other linguistic exercises.

The responses indicate that schizophrenics have mastery of the lexical micro-system of kinship, and that, if they do not give the 'correct' answer right away, it is not because they do not know the term requested.

Types of errors found in the responses:

(a) confusion of generations: one or two generations can be confused, merged with each other: *petits-enfants* → *enfants* [grandchildren → children]; *oncle* → *cousin* [uncle → cousin]; *neveu* → *cousin* [nephew → cousin], etc. These errors do not arise from the complexity of the questions; on the contrary, when the question implies a simple relation of filiation (father–son, for example), the answer is even more difficult for the schizophrenic.

(b) confusion of other distinctive traits: collaterality and consanguinity, collaterality and generations, for example; generational errors are almost always combined with these other types of error.

(c) responses with generic terms: this type of error, frequent among senile dementia patients who exhibit a loss of lexical specificity, is very rare among schizophrenics and shows up only among hebephrenics, or among respondents who resist the exercise.

(d) schizophasic responses: one could label as schizophasic such responses as 'elm striplings' (instead of 'twins');[2] responses indicating an attempt to restructure the kinship code, and to constitute a kind of neo-code through symbolic overdetermination of the kinship terms. For example: *Abraham* [Abraham] (for: *Le père de votre père?* [Your father's father?]); *un petit poussin* [a little chick] (for: *Qui êtes-vous pour votre père?* [Who are you to your father?]); *un 'Dieu'* [a 'God'] (for: *Le frère de votre mère, qu'est-il pour vous?* [What is your mother's brother to you?]). There is evidence that the respondent knows the requested term, but that he or she is questioning the lexical micro-structure, in the same way that he or she questions and reworks the language.

Errors in response to this exercise cannot be interpreted as the result of linguistic deficiency, or of the loss of lexical specificity (on the contrary, schizophrenics, who give 'first cousin' instead of 'cousin,' or 'nephews and nieces' instead of 'nephews,'[3] emphasize lexical specificity more than 'normal' respondents). The issue here is the relation of filiation. Utterances such as *'Papa et moi sont des frères'* ['Papa and I are brothers'], *'Le père ressemble au fils'* ['The father resembles the son'], *'Le fils et le père sont pareils'* ['The son and the father are similar'], show a flattening out, or even a reversal, of the *ego*–father relation. The generational axis, whose paradigm is filiation, constitutes the principal dimension of the kinship structure and the genealogical tree. When filiation is questioned, or impossible to establish, or perturbed, the result is the dysfunction of the kinship structure in schizophrenic discourse, which can also be detected in the spontaneous utterances of these respondents.

Paraphrasing of proverbs exercise

Respondents were asked to paraphrase three proverbs: *'Tel père, tel fils'* ['Like father, like son']; *'Ce que femme veut, Dieu le veut'* ['What woman wants, God wants']; *'Chacun pour soi et Dieu pour tous'* ['Every man for himself and God for all'].[4]

The choice of proverbs was determined by the responses obtained from other exercises (for example, the word definition exercise where the word 'God' appears, or the kinship structure exercise), and by certain themes found in the spontaneous discourse.

Comparison of comments about the proverbs made by male respondents on the one hand, and female respondents on the other, is interesting. In response to the first proverb (*'Tel père, tel fils'* ['Like father, like son']), 100 percent of the men respond with an utterance indicating either a reversal of filiation (*'le père ressemble au fils'* ['the father resembles the son']); or reciprocity in filiation (*'le père ressemble au fils et le fils au père'* ['the father resembles the son, the son the father']); or by elimination of the genealogical relation (*'Papa et Guy sont des frères'* ['Papa and Guy are brothers'], *'Le père et le fils, c'est la même chose'* ['the father and the son are the same thing'], etc.). The women give more diversified responses. Some go along with the expected response (*'Le fils a le même caractère que le père'* ['The son has the same character as his father'], for example). Others run counter to the message of the proverb, and make claims for resemblance between mother and son (*'Les garçons sont plutôt proches de leur mère'* ['Boys are more often close to their mothers'], etc.). Only three responses show similarity to the men's.

The divergences in the responses can be interpreted as the result of the difference of the relation of the speaking subject – male or female – to the message of the proverb. The answer changes according to whether the speaker can, or cannot, be represented as subject of the utterance in the proverb. The question is whether or not it is possible for schizophrenics to assume an utterance where they, or where their image, is represented as subject, particularly when the utterance is imposed by someone else – the researcher, in this case. In other words, what is the relation of the schizophrenic speaking subject to the referential, and, more precisely, the co-referential, function of discourse? The pertinence of the question thus framed is confirmed by:

- the comments given in reaction to the second proverb; the men's responses are more correct than the women's, the relation of the speaking subject to the subject of the utterance being the reverse of the one established for 'Like father, like son.'
- the problem the paraphrasing operation causes the schizophrenic. Relevant in this context are the types of comments given in response to all the proverbs; most of them do not consist of interpretations or explanations of the proverb, but of quotations from other proverbs, or aphorisms, etc.

Synonyms exercise

Respondents are given a certain number of substantives, for example: *peur, joie, maître* [fear, joy, master]; and a certain number of verbs: *parler, penser, vivre, exclure* [to speak, to think, to live, to exclude], etc., and are asked to supply a term with the same meaning or a very similar one.

The exercise was given to:

- the schizophrenic group (45);
- a group whose socio-cultural background is similar to the schizophrenics (15);
- a group of students in the humanities (36).

The specific characteristics of the schizophrenic responses are as follows:

(a) refusal to disambiguate the cue word or the response given: respondents ask the researcher to specify the precise linguistic term if the term exhibits any homophony or polysemy; they produce several responses instead of just choosing one, or preferring one as the most appropriate; they modalize their responses: *'on pourrait dire ça, mais encore autre chose'* ['one might say this, or something else'], *'par exemple'* ['for example'], *'je dirais effroi, mais je pourrais dire tout aussi bien autre chose'* ['I would say fright, but I could say anything else just as well'], etc.

(b) refusal to give synonyms: this refusal is particularly interesting due to the fact that schizophrenic language is almost entirely based on equivalences. However, the important thing for the schizophrenic seems to be the refusal of the meaning assigned by the language – more specifically by the language of the mother – and the attempt at elaboration of a neo-code whose rules he or she may or may not give. Hence the 'insane' character of this language for whomever does not know, or rejects, the specific code.

(c) diversity of responses: this characteristic could also be interpreted as a refusal of the most frequently used term according to the established linguistic code, and a questioning of the synonymic operation. Diversity has also been noted in the results of the opposites exercise.

(d) connotations of given terms: schizophrenics most often give a stylistically marked, rather than a neutral, term. Connotations can place the term in the colloquial, or even idiolectical, code: *peur* → *frousse* [fear → scared stiff]; *parler* → *parlotter* [to talk → to chat it up], etc. They can also signify the pursuit of lexical specificity, the intention to use only elevated language: *parler* → *articuler, disserter, discourir* [to speak → to articulate, to hold forth, to discourse], etc.

(e) systematic quantification: neutral terms are set aside in favor of terms marked '+': *peur* → *effroi, hantise, terreur* [fear → dread, haunting, terror], etc.; *joie* → *euphorie, hilarité* [joy → euphoria, hilarity], etc.

(f) tendency to privilege the signifier: the power of the signifier provokes aberrant responses: *maître* → *omettre* [master → to omit⁵]; *vivre* → *revivre, vivifier* [to live → to relive, to vivify], etc.

(g) responses with opposites: in the opposites exercise no responses with synonyms were noted, whatever the order in which the two exercises were given. Responses with opposites could be an indication of the schizophrenic's desire to distance herself or himself from the imposed utterance, from the researcher's discourse, and from the proposed code.

(h) tendency to operate across lexical classes, with preference given to substantives and adjectives, or to words having already undergone a transformation.

(i) schizophasic responses: there are few neologisms: *vivre* → *viviver, croisser* [to live → to vivivy, to grow]; *parler* → *défervence* [to speak → deffervescence]; etc. On the other hand, a certain number of deviant or unexpected usages are found that, outside the specifically framed context of the linguistic exercise, could be interpreted as schizophasic: *penser* → *voler, tricher, psychanalyser* [to think → to steal/fly, to cheat, to psychoanalyze]; *parler* → *transmission de pensée* [to speak → transmission of thought]; *vivre* → *profiter* [to live → to take advantage of]; etc.

(j) switch to another language: some respondents confuse synonymy with translation.

Singularities and errors can be interpreted in the same way as the results of the negative transformation exercise: refusal to assume an utterance as such, distancing with respect to the researcher, and to already coded language. These characteristics can be detected in the modalizations of the responses, the resistances to disambiguation, the multiplicity of terms given, the refusal to choose one as more appropriate, and the commentaries, etc.

Schizophrenics are more reticent in relation to synonymy than in relation to the negative transformations they can more easily convert into a formalistic play with linguistic forms, without having to take into account the content of the message. In this exercise, terms must be given with the same signification, the same meaning, as the one presented by the researcher. This seems to be more difficult and less acceptable to the schizophrenic whose language is elaborated out of specific, idiolectical equivalences, the goal being to restructure the meaning of the mother tongue.

Word definition exercise

Respondents are given a certain number of words and asked to supply the corresponding definition. The words were selected for their ambiguities: homonymy, synonymy, distributional polysemy (literal meaning/figurative meaning, for example): *mur, tuile, glace, corps, mère* [wall, tile, looking-glass, body, mother];[6] or for the thematic or semantic interest shown in them in the spontaneous or semi-induced utterances: *miroir, mère, dieu, corps, loi* [mirror, mother, god, body, law], etc.

The exercise was given to:

- the schizophrenic group (45);
- a group whose socio-cultural background is similar to that of the schizophrenics (15).

Characteristics of the responses:

(a) refusal of unequivocal definition, of one single definition, one single meaning: it is not only the terms chosen for their homophonic or polysemic ambiguities that provoke several responses, but almost all the terms. Comments emphasize the random nature of the respondent's utterance as well as that of the researcher.

(b) emphasis on the materiality of the object, along with, or contrasting with, predominance of the figurative over the literal meaning: this contrast, or opposition, emerges both in single answers given by individual respondents, and in the whole series of utterances produced by the schizophrenics. For example, we find, in response to *mur* [wall]: *'construction en terre, en argile préparée'* ['construction made of earth, or of prepared clay'], *'mur de pierres'* ['wall of stones'], *'il y en a en briques, en grillage, en tôle, en bois ...'* ['there are brick ones, wire ones, metal ones, wood ones ... '], etc., and on the other hand, *'c'est un obstacle'* ['it's an obstacle'], *'ça peut être une prison, un étouffement'* ['it can be a prison, a strangulation'], *'c'est un partage, une séparation'* ['it's a division, a separation'], *'quelque chose qui divise'* ['something that divides'], etc. All these responses imply what could be called symbolic overdetermination. The same for *corps* [body]: *'c'est des cellules, c'est du sang'* ['it's cells, it's blood'], *'c'est un ensemble d'organes qui permettent à un corps humain de vivre'* ['it's a set of organs permitting a human body to live ... '], *'c'est un ensemble biologique'* ['it's a biological unit'], etc., in contrast to *'c'est un embêtement'* ['it's an annoyance'], *'c'est une chose nuisible contre la vérité'* ['it's something harmful to the truth'], etc. For *mère* [mother], a response such as *'les eaux thyroïdiennes (amniotiques?)'* ['thyroidal waters (amniotic?)'), is opposed to a defini-tion such as *'c'est la plus grande partie de Dieu'* ['she's the greater part of God'], or *'c'est ce qu'il a de plus beau au monde'* ['what is most beautiful in the world'], etc.

(c) definition by connotation rather than denotation: respondents do not supply the denotation of the term, but rather express a certain number of connotations they think are appropriate to it. For example: *la loi* [the law]: *'c'est ce qu'il y a de plus magnifique lorsque c'est fait d'une manière absolue'* ['it's the most magnificent thing when it's done absolutely']; *la vérité* [the truth]: *'c'est la chose la plus belle au monde'* ['it's the most beautiful thing in the world']; *mère* [mother]*: 'c'est ce qu'il y a de plus beau au monde'* ['what is most beautiful in the world'], *'c'est quelque chose d'infiniment beau, de mystérieux'* ['something infinitely beautiful and mysterious'], etc. These types of response allow schizophrenics to avoid complying with the instructions, or to reject the coded referent.

(d) stylistically marked language: certain responses show the affectation of elevated style (schizophrenic mannerism?). For example: *'la vérité c'est ce qui peut être auguré avec la présomption, l'indice, et … qui finit par formuler une preuve'* ['the truth is what can be augured with presump-tion, the clue, and … ends up formulating a proof'], *'La vérité c'est un acte de prouvance'* ['the truth is an act of provance'], etc. The stylistic mark seems to take precedence over the pertinence of the definition, as if the exercise required a certain type of language, rather than the refer-ential function.

(e) responses with opposites: these responses are related to those given for the synonym exercise, and they share the same interpretation: distan-cing from the linguistic code, and from the researcher's utterance. For example: *la vérité* [the truth]: *'c'est le mensonge'* ['it's a lie'], *'c'est le contraire du mensonge'* ['it's the opposite of a lie']; *la loi* [the law]: *'c'est l'injustice'* ['it's injustice']; *le châtiment* [punishment]: *'c'est le contraire du bonheur'* ['it's the opposite of happiness'], etc.

(f) responses with translations: also related to the synonym exercise; For example: *la loi* [the law]: *'lei;' dieu* [god]: *'deo,'* etc.

(g) homophonic responses: *corps – coeur* [body – heart[7]]; *parenthèses – parentes; c'est des parents)* [parentheses – [female] relatives; it's the parents]; *tuile – tôle* [tile – sheet metal[8]]; etc. The choice of term seems to be determined by its phonic relation to the signifier given in the cue.

(h) schizophasic responses that can be grouped into three types of utterances:

● 'paraphonic' responses: *parenthèses: parents* [parentheses: parents], etc.
   where the definition, determined by homophony, is neological;

● responses with syntactical or syntactico-semantic neologisms: *dieu* [god]:
   'c'est comme moi, c'est le respecter dans sa personne' ['it's like me, it's
   respecting him in his person']; *le corps* [the body]: *'une chose nuisible
   contre la vérité'* ['something harmful to the truth'], *une glace* [a looking
   glass]: *'c'est un miroir ... Un mirage d'eau qui peut être miré, qui efface'*
   ['it's a mirror... a water mirage that can be reflected, that erases']; etc.

● responses with lexical neologisms: *dieu* [god]: *'ça vient peut-être par la*
   savanterie *cosmique de l'air ... Ça peut être qu'il est intéressé par l'*ostrument *du vide'* ['that comes perhaps through the cosmic *savanterie* of the
   air.... It could be that it is interested in the *ostrument* of the void']; *une
   tuile* [a tile]: *'c'est une plaque rendue mécanique, c'est-à-dire* agrippante
   qu'on a mise sur la toiture de la maison' ['it's a mechanical plaque, that is
   a *gripping* they put on the roof of a house']; *la vérité* [the truth]: *'c'est un
   acte de* prouvance' ['it's an act of *provance*']; *le corps* [the body]: *'c'est une
   matière* flanche' ['it's *flanch* matter']; *parenthèses* [parentheses]: *'je ne me
   rappelle plus... C'est un /égypt/ et un /drowl/'* ['I don't remember... it's
   an /aigypt/ and a /drool/']; etc.

It is significant that the schizophrenic rarely defines words, and instead
gives examples, expresses connotations, prefers symbolic or figurative interpretations. In addition, the schizophrenic never pleads ignorance of the
meaning of the proposed term. For example, it is obvious that a certain
number of respondents do not know the meaning of 'parentheses,' but
they do not say so, and prefer to invent a definition. This exercise, not
rejected by schizophrenics, but giving them more problems than the
opposites or the synonyms exercises (they respond just with syllables,
constantly interrupting their utterances, etc.) is undoubtedly the most
effective one for examining the problem of reference in schizophrenic
language, and for analyzing the articulation of the coded linguistic
meanings of words with whatever meaning these same words have in
schizophrenic language. One is able to grasp and perhaps interpret more
accurately what has been called 'reification,' 'mannerism,' or 'symbolic
language.' It is also interesting to note that it is among the responses for
this exercise that one most frequently finds neologisms and schizophasia.
Whenever the meaning of a word, an utterance, or a message, escapes the
respondent, she or he is likely to respond schizophasically, or with a neologism elaborated according to the morphological procedures of her or his
own language.
   One also finds the same specific characteristics of schizophrenic

responses as in the other exercises: refusal to disambiguate a message (sent or received), predominance of the signifier, homophony, stylistic singularities, etc.

Personal pronoun exercise

This exercise is used to verify the formal and pragmatic framework of enunciation, constituted by interrelations among persons, and specifically the *I–you* relation.

Respondents – the schizophrenic group and the control group of similar socio-cultural background – were asked to integrate personal pronouns, in various combinations of twos, into a minimal sentence pattern. For example: I–me, I–him/her, you–me, you–him/her, he–me, he–you, etc. The goal is to cross-check the economy of personal relations detected in the spontaneous and semi-induced discourses.

Characteristics of the responses were that responses exhibit the same avoidance of establishment of relations between the persons specific to the enunciation (I–you) that was observed in spontaneous language. This avoidance can go so far as to substitute for the pronoun a homophonic term belonging to another grammatical category. One does obtain utterances integrating they–me, one–me, they–them, one–them, etc. This can be interpreted as showing that schizophrenic language is a language of citations, of utterances of utterances, but that it cannot be understood as a practice, a pragmatics, of conversion of language into discourse. The pronoun *I* is found in the utterances, showing specific functional characteristics: either it designates the formal paradigm of all speaking subjects (it is then a kind of citation of the linguistic form of the speaking subject), or it represents the subject of a narrative of narrative, a type of reported utterance. It does not signify the first person, the speaker, in an actual process of appropriation of language. *You* and *you (plural)* are not found in the subject noun phrases of the utterances produced.

For further discussion of this exercise, see Chapter XIII, 'Does Schizophrenic Discourse Exist?'

Sentence production exercise

Orally, respondents are given, in a definite order, two, three, or four morphemes, and the instructions to integrate them into a minimal sentence pattern: 'Make *one* sentence, the shortest, simplest possible, with the words I indicate.' The cue words correspond to several different syntactic functions, belong to different lexical classes, and exhibit limited compatibilities for combination. The exercise requires the use of three types of linguistic rules: syntactic (intuition of the minimal sentence pattern, with its possible expansions), lexical (respect for syntactico-lexical correlations, disambiguation of proposed morphemes, and eventual selection of a verb), and semantic (establishment of the compatibility or incompatibility among the suggested morphemes and certain messages, as well as among the terms themselves). The instructions are given with an example demonstrating the definition of the minimal sentence, and implying that the respondent should rectify any agrammaticality or anomaly in the message constituted by the cue words.

The exercise was given to:

- the schizophrenic group (45);
- a group with a socio-cultural background similar to the schizophrenics' (15);
- a group of students in the humanities (49);
- other 'pathological' groups: senile dementia patients, aphasics, etc.

Strategies adopted by the speaking subjects with respect to the linguistic rules show up both explicitly, in their verbal and non-verbal behavioral reactions to the cue, and implicitly, in their linguistic performances.

The behavioral reactions of the schizophrenics can be grouped as follows:

- comments emphasizing the ambiguity of the received message;
- comments emphasizing the ambiguity of the message carried out. These comments would seem to indicate that the utterance produced by the schizophrenic is some kind of game played with linguistic rules, carrying no message assumed by the speaking subject. All modalizations of the utterance also indicate this: *'on pourrait dire ça ...;' 'par exemple;' 'je dirais ça, mais aussi bien autre chose'* ['one might say that ...;' 'for example;' 'I would say this, but anything else too'], etc.

The characteristics of the sentences produced can be analyzed:

1   from the syntactic standpoint, in:
    - the specificity of the verbs used (for example, attribution verbs, verbs referring to the Greek 'mean') and their modal and temporal aspects;
    - relational elements used to establish equivalents that are 'paradigmatic' as opposed to 'syntagmatic;'
    - aphorisms, single word discourses, holophrastic expressions;
    - the availability of pronominal and negative transformations (unlike the senile dementia patients, for example).

2   from the lexical standpoint, in:
    - the specificity of the terms used;
    - the perception of ambiguity in the morphemes of the cue words, often followed by refusal to disambiguate;
    - the scarcity of neologisms and schizophasic expressions, and the presence of singularities and improbabilities in the semantic compatibilities, and in the established syntactico-semantic correlations.

3   from the syntactico-semantic standpoint, in:
    - the subject noun phrases, most often animates or specific inanimates;
    - the preferred personal pronoun *I*, functioning as formal paradigm of the speaking subject, often interchangeable with the impersonal *one*;
    - the intransitive verbs; intransitive construction is in any case preferred.

4   from the semantic standpoint, in:
    - utterances that most frequently make no sense, except as play with the linguistic code, but that avoid major linguistic anomalies (cf. responses to the cue: *red–see–horse* in Chapter VII, 'Sentence Production among Schizophrenics and Senile Dementia Patients').
    - These characteristics can be interpreted as indicating that schizophrenics never really articulate the subject of enunciation with the subject of the utterance. They refuse to, or cannot, emit or transmit, a message. They refuse to, or cannot, communicate. What they say is a manipulation of the code itself, and their utterances lack 'content.'

STUDY OF SPONTANEOUS OR SEMI-INDUCED LANGUAGE

The difficulties of approaching schizophrenic language, and the still fragmentary character of enunciation theory, led me to treat this data according to different methods.

Discourse analysis (Z. S. Harris's method)

Twenty fragments each of about one and a half typewritten pages were isolated. Selected from the beginning of the recordings, the fragments included only minimal interventions on the part of the researcher. Ten fragments were produced by male respondents and ten by females. They were analyzed in tables broken down under the rubrics NP1, VP, NP2, NP3,[9] adverbs and adjectives. The tables also show the clauses (C). Each line of the table reproduces C1, or C2, or C3, etc.

Interpretation of the tables shows the specificity of syntactic and syntactico-semantic construction among schizophrenics. This analysis permits extrapolation of a model for the kernel sentence, which varies according to the evolution of the illness. It should also be noted that male and female respondents do not make the same types of sentences.

Grammatical case (Fillmore's method)

The 20 fragments defined in Part 1, above, were analyzed according to grammatical case. This type of analysis delineates specific grammatical competence. In Fillmore's terms, it can be expressed as follows: 'I' (A) is constituted as objective (O) by an counter-agent (CA). The operation of the counter-agent shows up particularly in the locative (L): A is placed by CA in an L connoted harmful because A lacks an instrument (I) to carry out the action (therefore the discursive process) he or she wants to carry out.

Interpreted in terms of the functioning of enunciation and of its relation to the utterances produced, there is no possible 'I, here, now' for the schizophrenic. The frequent use of the locative is a substitution for the 'here' of the process of enunciation, and it demonstrates that 'here' is impossible. The number of temporal transformations signifies the impossibility of 'now' in the production of discourse.

From this analytic perspective, I attempted to interpret what appears to be a 'discord' in schizophrenic language: the presumed lines of selection for syntactic structuring are not respected. There is therefore a clash between grammatical competence and lexical competence; hence, the anomalous character of the denotation, the impossibility of identifying the referent.

Flow-chart analysis

I attempted to account for the specificity in the embedding of clauses for the 20 fragments defined in 1 and 2, above.

This type of analysis demonstrates:

- that schizophrenic language is often constituted by a proliferation of parentheses, opened up one inside the other, but not closed;
- that these parentheses are most frequently appositions serving to connote differently a noun phrase or a predicate, and have no denotative or referential function;
- that the parentheses also correspond to the complex intermingling of

enunciative processes attributable to *x* speakers in *x* places and at *x* moments of production of discourse;

- that the order of transformations is not respected; hence the incomplete character of the clause;
- that clauses develop a series of transformations of the types preferred by schizophrenics, but do not, however, constitute an utterance.

Analysis of two corpora of spontaneous language

This analysis is carried out on the entirety of the spontaneous language recorded for two respondents. Since sexual difference was a pertinent criterion in the results obtained, I selected a male's corpus and a female's.

This type of analysis raises questions about linguistic and psychiatric methodologies, in addition to the question of sex markings. For example: how does one define the signifying unit in schizophrenic language? Is delirium within the province of thematic analysis, of syntactic analysis, or both? How might one analyze their articulation? In addition: can one speak of 'schizophrenia' as a nosological entity? If schizophrenia is defined according to chemotherapeutic criteria, what does the functioning of language indicate about the effects of those criteria? Does the analysis of schizophrenic language open up the path for a verbal therapeutics elaborated on a scientific basis? Would it be preferable to chemotherapeutic, or to more immediately biological, methods of treatment?

Research on the indexical aspects of language

Analysis of the indices of person, time, place, and mode (cf. 'Does Schizophrenic Discourse exist?') shows a specific functioning that calls into question the constitution of discourse in the language of schizophrenics. They do not actually convert language into discourse; hence the singularity, the strangeness, of a language that mobilizes the linguistic signs of passage from code to message, but diverts them from their path. This problem concerns the functioning of the process of enunciation, and its relation to performed utterances in schizophrenia.

Analysis of schizophasic mechanisms

All the neologisms in the corpora of spontaneous and semi-induced language were isolated, and the procedures for their formation examined.

I noted:

(a) that they were almost all elaborated according to processes of deriva-
     tion appropriate to the French language; non-coded forms, or
     morphemes, were created, but that is not to say that they could not
     have been coded. For example: *psycher, luminer, programmique,
     prouvance, senserie* (to psyche, to lumine, programmic, provance,
     sensery], etc.

(b) that they sometimes constituted paraphonic errors. For example: *lésion
     conjugale, amnosphère vitale, instrallé en France, des gens qui m'électru-
     quent, j'avais des formes de chèques* [conjugal lesion, vital amnosphere,
     instralled in France, the people who electruck me, I had forms of
     checks], etc. It is not always possible to determine what, in these
     'errors,' might signify overdetermination in the meaning of a word
     (conjugal lesion), or what might be just a simple substitution for a
     forgotten term.

(c) that they were sometimes formed as hybrid words, a kind of stylistic
     procedure producing effects on meaning. For example: *horriable* (horri-
     able [horrible + abominable]); *gourderie* (dumceitfulness [dumb +
     deceitful]); *faribandelles* (nonsensinesses [*faribolles* + *bagatelles*
     (nonsense + trifles)]), etc.

(d) that they sometimes signified the idiolectical symbolic overdetermina-
     tion of a word or an expression.

(e) that they were often formulated using anomalous syntactic construc-
     tions or anomalous syntactico-semantic compatibilities. It is not the
     words here that are to be understood as neologisms, but rather the
     oddity of their functioning in the utterance. For example: *'frottez pas
     vos yeux, on va vous les coulisser'* ['don't rub your eyes, they will slide
     them open for you']; *'nous faisons le mouvement des élèves'* ['we are
     doing the movement of the pupils (=watching over the rows')]; *'si nous
     avons des économies garantes'* ['if we have guarantor economies']; *'nous
     sommes rentrés en normal'* ['we came home in normal']; *'on a dit notre
     victime'* ['they said our victim']; etc.

This work should be carried on with research into the referential function:
the function of the proper name; interpretation of the large numbers of
deictics; and interpretation of the substitution of connotative for descriptive or denotative traits allowing identification of the referent.

*

In conclusion, the following questions could be formulated:

- For the schizophrenic, is there a possibility of what is called discourse? This question takes up the results of analyses done in the different chapters and puts them into perspective, based principally on theories of the practice of discourse, or on the pragmatics of enunciation (cf. theories of Jakobson, Benveniste, Austin, Searle, etc.).
- How might we determine the specificity of schizophrenic language in relation to other groups of respondents defined as pathological?
- How might we analyze the characteristics of schizophrenic language in relation to so-called normal language? What *normal* language would be closest to schizophrenic language?
- Does schizophrenic language represent an idiolect of so-called normal language? How is that idiolect formed and how does it function? Or: is it really a stratum of language functioning habitually hidden under a certain kind of logic? Which logic?
- Do linguistic methods allow us to interpret schizophrenic language? Or are they powerless to account for the way it functions? Can psycholinguistics make a contribution to linguistic theory, which currently pays insufficient attention to the mechanisms of enunciation, and is founded too extensively on criteria of language production considered as universal norms?
- At the other extreme of the socio-cultural model, are psychiatrists ready to base their therapeutic methods on analyses of language? Are they prepared to listen to what can be creative in expressions considered atypical in relation to an often stereotyped and impoverished norm?

XIII

Does Schizophrenic Discourse Exist?

When I switched from analysis of the verbal productions of patients with senile dementia to analysis of the language of schizophrenics, my work began to require different methods, and instruments capable of accounting for singularities in discursive practice, or pragmatics, and in modes of enunciation. Problems in schizophrenic language are related more to the dynamics of enunciation, of 'putting language into operation through individual acts of utilization' (according to Benveniste's definition of enunciation), than to any eventual symptoms or deficiencies, the problem that always underlies the study of the language of senile dementia patients or aphasics.

The linguistic characteristics of enunciation, or the types of relation of the speaker to the language she or he uses, can be studied in different ways, some of which I analyzed with respect to the language of schizophrenics.

THE INDEXICAL ASPECT OF LANGUAGE

Language includes a class of elements that permit passage from, or conversion of, language into discourse. These elements have a double function: on the one hand, they are part of language defined as a system of signs, and as the syntax of their combinations; on the other hand, they belong to language as activity manifested in instances of discourse. These elements are called *indexical*, or pragmatic, as opposed to the denominative, or referential, elements of language. Analysis of the indexical aspect of language constitutes a chapter of enunciation theory to which E. Benveniste and R. Jakobson made significant contributions.

The indexical elements can be subdivided into four types.

PERSONAL INDICES

(a) The I–you relation constitutes the formal framework of interlocution. It is produced only in and through enunciation, and its variants can be analyzed to characterize specific forms of enunciation. In order to study the process of interlocution in the language of schizophrenics:

(i) I analyzed the spontaneous or semi-induced discourse of 50 respondents. I noted the near absence of I–you interrelations in the utterances produced. Relations among the partners of enunciation are represented only in reported discourse. In direct utterances, only I–him/her, they–me, one–me, they–them, one–them relations are found, and can be interpreted as a depersonalization of discourse through the use of utterance of utterance. *You* (singular or plural) is not found in the noun subject or object phrases of direct utterances. *I* appears, but functions in specific ways: either it designates the formal paradigm of all speaking subjects (it is in some ways the citation of the linguistic form designating the speaking subject), or it represents the subject of a narrative of narrative, a form of reported utterance. It does not signify the first person, or speaker, in an actual process of appropriation of language. It is a common noun, an *it* (a non-person), taken up from a prior act of speech production to designate the subject who speaks in the discourse. These few conclusions already indicate the singularity of schizophrenic discursive practice.

(ii) In the recorded corpora, I also considered the preferred forms of utterance, and analyzed their relation to the conditions of interlocution. For example, interrogation and direct address (imperative, vocative) can be interpreted as transformations implying an actual relation between speaker and addressee. They are very rare in the dialogue between schizophrenic and researcher, and appear only in reported utterances. Assertion must also be viewed within the context of interlocution. It is the commonest form of intervention of the speaker in enunciation, and, its aim being to impose a certitude on the interlocutor, it has at its disposal specific instruments manifesting that intervention: the words 'yes' and 'no.' In schizophrenic utterances, assertion is modalized in such a way that affirmation or negation are suspended, maintained in ambiguity. A questioning of the very process of assertion is verbalized. For example: 'Whether one eats or not, it's the same thing,' 'Whether he bets or not, it's the same,' 'Whether they know it or not, it's the same thing,' 'He wants to stop me from speaking or from not speaking,' etc. Schizophrenics' use of the logical operation of negation (do … not) can be interpreted as an aptitude for manipulating the linguistic form, without direct reference to the pragmatic context of interlocution (cf. 'Negation and Negative Transformations in the Language of Schizophrenics').

(iii) I administered an exercise dealing with the structuring of relations between persons in discourse to groups of respondents of differing diagnoses. Personal pronouns were presented two by two in various combinations, and respondents were asked to integrate them into a minimal sentence pattern. The goal of this exercise is to cross-check the economy of personal relations observed in spontaneous or semi-induced discourse. The responses obtained show the same avoidance of relations between the persons specific to the enunciation (I–you), which can go so far as to substitute a homophonic term belonging to another grammatical category for 'you.'[1] One does find, however, utterances integrating the pronouns *one–we*, *she/he–them*, *he/she–me*, etc. This exercise is not so well received by schizophrenics as those dealing with denotative elements of language.

(iv) The relation of schizophrenics to interlocution can also be analyzed in their reactions and responses to verbal exercises requiring negative transformations, the disambiguation of utterances, or the production of sentences, of synonyms, and of word definitions. Schizophrenics consistently call into question the types of assertion, direct address, and interrogation that are required by the instructions. Respondents either emphasize the ambiguity of the cue words, or try to reduce the implied message to its linguistic forms and rules (the answer then becomes a formal exercise with the linguistic rules and elements), or answer with a series of transformations and comments on the instructions or the expected answer. All of these types of reaction can be interpreted as ways of rejecting the interlocution initiated by the researcher. The same remarks apply to the way schizophrenics answer questions during the recording of semi-induced language.

(b) In interlocution between *I* and *you*, language is used to express a certain relation to the world (he/she/it). This implies, in the locutor (*I*), the need and the capability of making a *reference* through discourse, and in the addressee (*you*), the aptitude for co-reference, according to the terms of a pragmatic agreement making each locutor a co-locutor. The referential mechanism can thus be studied as the integral part of the process of enunciation. The perturbation of interlocution in schizophrenia affects aptitude for reference and co-reference in the practice of discourse. From this perspective, I began to examine, in the recorded corpora, the function of denotation, in particular with respect to proper names. To approach the problem of reference, I used the works of the logicians Russell and Strawson, in particular their texts *On Denoting* and *On Referring*.

DEMONSTRATIVE AND PLACE INDICES

Indices like 'this' or 'here' refer to the place where enunciation occurs. They have meaning only within the context of the actual practice of discourse, and their signification is correlated with each new process of enunciation, unlike nominal terms that refer to concepts defined in and by the language. The indices of place are closely associated with the partners of discourse (*I, here/you, there*). Interpretation of their occurrences and of the roles they play in the recorded fragments reconfirms the analysis of the personal indices.

INDICES OF TIME, OR TEMPORAL FORMS

The paradigm of temporal forms is determined, in many languages, in relation to the present, the time of enunciation, renewable for each production of discourse. This present coincides with the moment of enunciation – whose center is *ego* – and it forms the axis for the definition of verb tenses. Discourse and its relation to the present have been analyzed by Benveniste, Austin, Searle, Strawson, and Vendler, in particular. I referred to their work (cf. *Problèmes de linguistique générale, How to Do Things with Words, Speech Acts, Intention and Convention in Speech Acts, Les Performatifs en perspective*) in order to analyze temporality in the language of schizophrenics.

Benveniste divides French verb tenses into two distinct and complementary systems, revealing two different levels of enunciation he defines as *historical enunciation*, on the one hand, and *discourse*, on the other. A third type of enunciation, a means of articulating the two others, would be *indirect discourse*, where discourse is reported in terms of events and transposed onto the historical plane. The characteristics of historical enunciation and of discourse, as described by Benveniste, are pertinent for interpreting temporal forms in the language of schizophrenics, who prefer certain tenses typical of historical enunciation – the imperfect (including the conditional form), the perfect and the pluperfect. The present does play a role, but as atemporal present. Furthermore, the historical plane of enunciation establishes a particular economy in the reciprocal relationship between the two verbal categories of tense and person. Historical enunciation never adopts the formal apparatus of discourse whose essential framework is the *I–you* relation. Historical expression never uses *I*, nor *you*, nor *here*, nor *now*. Only 'third-person,' in other words non-person, forms are found in historical narrative, and discourse is produced without direct intervention of the locutor into the narrative. One might even say that no one speaks.

Interpretation of fragments of discourse has shown that the interpersonal relation (*I–you*) is all but missing from schizophrenic language, that *she/he/it* is the preferred subject of the utterance, and that *here* (or this/that) are extremely rare.

Now – either explicit, or conveyed through the present tense, the time of the process of enunciation – is not found in the fragments. However, attenuating these observations is the fact that the aorist – the preterite or the past definite – preferred tense of historical enunciation, plays almost no role, except in reported discourse. The preferred temporal forms are the imperfect, the conditional, the pluperfect and the atemporal present. It is also true that *I* is found as subject of the utterance; however, it is not associated with the first person, and should rather be interpreted as a cited paradigm for the speaking subject, an *it*, the non-person of interlocution.

The characteristics of temporal indices in the language of schizophrenics are more closely related to historical enunciation than to discourse. They cannot, however, be entirely identified with them, any more than with those of indirect discourse, with which they show some analogies, without, however, conforming to the temporality required for transposition of discourse onto the historical plane.

In the recorded corpora, temporal forms were also analyzed according to theories on performatives (cf. works of Austin, Searle, Strawson, Vendler). The conditions required for classification of the temporal form of a verb as a performative are almost never met. Verbs that could be classified as performatives are rare in schizophrenic language.

If such verbs are used, the syntactic conditions, temporal forms, and personal indices do not correspond to the characteristics of performatives. Performatives are the markers of discourse; they emphasize, or make explicit, the illocutionary force of an utterance. They are another way of examining the pragmatics of language. Their absence from the language of schizophrenics emphasizes, from yet another angle, the singularity of their discursive practice.

MODALIZATION

I also took up the problem of modal forms in schizophrenic language, both the modes of verbs (optative, subjunctive), and locutions modalizing the relation between the utterance and the locutor: *maybe, no doubt, probably*, etc.

Neither the optative nor the subjunctive, modes marking the attitude of the speaker with respect to what he or she says, and requiring a distancing from the moment of speech, are found in the recorded corpora. As for locutions found in the utterances, they differ from *maybe* or *no doubt*, which express, in the discourse, the way the subject of enunciation assumes her or his utterance. In schizophrenic language they would be better interpreted as the sign of a refusal, or of an incapacity for assertion on the part of the speaking subject: 'for example,' 'one could say that, but other things as well,' 'possibly,' 'probably,' 'I could say it completely differently,' etc.

Phrases of the same types can be found in the responses to the verbal exercises. They confirm the schizophrenic's insistence on emphasizing the ambiguity of the cue words and of the answers he or she gives, emphasis which at times consists mainly of an enumeration of the ambiguities and the variants possible in response to the cue words.

This manipulation of the ambiguities of the terms used in certain exercises (opposites, synonyms, sentence production) prompted me to administer an exercise with *ambiguous phrases*, where the respondent was asked to resolve the lexical or syntactic ambiguity of a given utterance. The responses obtained are, for the most part, paraphrases or comments. Schizophrenics manipulate ambiguities in the elements of language, but do not easily perceive the ambiguity of an utterance, and do not really understand what would need to be done to disambiguate it.

THE SEMANTIC ASPECT OF LANGUAGE

The question of how language is converted into discourse, in particular with respect to the formation of meaning in words and in syntactic structures, is a difficult one. I approached it as follows:

- by examining the functioning of the lexicon and of transformations. The symptomatic aspect of meaning, lexical meaning in schizophrenia to be exact, can be apprehended from several different intersecting angles: refusal of the mother tongue as it has been transmitted; a linguistic or a metalinguistic attitude with respect to that language, whose lexical and syntactic forms are taken as objects for manipulations resulting in idiolects and neo-codes; lexical or grammatical schizophasia; procedures of derivation imposed on the lexical elements of the mother tongue; constant transformational activity. Spontaneous or semi-induced discourse, as well as responses to certain verbal exercises (sentence production, opposites, etc.) served as source material for these analyses.
- by analyzing the procedures used by schizophrenics to maintain *ambiguity* in their utterances: modals, paraphrasis, temporal forms, and metalinguistic activity.
- By examining presuppositions in schizophrenic 'discourse.'

XIV

Schizophrenics, or the Refusal of Schiz

When applied to the language of an individual designated, in psychiatric nosology, as schizophrenic – a term whose most common rendering would be 'mind split in two,' or 'divided in two' – a certain number of instituted dichotomies are revealed to be ineffective, and even outdated. One might object that these dichotomies are metalinguistic, that they belong to discourse about language, to the science of language, and not to language itself. That presupposes, however, that linguistic methods can be heterogeneous to language, or that linguistic discourse is in no way marked by the language it uses: hypotheses that are hardly defensible, and that immediately raise the question of the very possibility of a linguistic metalanguage, and of its pretentions to establishing rules with respect to natural languages. However, that issue will not be addressed here, at least not explicitly. We will examine the economy of schiz in the verbal productions of schizophrenics, and consider the functioning of their 'discourse' with respect to certain dichotomies used in the analysis and interpretation of language. These dichotomies are disparate, but intersect with each other. They were chosen intentionally, in order to examine in several ways – insofar as that is possible in a few pages – the singularity of schizophrenic language.

LANGUAGE/SPEECH

In structural linguistics, *language* is conceived as a system of signs, an inventory of elements, each defined by its position relative to the others, or as a system of values determined solely by their mutual relations. It should be added that language exists 'in the collectivity, in the form of a set of imprints in each brain, almost like a dictionary, of which every individual would have a copy. It is something that is within each of them, while at the same time common to them all' (F. de Saussure, *Cours de linguistique générale*, Paris: Payot, 1962, p.38).[1] *Speech* consists of 'individual combinations,' through which the speaking subject utilizes the language system in order to 'express his or her personal thought,' combinations 'dependent upon the will of the one who speaks,' as well as on the 'acts of phonation necessary for the execution of these combinations.'

This restatement of the definition of the language/speech distinction, which could be termed axiomatic for the structural linguistic method, may cause some amusement. Nevertheless, the authority of this distinction at least partially explains our resistances to schizophrenic language, and the fact that we characterize it as strange, or foreign, or mad. Perhaps the same could be said of any questioning of a binary systematization? In any case, schizophrenics can be said to have neither language nor speech, in Saussure's sense of the terms, and there is no dictionary identical to that of all other members of society printed in their heads. Even if it were a schizophrenic society! The schizophrenic's glossary is neither within her or him, nor common to all, but is defined by a specific set of relations to the *language of the mother*. The socially determined characteristics of the mother tongue that are particular to a given society are re-marked by the singularity of the language of the mother. Language is no longer a neutral code, a set of conventional signs and rules, set down in dictionaries, available for everyone to use. It is a sub-code, an idiolect with no laws common to a group of speaking subjects, an avatar of the speech of the mother, or of her substitute. It is private, and, in addition, its inventory, the taxonomy of elements that constitute it, is also more limited, more restricted, than the mother tongue. Furthermore, the ways in which these elements are related to each other, and are determined by their mutual relations, are not neutralized by usage, or by the wear and tear of a linguistic practice experienced and systematized by a group of individuals, but are rather prescribed by the syntax regulating the discourse of the mother. *Language* here is not a network or a net, without central control, that functions as a system of in-finite references among distinct particles; it has become an interlacing of threads whose weave follows a certain pattern emanating from a center, which in this case happens to have a hole in it.

Meaning, rather than becoming manifest through specific relations of difference established in a message, is from the very start assigned by language. It can only repeat, contradict, refute, or dislocate itself, etc. It is not created, as Saussure maintains, in the act of speech. Speech loses its function and, furthermore, the possibility of its realization. The schizophrenic's code is not a social code, any more than his or her speech is individual or personal speech, 'consisting in freedom of individual combinations depending on the will of the speaking subject,' 'with the goal of expressing his or her thought.' Schizophrenic language cannot really be described as the actualization of a system of conventional and abstract signs within concrete, always differing, acts of speech. What the schizophrenic does is to repeat, with a certain number of transformations and adjustments (almost foreseeable if the rules of operation are discovered), sequences of already programmed signs, 'concretized' in a discourse. Due to their reiterations, reproductions, and transformations, bearing no relation to an intra- or extra-linguistic context or situation, they appear to be abstract, but their abstraction is not comparable to that of the elements distinguished and defined by linguistic analysis.

In any case, for the schizophrenic, the sentence does not belong to the register of speech, as if it resulted from an act of individual creativity on the part of the speaking subject. The grammar of what takes the place of language for the schizophrenic cannot be described, as in a structuralist conception of language, as a taxonomy of minimal elements, paradigmatic classes, and certain types of syntagma (as in Nicolas Ruwet, *Introduction à la grammaire générative*, Paris: Plon, 1967, p. 51). It is from the start syntactical, and even always already in phrases. Would generative grammar be a more appropriate means for theorizing the language productions of schizophrenics? Would other types of binary oppositions – competence/performance, deep structures/surface structures, etc. – be isomorphic with the principles in operation in schizophrenic language?

COMPETENCE/PERFORMANCE

This new linguistic dichotomy takes up the classical opposition of language/speech, but differs from it where grammar is concerned. Language is no longer defined inductively as an inventory or taxonomy of elements that are related to each other, associated into sentences, or syntactically combined, through speech. It is conceived as 'a system of general rules permitting the enumeration of all grammatical phrases' (Ruwet, pp. 45–6);[2] in other words, as a 'finite mechanism capable of generating an infinite set of phrases' (Paul M. Postal, *Limitations of Phrase Structure Grammars*, cited in Ruwet, p. 46). *Competence* designates the implicit 'linguistic knowledge' of speaking subjects regarding these rules, knowledge that would allow 'any adult subject speaking a given language … to transmit spontaneously, or to perceive and understand, an indefinite number of sentences that, for the most part, she or he would never have pronounced or heard before' (Ruwet, p. 16). *Performance* puts the abstract, finite rules of competence into operation; it is the manifestation, realization, or actualization of the rules, in an indefinite number of grammatically correct sentences. It should be noted that this definition of language modifies the role Saussure attributed to creativity in linguistic activity. For Saussure, there is creativity only at the level of speech, in the singularities and individual deviations of the speaking subject combining the elements of the linguistic system in order to form messages. This conception of creativity remains valid with respect to performance in generative grammar, which also posits a second type of creativity related to competence, and based on the recursive power of the rules that constitute the language system.

This emphasis on syntax and on its generative powers would seem to be an effective instrument for the analysis of the verbal activity of schizophrenics, despite the fact that the latter is in large part deconstructive of syntax. However, the categories defined by generative grammar do not really apply to schizophrenic language. The grammar manifest in schizophrenic utterances cannot be formalized as a finite set of rules, general rules that can be represented as logical relations among abstract symbols. The rules of schizophrenic 'discourse' are pre-determined by the mother tongue as it is brought forth in the language of the mother. They have always already been actualized. One might object, with reason, that it is in truth the same for anyone else as well. However, the power of the mother's language over that of the schizophrenic is such that overdetermination becomes assignation. Due to the specificity of their usage by the mother or her substitute, the grammatical rules have become, rather than mechanisms for the production of an infinite number of sentences, machines programmed once and for all, generating only a finite 'discourse,' closed off, at once limited and enveloping. Actual concretizations in syntax are not in-finite in number; there are no transmissions or receptions of new, never before pronounced or heard sentences. In a certain way, everything has already been set down ahead of time. This does not mean, however, that it is not radically impossible for speaking subjects with knowledge of the same mother tongue – supposedly – to anticipate or automatically to understand schizophrenic utterances. Why? Notably because they have never questioned the functioning of the code or the sub-code that they use. Schizophrenic language, constrained linguistic activity where naive usage of the language is suspended, keeps the question open. Enigma, word puzzle ... Should it be designated insane, and classified in reassuring nosological categories? Or questioned as reservoir of meaning, or for meaning?

In any case, schizophrenics do not escape the problems of the functioning of language. As soon as they try to speak – instead of just being spoken – they become linguists; they produce only language about language, or about what constitutes language for them. They continuously rework the rules of 'their' language, trying to re-establish their potentiality beyond linguistic performance of the language of the mother, trying to extricate them from maternal phraseology, from her psychological or socio-cultural determinants (to mention only those admissible in linguistic theory). A linguist in quest of the lost object – language – the schizophrenic tries to re-suscitate it at every turn by freeing grammar from its rigid and rigorous machinery. Hence, the apparent syntactic games, or the

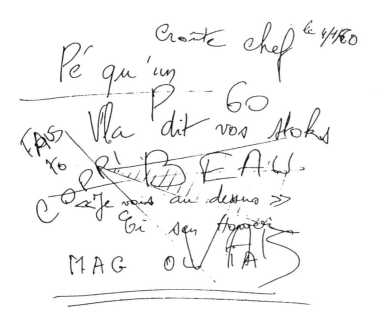

fact that the schizophrenic is perhaps the most rigorously 'syntaxifying' (to use Mallarmé's term) of all linguists, and all 'speaking subjects,' with plenty of intuition of the language, and to spare. Syntactic operations are the surest way for schizophrenics to carry out verbal, or more precisely morphological, or scriptural, activity. They control language only in finding and playing with the articulations and joints of syntax, in deconstructing its concatenations and fixed sequences, in attacking sentences, and even words, and unlinking their elementary particles. They disjoint them, break them down into their minimal components, their polyvalencies, their possible variants. They challenge their codified, unequivocal functioning, and produce all kinds of associations and unforeseen combinations with partially fabricated elements or morphemes, caught up in the play of unexpected substitutions and groupings. The morphemes are sometimes borrowed from foreign languages and reintegrated into the grammar of the mother tongue through addition or modification of its rules (cf. Louis Wolfson, *Le schizo et les langues*, Paris: Gallimard, 1970). Thus schizophrenics elaborate sentences, syntagmatic sequences, and word-phrases that are not necessarily understandable or acceptable for a subject supposedly speaking the same language.

Having already questioned schizophrenics' use of the same code, we must now keep in mind that it is only erroneously that we say that they speak. We might rather say that they *unspeak, reversing the process of formation of utterances.* They try to break through the closure of constraining discourse, in an attempt to find the laws of its engendering. They move away from phonetic realizations that harass with their insistent, repetitive noises – sonorous actualizations of significations that bind the listener without his or her consent – and move toward what would be the key to their power, the secret of their formulation; that is, their 'fundamental structures.' They destroy imposed speech, which is violating in its claims to proper, exclusive, totalitarian meaning ... They explode that meaning – which for them had always been meaningless – in order to get back down to, and play around with, its categorical and lexical components, its underlying articulations. Everything happens in reverse *between* 'surface structures' and 'deep structures,' but this *between two* is per-verted by the fact that the domination of the language of the mother denies free access to the 'deep structures.' Schizophrenics are able to perceive them to some extent, because the mother tongue is, after all, spoken by the mother. The fact remains that what is missing is the articulation of the code with its sonorous signifying realizations.

This could be one possible explanation for schizophrenics' syntactic behavior, their transformational activities, their incessant manipulations of the sub-code in search of a subtilized code that would allow them access to speech. However, it is not the only possible hypothesis, and is, moreover, as questionable as the linguistic categories on which it is founded, in particular the authority of the theory of the sign, a theory that has never been seriously called into question.

SIGNIFIER/SIGNIFIED

Schizophrenic language also raises the question of the sign. The empire of the sign goes back much farther than Ferdinand de Saussure. His linguistic interpretation conforms to the definition already at work in Stoic philosophy, as Roman Jakobson reminds us in 'A la Recherche de l'essence du langage' *(Diogène,* 51: 22). We will consider the ways in which Saussure's theory might, or might not, be applicable to schizophrenic language.

The *sign,* or 'linguistic unit, is double, made up of the connection between two terms' (Saussure, p. 99). 'The linguistic sign does not unite a thing with a name, but a concept with an acoustic image.' 'The linguistic sign is therefore a psychic entity with two faces.' 'In current usage, the term sign generally designates the acoustic image alone.... . The ambiguity would disappear if one designated the three notions involved by names that, while in opposition to each other, resembled each other. We suggest conserving the word *sign* to designate the whole, and replacing *concept* and *acoustic image* by *signified* and *signifier* respectively; the latter two terms having the advantage of emphasizing the opposition separating them from each other, and from the whole of which they are parts' (Saussure, p. 99). The language of schizophrenics, or their relation to what are 'signs' for them, calls into question almost every one of the terms of these statements. I will examine only some of them, playing the game of this definition of the sign.

Meaning, for schizophrenics, is constituted through the signifiers, which are meaningless for them, of the mother's discourse. That is to say that they are marked by 'sounds' whose 'concepts' remain hidden, veiled. Stolen? The result is their simultaneously fascinated and painful relationship with signifiers, that they repeat, transform, disjoint, fracture, break down, and rework, as if they wanted to destroy them and seize some of their power. The signifiers they enumerate, associate, pulverize, and reconstruct, come flooding to the surface to be passively transmitted, or utilized as material for refashioning or re-elaborating; they evoke no specific concept or signified, nor are they simple acoustic images. They produce themselves, reproduce themselves, unlink and relink themselves together, like re-markings of *traces*. The signified is an effect of the power of the signifiers of the mother's discourse. There is no double-faced sign in schizophrenic language, but rather cryptogrammatic writing or rewriting of sonorous inscriptions.

The signifier, if we may keep the name, is emancipated from the power of the sign. The dichotomous constitution of the linguistic unit, wherein a signifier represents a signified, is broken up, dislocated, dissolved, called into question. The signifier no longer represents a meaning that the speaking subject assigns, or re-assigns, to it. It repeats imperfectly, in an 'imperfect' tense, a signification whose 'concept' neither the mother, nor the schizophrenic, has ever mastered. As opposed to the sign, which supposedly exists in an eternal present without a past, the schizophrenic signifier evokes a kind of imperfective past that never was and never will be present. Meaning is always in the process of trying to produce or to reproduce itself in that signifier. It cannot be detected in any one single term, any more than in the totality of *one* discourse, but in the repetitions, transformations, *derivations, deviations* from one discourse to the other, in one discourse by the other.

Processes of derivation/deviation are prevalent in the linguistic activity of the schizophrenic, in the formation of new words through addition, suppression, or replacement of 'morphemes' (either already existing in the language or elaborated according to codified derivation processes), and in the transposition of words from one grammatical category to another without changing their forms. These derivations eventually stand on their own, and are used to subvert all references to radical, base, root, or fixed

Depuis quelques jours,
je TOUS sérieusement

La Chose est sans
importance pour moi ...

'Elle a commencé par un Rome
et continue ... !!! 999 ... par
une espèce d'insignifiante bronchite
✳

LA LÉGION «MARCHE
| 20 | 30 | 40 | ou
          CRÈVE »

category. Schizophrenic language thus consists of an unending process of derivation without represented or representable axis – *ex-centric, unhinged, cut adrift.*

Could this constitute a laborious response, or a parry, to the fact that the schizophrenic functions as signifier, in derivation/deviation, in the economy of the discourse of the mother? Ex-orbitant signifier: circuit derived from the play between signifiers in the language of the mother, ensuring that their circulation does not open up onto some gaping hole, some void. Signifier that occults, bars, blocks, occupies the space of a gap or a hole, or of the unspeakable, like a linchpin that assembles, fixes, and connects the signifiers of maternal discourse around a void, of which it takes charge. The schizophrenic is implicated in and by the discourse of the mother as signifier of an unnameable signified: *rather than as lack of signs.*

Playing, yet awhile, the sign theory game, one might interpret the sign's linguistic function as the *signifier-symptom* of the inadequacy of (codified) signifier to (codified) signified, as signifier of the *excess* of signifier or of signified with respect to instituted signs. This excess is experienced through the mother and through the mother tongue, not as a question about meaning, as reservations on or about meaning, but as the threat of meaning's collapse, disintegration, or decomposition. The excess becomes closure: signifier that blocks, seals off, and closes up investigation into the constitution of the sign, notably in its bipartite, dichotomous combination.

The schizophrenic takes the place of the signifier of a discourse skidding out of control toward its elsewhere, its other, its outside, a discourse that projects itself, assures itself, re-assures itself through the *in-fans*. This is the source of the hesitations, the oscillations between extremes. Could the schizophrenic be God? Representative of a transcendental signified he or she furtively guarantees, through mutism: silent cornerstone of language? Or could the schizophrenic be nothing? Signifier of a vacancy, a gap, a blank, a fracture in discourse, or risk of blackout, of drift, of slippage in signification. Let us rather say that the schizophrenic supports the faltering relation between two abysses, and has for that reason been reduced to the role of a magic word, a key word, a signifier both unique and ambivalent. The schizophrenic will forever be in the process of disengaging from this reified status. She or he enters discourse as a sign, if we can still use the term, of the inadequacy of signs, of their failure, and in order to guarantee their perpetual functioning as signs. Alien in, or of, a discourse that refuses to consider the strangeness and dementia of its own process, to pay the price of madness for its own reason, to underwrite the anomalies of its fixed and rigid norms. Signifier of this deficiency, of this swindle, the schizophrenic, as in-fans of his or her mother and of society, remains as security, in trust, on notice – incarcerated, legally neutralized, codified symptom of the deadly (and yet always threatened with derision, or dereliction), law of power of the signs in power. *Signifier of the omnipotence and the impotence of discourse*, the schizophrenic in-fans is at one and the same time necessary to and banished from the process. Out of the I-position, out of the game, of language which claims to take place now, to communicate something here, to signify in the present, in all codified normality, intelligibility, communicability, and security. Like a sign exiled from discourse, but nonetheless necessary for the functioning of language, rejected and required, heterogeneous to the system, but guaranteeing its homogeneity.

We can thus understand that for schizophrenics words are the much sought after and much feared ciphers of their enigmatic aphasia, of their irreducible alienation and lack of common sense. Their linguistic activity consists of fracturing, along every possible angle, the envelope that enacts and harbors the meaning of the language of the mother, the nicely reassuring value of its signifiers, and the proper and paralyzed syntax that produces limited and repetitive sequences. Caught between the vertiginous fault in discourse, of which they are effigy and emblem, and its closure which they guarantee, schizophrenics cannot be read as signifiers representing a signified, or even several signifieds, but rather, since we are using this terminology, as what Saussure rejects as definition of the sign: a *name* designating a non-codified, non-codifiable, unnameable *thing*.

Nor do schizophrenics have at their disposal the conventionally structured system of the signs of the language. Words are not discrete and distinct elements, able to be mobilized and combined for the transmission of messages, because they are always already captured, prisoners of programmed sequences. The association of signified and signifier in the sign no longer obeys the law of the arbitrary. The play, the free will, of the law of the arbitrary, is missing from schizophrenic language. Paradoxically, this results in the interpretation of what the schizophrenic says as unmotivated, gratuitous and unfounded. In fact, schizophrenics' signifiers are rigorously prescribed by a meaning that is never subject to the arbitrary law of the sign, whatever their attempts at reintroducing conventions and rules that might resemble its function. These schizophrenic conventions do not, or no longer, govern a link between a sound and a concept. They seek to eliminate, or tame, or even seduce the violent force of sounds. They attempt to develop an economy of signifiers, a signifying economy, where signification can be produced and partially controlled through a system of rules seeking to organize the power of (the) signifier(s), either linked in sentences, or detached from one another. By reassembling them in a grammar they can manage?

The 'signified' can no longer be detected at the level of the sign, but in the elaboration and functioning of an idiolectical syntax, or perhaps only in the reiteration or the deconstruction of maternal syntax. In schizophrenic language, 'difference' is not to be found between the signs, but rather in the processes of dissolution, distortion, derivation/deviation, and recoding the maternal language undergoes as the schizophrenic tries to distinguish herself or himself from it. It is the undoubtedly rather singular syntactic work that maintains, in his or her language-producing activity, the play and the articulation of differences. The *arbitrary* and the *differential*, essential attributes of the constitution of Saussure's linguistic sign, are inappropriate to describe schizophrenic signifiers.

In addition, the representation of the double-faced sign as a signifier separated from a signified written underneath a bar or a horizontal line is inappropriate, as is the layering of the linguistic unit, dichotomized by a plane, split, cut. 'Language is also comparable to a sheet of paper: the thought is the front and the sound is the back' (Saussure, p. 157). The virtuality of the sheet of paper, its plane surface, cuttable and cut up into double-faced units, is missing in schizophrenics. In their language there is neither plane nor bar separating 'signifier' from 'signified,' which is perhaps precisely why there is none between present (participle) and past (participle). The 'signifier' repeats and reinscribes the 'signifier,' while transforming it. It re-manifests its power, attempts to elaborate and re-elaborate its strata and sedimentations in multiple redistributions, without detectable or institutable distinctions in or between signifier/signified, present (participle)/past (participle). This operation more closely resembles an effort to modulate, articulate, or sometimes simply neutralize the power of sounds.

Thus, in schizophrenic language, none of the linearity or the arbitrariness of the sign, its primordial characteristics according to Saussure (Saussure, p. 103). Schizophrenic signifiers are not produced 'along one single dimension ... a line' – far from it (Saussure, p. 103). What Saussure has to say on this subject, practically contested by himself in *Anagrammes* (cf., for example, *Mercure de France*, February 1964: 242–62; *To Honor Roman Jakobson*, Mouton, 1967, pp. 1906–17; 'Lettres de Ferdinand de Saussure à Antoine Meillet,' in Cahiers de Ferdinand de Saussure, 21: 89–135), should be re-examined with respect to the conception of time prescribed by classical philosophy, where time is determined as a succession of points, as a line, or as a circle. Saussure's theories should also be questioned regarding their lack of development of the economy of space, of space-time, and of spacing in the articulation of signifiers. From the beginning, Saussure's reductive, repressive, 'flat' interpretation of writing prevents him from thinking about the economy of the *blanks* in discourse (cf. the analyses of J. Derrida, in particular *De la Grammatologie*, Paris: Minuit, 1967).

Schizophrenics ceaselessly and irrepressibly contravene this classical concept of temporality. The linearity of the signifier is broken up into fragments no longer recognizable as elements, as 'points' of the language or of speech. Schizophrenics multiply the blanks by fracturing the discourse. They refuse to produce or to inscribe it onto one single page, or one single medium, or into one single blank. There is no one appointed, fixed sheet on which they write, or rewrite, a text. The pages are strung together, but come unstrung, slip away, fly away. The planes flatten or collapse into each other. Neither discourse, nor the message, is pronounced or articulated at the point of intersection of two axes of co-ordinates, two lines defining a plane – even a blank plane – those two dimensions designated as language/speech, paradigm/syntagm, signifier/signified, etc. Discourse and messages accumulate like innumerable, uncountable fragments – that do not add up – of heterogeneous blanks, and sounds, and voices: the ones programmed in the language of the mother and in the mother tongue that they break up and remanipulate; the one that sustains and organizes that tongue and that speech as such, as systems, or as systematic; the one that guarantees the circulation, or indeed the circularity of (the) signifier(s). Which might correspond to an exiled signified, or to the functional law of the system (which for structural linguistics is fear of the blank space), its denomination, its proper name, and even its flaw, its lack of signs. These blanks, these functions of the blank supported by the schizophrenic in-fans, are the very ones she or he seeks to deconstruct as entities, to fragment into disparate chunks of debris, defying any possibility of their reconstitution into a unity. The unity of the blank in all of its privileged roles? Especially its role as support for the system of language, ensuring the circle of maternal, familial, and social discourse underlying the plane (possibly even the blank plane), the line, the point, the present, the sign, the time, and the space-time of the sign.

There are other dichotomies called into question, or destabilized, by schizophrenic linguistic process that must be examined, even if they intersect, at some angle, the dichotomy of the sign. To mention only a few: locutor/addressee, speech/writing, enunciation/utterance, literal/figurative, original/derivative, subject/object, active/passive, etc. And we must ask ourselves how to understand this process. It can, on the one hand, be interpreted through a language that never questions its constitution or its functioning; the verbal activity of the schizophrenic then appears insane, incoherent, dissociated, unmotivated, gratuitous, etc.; it is defined by a lawmaking discourse as foreign to its laws, outlawed, to be subjugated to instituted norms. Or, on the other hand, schizophrenic logic can call into question the normative conventions of language, along with their implications and correlates. We might then hypothesize that schizo-phrenia, as seen in certain individuals, is the name of a projection of the dichotomous

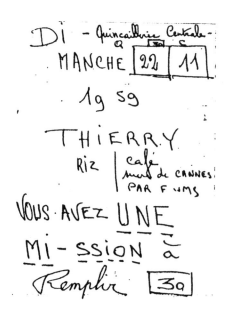

mechanisms at work in the discourse of those who *name*, those who speak *literal meaning*, onto those who reveal *the remainder*, that which is left over from the binary divisions of discourse. Schizo-phrenia could be the symptom of a certain type of language-functioning, unrecognized by its locutors, and for that reason attributed to the in-fans of the language of the mother, of the mother tongue. A schizophrenic would then be someone who could not, or who would not, play the game, who recalls what lies underneath, the reverse side, the prerequisites, or the balance, lack of recognition and the price to be paid for it. The schizophrenic would signal (the way toward) the above or the beyond of signs.

XV

The Setting in Psychoanalysis

The setting of the analytic scene may not be just another empiric, or just another psychical application, an experience like any other. Who knows? It may be a setting that disorients, disconcerts, and destabilizes the scene of representation.[1]

I am not returning, or regressing, to this scene insofar as it is medical act, or praxis, whose distance from what is going on here would guarantee the safety of some kind of secret I am keeping, that any analyst keeps – just another hermeneutic obstacle. The psychoanalytic setting has no secrets other than the one that psychoanalysis and its readers, including those on the outside, have neglected to interpret – that is, the theoretical impact it might have. To investigate psychoanalysis as text only, to apply only the text to other cultural domains, is to treat as negligible this setting that is at work in representations of psychoanalysis, as well as in its theoretical texts, determining their incoherence, or their other kind of coherence – that is, the fact that Freud's text does not answer to the same systematic criteria as a philosophical, or a scientific, or even a literary text. This does not mean that it does not convey certain postulates, fragments and sequences. . . . however, they are not anchored to a domain, a method or a system. One argument that could be made against psychoanalysis, and against its eventual diaspora, is its lack of recognition of its setting. As if it nostalgically wanted to lock up in the text, in theoretical and scientific interpretations – even those made while 'in session' – a scene that calls the very condition of representation into question. As if psychoanalysts, or their readers, could not stop themselves from reframing within classical representation everything about psychoanalysis that does not fit in, trying to re-master in the utterance the drama of enunciation that is played out there. Everything that is said and written about psychoanalysis bears witness to this. Writing *on* psychoanalysis always runs the risk of downplaying the efficacy of the scene.

How can we speak of analysis from within its setting? From inside the scene?

*

Do you think you can put the beginning in front, and the end, the culmination, in back? Is the former not always intuited, rationalized, as the past

– already left behind, even when you try to get back to it (and not by walking backwards) – and the latter as the future, up ahead even when implying a detour through the past?

Try to imagine the beginning ahead of you, and the end behind you, and the habitual scene of representation starts to vacillate. Try to imagine it with no way out, and no hidden agenda, in the following scenario: in an eternal present, in the future perfect, in a futurable conditional – not some eternal return of the same – and with absolutely no reappropriation of the beginning in the origin. What vertigo without our reassuring representation of space! What direction do you move in? How do you begin speaking?

What do you say anyway? What meaning can language still have?

The subject is often imagined as source, with nothing behind him or her. As if he or she had their back to the wall. If there was anyone back there, it would be God: the creator of everything. Back turned to everything that went before, does the subject imagine she or he is protected in front and up above?

In back of the subject who speaks in analysis, there is the analyst. Of course, it is not quite so simple. Underneath the backside[2] of the analysand, there is the couch. The reality of having actually to lie on the couch makes it more difficult to believe he or she has no backside, or to imagine some God back there. Under the couch maybe? Too humble a position for a God. Obviously, there is also the analyst, in back. But there's not supposed to be anything back there. Is the analyst going to function as God? At times, perhaps when she or he is silent and seems all-powerful. It becomes more difficult when the analyst admits something about her or his own desire – in interpretation, for example – or when seen face to face before or after the session, or when touched. Is the analyst going to function as 'wall'? Here again, not always. In any case, yes, in the phantasms of the subject. But maybe that is where the analyst discovers the wall he or she was leaning up against.

And what if this wall speaks? Where is the source now? In the analyst, the only subject? If she or he claims absolute knowledge – then, yes, possibly. If the analyst plays the hermeneut – yes, maybe, at least for a time. But when the analyst's own transference and desire dictate what he or she says, things are a lot less simple. The source is no longer simple. In the scene, it is at least double. Which is strangely disturbing for the proper ...

The position of the analyst has several other effects. Discourse is actualized at the intersection of two axes. The subject of representation has a front and a back, an up and a down, and is supposedly upright, forming a right angle with the plane supporting her or him. What happens when the subject lies down and speaks with someone in back?

Imagine the scene. The cardinal points flip over. Where is the subject with respect to front, back, up, down? What becomes of the horizon, for example? The subject's intersection with it is infinite: analysis is interminable.

In the scene, right and left are precious co-ordinates for orientation. When right and left are missing, Plato's demiurge cannot make the world turn; Kant can no longer be found in his room, etc. At the analyst's, the analysand is not in his or her own environment, among familiar objects, and the analyst, from one visit to the next, could very well move all the objects in the office around. The reference point formed by the analyst's body when the subject enters the scene disappears all at once, due to their respective positions. The analysand misses the analyst's body. All reference points are reversed; face to face, right corresponds to left and left to right. Here, they are one behind the other; left corresponds to left and right to right. As if they were looking at themselves, at each other, in the same mirror. Besides, if you walk up to a bed and lie down on it, you will yourself have modified left–right orientation. However (and this deconstructs representation), it is the analyst who directly maintains certain co-ordinates for the subject: is the analyst then imagined to be holding up the vertical axis, while the subject is lying down? The junction point of the two axes is no longer *within* the one who speaks. That which guarantees the present splits in two? Opens up an abyss between the two? The right angle is, at least for the time being, lost to the subject?

In this between two, the accordance of reflection with representation is also lost. Even if subjects can reflect 'within themselves' on the conformity of the representation to the thing itself, and even if they have in some ways introjected the specular, the specular matrix of everything they were representing, it is the analyst who fulfills the function of the mirror. Of course, the thing in the mirror is not the same thing any more, never was the same thing, and never was actually there. The identity between a thing and its representation holds no assurances. The distinction itself is highly problematic. The representation is not necessarily different from what it represents, not because the thing is nothing more than a memory, but because the memory itself might not have a reference, or a model for memory. There is no rating scale for the appropriateness of memory, no right or wrong memories, nor even any 'thing' to remember; there is never any painting of the real thing hung up on the wall in front of the subject.

Memories as such are not the object of analysis. And remembering is not about bringing memories back in order to show or to demonstrate their conformity, or lack thereof, to some abstraction of memory.

Memories emerge as the privileged – not always – mode of expression, no doubt because of the supine position, and because of the absence of immediate perceptions, notably visual ones. But they also signal a mode of defense: inertia, the filling-in of an invisible frame of representation with a content the subject thinks appropriate to it. The 'object' would really be the framework of all representation, the imperceptible, unrepresentable construction of the phantasm that dramatically reappears because no objects are perceived, because 'say everything' results in meaningless discourse, and because there is no guarantee that what is said is truthful, etc.

The object of desire does not simply conform to the same teleology as the object of representation, nor to the same methodology. And it often outwits all intuition. Here as well, the subject must be at least double, because if something can be signified about the 'object,' it is as the result of its projection in analysis onto the analyst. The form-content (if we can use these terms) of what is to be represented – impossible aim in the classical sense of the term – is produced between the analysand who speaks and the analyst who sustains the setting of his or her word. And, of course, there will almost never be discovery of the setting, or unveiling of what seduces and maintains the word within this framing. The frame, or the window, determines the form of the apparition; they themselves do not appear, any more than they exist outside the session.

Let us also note that the object is usually in front of the subject, but in this case it is in back. When the subject – accustomed to a certain practice of representation – seeks the object 'before' her or him, who is the source, the object has already moved to the back. And what comes to the 'forefront' masks the object: profusion or excess of meaning, or of literal meaning, meaning's elusive above or beyond. The subject is *overwhelmed* by language, and, consequently, all signs or signifiers appear, at least for a time, as equally contingent, inappropriate, lacking in specificity, etc. The scene of representation dissolves into confusion. It empties out, even as it loses mastery, both at the same time, within an ever more profuse enuncia-tion. The subject no longer knows where to begin, what goal to aim at, what type of utterance or enunciation to articulate here and now. It is the transference, the projection onto the analyst of what causes the word, or the desire, to reclaim its framework, that maintains what is spoken, the id that is spoken . . .[2] But in what time? In what confusion of times?

How? By assigning to the analyst the simple function of reflecting screen? Of mirror? Thus allowing the subject to read the secret cipher of his or her desire? By watching for signs of her or his image to appear on the analyst in order to introject it? But since it is not really about the image, but rather about its framing, how to distinguish 'me' from 'him' or 'her'? Me as the same as him or her? Especially since about the analyst himself or herself (as same) few clues are given. The subject would have to introject the whole analyst? The same questions subsist. Who is *I*? Who is *you*? And furthermore, the subject leaves whatever he or she does not want to be, to have, or to know, to the analyst, and wants nothing more to do with it. How to distinguish between a good and a bad projection? A 'good' or a 'bad' copy of oneself?

This quest for the appearance in the mirror of the cause of language, of desire, is yet another illusion caused by their reappropriation in representation. The analyst signifies this by functioning as mirror as well as by eluding this function. Undoubtedly, the subtlest articulation of the analytic scenario, and the most insidious question it raises about representation, are the distinctions among *projection, identification, identity to self*, and *desire for the same.* These functions become confused due to the inexplicit, uninterpreted postulate that representation has only a *front*, and no back, and that it does not undergo the inversion produced in the mirror. The setting of psychoanalysis, its unfolding, contradicts this pretension concerning representation's 'front.' Let us remember the respective positions of the protagonists, their evolution, the preoccupation with the backside of the subject (no acting out – that would confuse phantasm and reality, and avoid questioning the status of representation itself; with no exceptions, the backside of the subject is situated over on the couch), the non-face-to-face with respect to the object, the non-face-to-face with respect to the mirror, etc. Representation submits to a certain number of swivels and turns, or leaps, that elude common sense, leaving, behind the face that is exposed, the secret, hidden reserve of its back side, hermeneutic resource, and this is not one of the least disconcerting aspects of the practice. In the front-to-back about-faces of representation, subjects find their 'volume,' not only the volume of soul, or of mind (circle never constituted except in the face-to-face?), but also of their body, flesh, and story.

This is not to say that there will not be, in the language of the analysand, preferred signs, words, and sequences. When they are interpreted as such, the fascination they momentarily exercised in the face-to-face is reinforced with meaning, so-called secret meaning that the analyst unveils. These are the key semantemes of the analysand's language-desire, the main points of her or his meaning system deciphered by the analyst, new high priest of hermeneutics.

No sign is worth being singled out and interpreted as such in analysis. Such a gesture would resubordinate the setting to the scene of representation that brought on the neurosis. Which means that no projection, no identification, no mimeticism, should be pinned down to the truth of *one single* meaning. One has to wait until, breaking off from their support, these diverse modes of identity – that is, projection, identification, and mimeticism – teach the analyst and the analysand that they have a back side. What maintained their fascination and their privilege was the security of the only face possible, the face-to-face, along with the hidden support assuring their presentation: that surface whose back never appears, and that must be penetrated until infinitely pierced by a final inaccessible meaning.

Since all representation can be turned around, its value becomes part of an economy, and furthermore an echo-nomy, which needs no ultimate anchorage in order to have value. The signs play off each other without some Master, Father, or Analyst, who would answer for their ultimate meaning: no all-powerful mirror, no guarantor for the functioning of the totality of the set of signs or signifiers, no legislator of suitable meaning. Dancing while writing, no doubt, evokes the pursuit of a similar practice, at least for whomever does not dance always in the same direction, or pirouette around the same axis, but turns round without depending on a fixed plan. The problem remains: can one get there alone?

We have known for a long time that the language spoken in analysis leaves considerable room for the past, and that the present is immersed in the past: a past that was never present – in the sense of a representable thing – and that never will be. Representation is thus disengaged from its pretension to a univocal here and now, even an eternal here and now, because, once again – despite the hopes of the analysand – there will be no model for memory, nor discovery of a memory that would equivocally give weight to representation, overdetermining it with temporal stratifications whose different impacts could be interpreted, giving meaning to every moment of the past, up to the present. The facilitation of the trace has no term that can be appropriated, in either direction. It writes, rewrites, inscribes, reinscribes, but does not offer itself up to be seen, intuited, reintuited, remembered. So what happens to it in the analytic setting? Where will its tracing be marked, re-marked? Against what will it exercise its strength? What will the medium for its writing be? What or who will keep its memory? For a time, the analyst fulfills these different functions. More precisely, the analyst's body? For either the memory is repressed in the present, or it is assisted by already written 'things,' texts, as well as laws, or else it needs a corresponding material in order to be inscribed and kept, at the time of each displacement, and each reworking of the economy. What the analysand asks of the analyst, at least implicitly, is to ensure that her or his memory traces are maintained. And the analyst has no other choice but to refer to an already written text and submit them, compare them and evaluate them according to it – text-book, or text of his or her own personal economy – or to make himself or herself, insofar as that is possible, into the available medium for the inscription of the traces of the analysand, for the time of the drama of analysis, and thus to become what is unfit for all effective presence, unfit for all the edicts of common sense, and unfit for attestations to truth of any kind, etc.

Who ensures this keeping of the traces in theory or in writing? And what price is to be paid by someone who renounces the appropriation of her or his own meaning, or of the other's. The appropriation of her or his own desire, or of the other's? The analyst is paid for this function, for this forfeit, or this infamy, which is in any case unrepresentable in the estimate of the debt. In any case, the analyst is paid, sometimes too little, sometimes too much.

However, some other criteria do come into play here. How, how much, whom to pay for keeping the traces outside of this scenario? What is the relation between guilt, the debt owed to the father, or to the truth of the word, and the one who is unpaid and who functions as memory? It is to the father, no doubt, that we owe the transmission of the text of the law, but is he not the very one who forces into a representation the traces that do not remember him? The father is not the keeper of the traces: he erases them in the common sense of the present. But they want to be about their work, and can do so only if reinscribed onto a readable medium. What or who will fulfill this function without appropriating the traces? What will he, or she, be paid for this service? And does the secret of meaning – in the text as well – not come from, does it not in large part come from, this unavowed medium that does not even know itself, and to which the meaning owes the investment of its present meaning, or even its force, and the tracing and design of its writing? For re-marking the facilitated pathways, the scribe is not sufficient unto himself or herself. Even were the scribe, in some privileged way, medium, the strength would have come from some other, whom she or he would rewrite.

In the scene of presence, the *voice* is the most subtle means of auto-affection, or of auto-reaffection for the subject in his or her interiority. The voice, in the analytic setting, runs through an additional circuit. Auto-affection imposes itself from the very beginning as relayed through hetero-affection. The illusion of simplicity in the return to self, in identity to self, is blurred by this doubling of circulation. *I* returns to *itself* thanks only to the detour through the other. *I* thinks itself only after having passed through the other. The *I think* that accompanies all representation is already the other's thought. The voice returns to the subject only through the voice of the other, including the voice of her or his internal speech and thought.

Since the determinant is not so much what is said here and now, as it is the phantasmatic framing that dictates that nothing else can be said, a framing that the analyst has already heard, analysands can carry on a silent monologue with themselves, and they will be listened to. They know it too, without knowing it: from their discomfort at keeping quiet, from their anger at being heard in spite of everything, from their irritation if the analyst begins to speak, reactualizing the fact that there have always already been two voices, and that if there had not always been two, they would not hear or understand themselves, and that, if priority must absolutely be assigned, it would go to the other who spoke before them, in them. It is when they believe they are auto-affecting exclusively, that they are trying most purely to re-hetero-affect – but that, they do not want to know.

It can result in all kinds of murders – real, imaginary, symbolic. Nonetheless, within the autarkical pretension to current common sense, it seems the murder succeeded in part, that it formed one body with a so-called proper word, with a realized identity to the self. Which does not prevent fights to the death from persisting among theoreticians, or even writers, in order to appropriate the proper signification. The various interpretations do not change anything; the war goes on, with other weapons, perhaps.

The war is also waged in analysis. When it comes to meaning, analysand and analyst do not surrender unity of voice easily. But the voice that comes from behind the one who thought herself or himself the origin of meaning confuses the geography of auto-affection. It is not a confrontation of voices, or a crossing of voices, like a crossing of steel, nor is it violence, even though there can be violence in the contest to see who speaks louder, or more appropriately. One of the voices comes back to the subject from behind. If he or she silences it, then he or she risks losing his or her own.

How are these two irreconcilable voices represented in theory, in the text? In theory, in philosophy at least, we know a little about it: the son forces silence on the father, steals his voice by force.

But are we still really talking about voice? Or is voice not dead as well – except in some delirium of internal speech, some hallucination, some so-called divine revelation or inspiration – in this takeover of the voice of the one by the other? Sense, meaning, have no more voice. A connotation that risks making them unfit for truth.

And what about in writing? How to retrace simultaneously the two voices, together and apart? Without privileging either one? Without some forced analogy that, in some ways, reduces them to the same? Is it possible to write in two voices? If not, what unity of the subject re-forms in writing? Or: does writing renounce the voice? Why? Where can the traces of its effacement be read in the text?

*

And the gaze? It has always been the gaze that commands object-representation; the gaze that intuits, exposes, reassembles the represented in front of itself, giving it or recognizing its form; the gaze that maintains the privilege of the face-to-face. It is difficult to look at one's backside, unless it is projected to the front by a play of mirrors. The backside is the impotence of the gaze.

Analysands have nothing before their eyes. In the view of their habitual view, they are plunged into blindness. They see nothing but nothing-to-see, apart from a minute inspection of the analyst's furniture, perception that's soon exhausted. As for the face-to-face of representation, the supine position disrupts it. In analysis, what happens to the gaze, privileged organ of representation? Perhaps it is abandoned to the analyst for a while. Perhaps analysands temporarily experience themselves as object of the other's perception. But the scene cannot be reduced to that. So? Subjects re-vision their memories? How to be sure that perception, or the relation to perception, is right? They tell what they have seen, here or there. They re-see and replay what they saw for the other? They have no idea what or whom to look at, or look upon. The perspicacity or the acuity of the gaze overflow. They tell what they do not see, have not seen, saw without seeing – beyond the horizon – think maybe they saw. Should have seen? How can they know? Where do we make the distinction between seen and not seen, visible and not visible? Hallucination and reality of perception? Perhaps, what the subject sees there most clearly and most surely, is precisely hallucination. And if we had to declare what is most distinctly recognizable in analysis, would it not be a language of hallucination? But what happens to it in the scene of representation? Where is this underside of the perceived, the perceptible, or the recognizable hiding? Could it be in the fact that the chain of meaning is somehow closed off? Or in the fact that all there is to see is already given in representation, and that there is no room for another seen? Or in the fascination with literal meaning? Or in its authoritarian power of conviction that captures the conviction of hallucination? Or in the postulated imperceptibility of ideality? But from what then would ideality have taken its framing? What relations are sustained between ideality and hallucination? Is each the underside of the other? Unless ideality is an hallucination that repeats itself in representation, if the treatment does not bring out their intervals, their alternations, and even their reconciliations?

The psychoanalytic setting makes it obvious that the hierarchy of values of representation corresponds to a perspective, even to an optical illusion. Mastering all representations in the face-to-face, organizing them into the same time-frame, onto the same plane, while maintaining the pretense of respect for their spatio-temporal differences, requires that they be ordered within a perspective with differing degrees of presence, propriety, and proximity, in accordance with the rigidity of the proper, a perspective that damages, infinitely, through loss of volume.

The privileging of the gaze and its face-to-face is allied with an economy of the sexual: privilege of the visible sex, but also of all tropism of the front. Freudian sexuality is perhaps, at the same time, a negation of the sexed body. It leaves woman as guardian of a body without a sexuality of its own? Castration is reduced to nothing to see? In the other? Hence, the Other?

Concerning the privileging of the visible of and in representation, the following questions can be raised:

- Is what makes us laugh in a play on words not the revelation of the back side of the words, the things? The incongruous discovery of a part of that back side that is supposed to be hidden by common sense?

- Would *repetition compulsion* not be that which remains of an insistent left-behind? And the death at work there, does it not really mean that it/the id[4] is still, and always, repeated, or that it/the id is still, and always, trapped in the mirror-surface of a present, leaving life drives left-over, or behind?

- Couldn't *deferred action* be interpreted as what is imposed by the under-side of things, after the subject has charged ahead, projected himself or herself forward, seduced by the fascination of the face-to-face?

*

Why and how did Freud get the ingenious idea of this scenario? Because he found himself facing a sign undecipherable except in its paralysis? A sign whose only representation was paralysis? Of course, all representations are paralytic, but they do not know it. Whereas hysteria, deprived of its own sense, of common sense – of all sense? – presents in its miming only this remainder of the meaningful sign: its paralytic setting. Is that what empirically pushed Freud to deconstruct the frame of the proper, of so-called objective reality, in search of conditions that would permit every-thing to be said without hierarchical judgment, without *a priori* appropri-ateness or truth, plunging sign and sense back into their sedimentations, their waste products: the little stories of his patients (male and female), the beginning *plus* the origin, phantasms, dreams, hallucinations, perceptible transference, etc.? Why then does he *also* resubjugate it to the traditional logic of representation? Not only just that, but *also* that? And why the lag in theory that could very well re-establish the authority of the *a priori* of meaning over a setting that calls them into question; a lag that could reduce psychoanalysis to a science pretty much like any other, a *theory* pretty much like any other, an *empiric* like any other. Whereas psychoanalysis, since its setting is not an empiric like any other, has the power to question the dichotomy. In other words, could this empiric undercut certain *a priori* governing the scene of theoretical representation, including the divorce between its oppositions?

If we invoke the fact that Freud knew only the analyst's position, and not the analysand's: armchair/couch, seated/supine, face-to-face/no face-to-face, etc. it might be objected that the argument is much too empirical. The only decisive response might be that is how he missed the relation between the two positions and its possible interpretation. However, the hypothesis cannot be verified; nor should it be. That would be reprivileging one position over the other.

What can be known, on the other hand, is that the setting was imposed by a *practice* of sexuality, and that it inspired a *theory* of sexuality. But has that theory of sexuality not come to be an obstacle for inquiry into representation? Is the *theory* of sexuality not Freud's most regressive contribution? Can we negate or deny the *phallomorphic, phallocentric* character of this theory? – even though, as far as the logic of truth is concerned, Freud's practice does raise certain unavoidable questions: dreams, phantasms, deferred action, overdetermination, etc. How is it that he missed the articulation between his theory and his practice? Was it an ideologically marked social sexual practice that created an obstacle to theoretical progress?

Why all these questions? They interrogate the sign and the text. They ask how we might move beyond their 'true' meanings, their 'right' meanings, their common-sense meanings, without ending up in some other mode of fascination, or of paralysis, or excessive repetition of what has been neglected about the backside, and without crossing over into disorder, simple anarchy? How can we turn the sign over, even in the text? Turn it over so that one side no longer has the monopoly on its value? Turn it around in several different ways: looking into the inversion of all specular operations that projection – confusing that which is projected with identity – has never wanted, or been able, to see, the other being no more than the medium, surface, mirror ensuring the projection of the same. Turning it over also so that its back side need not stay hidden, secret, sacred. This means that the linearity of the utterance, whatever the force of its demonstrations, is no longer sufficient, and that all of its pornographic attestations and transgressions are not sufficient. They lead the sexed body back to the privileging of the projection out in front, even if what is really out front is the backside itself. Fragmenting the text is not enough either ... We need to regestualize the sign, but not within an already prescribed – by the *a priori* of the sign – semiotics of gesture. We have to turn signs over and over in every direction, shake them up well, and not repeat or confirm them from memory, adhering to a medium for identity that cannot recognize the other side of a backside.

And I might express regret that today, even here, the face-to-face was privileged; not that I believe that pirouetting around a classroom or a conference hall can ever eliminate the obstacle of such an old, old story.

XVI

The Poverty of Psychoanalysis[1]
On Some Only Too Pertinent Considerations

In memory of Juliette L.

Gentlemen, psychoanalysts . . .

Why 'gentlemen' only ? Adding 'ladies' changes not a thing: in language, the masculine rules. The subject is expressed in one gender only (unless he discovers the flaw in his truth?). The phallus – and what is more, the Phallus – is the emblem, signifier and production of one single sex.

Therefore, gentlemen psychoanalysts, most of you – if I go by what you say, and write – will not be able to understand my title, what it evokes, what it refers to, in whose memory it is formed, in whose history it is inscribed, in which discourse it has already taken place, what desires it speaks of, or imitates, etc. Most of you will not know how to interpret it. And your attention will be blocked by at least two systems of screens, censorship and repression:

- a psychic reaction of rejection, at first individual, and then collective. Psychoanalysis poor? Psychoanalysis petty or mean? Psychoanalysis pathetic? What is that all about? The phallo-narcissistic investment you have made in your function as analysts will not allow you to tolerate expressions like that, even in questions. You will protest, more or less consciously, like those who wish to keep some desire repressed: psychoanalysis is certainly not in the poorhouse, or petty, or pathetic. That will even strengthen your resistance. Let us hope that it will last only so long as it takes you to understand, and that your institutions themselves are not founded on ignorance of your poverty, of your pettiness, and of how pathetic you are. . . .

- a desire to know, at least for those who still have it. Go ask some professor of philosophy or mathematics, or some political militant or ex-militant (male or female), what I am talking about here. As 'subjects presumed to know,' they will perhaps get the benefits of your transference . . .

To know what exactly? Something about philosophy? About politics? Or something about the way the unconscious functions? You intend to separate philosophy and politics from the unconscious, but you have been mercilessly misled, since in reality they are mutually determining in the history of knowledge. You do not want to know that the unconscious, your own concept of the unconscious, did not shoot up fully armored from the head of Freud, that it was not created *ex nihilo* at the end of the nineteenth century, springing forth in order to impose its truth on the whole of history – including world history . . . – past, present and to come. The unconscious was discovered, and should be understood, spoken about, and interpreted, within a tradition. It exists within, through, and for a culture. Failing to put it in its proper place, you reduce it to . . . ? A goal or object of your desire whose truth still escapes you, some object 'O' or 'o' that maintains your drives in effervescence, keeps you on the run, impassions and terrorizes you, turns you on, and makes you all band together, all stick together, all resemble each other . . . Economic solution – in every sense of the term – to the general crisis of indifference hanging over the Occident. Perhaps you did not know about that?

In your contempt for culture – which is very profitable for you – you resent some men's and women's questioning of the consecrated values of psychoanalysis. A psychoanalyst, male or female, who examines the history, culture, and politics into which psychoanalysis is inscribed, is supposedly not one of you any more. Psychoanalysis must remain closed in, without limits or determinants other than itself, with no authorizations – of existence or essence – other than its own. In a word: *whole,* absolute, and without historical foundations. Its theory and practice are founded on just a little dab of history. It is enough to have read Freud and Lacan – even better to stick to the latter only – to be a real analyst.

But how is it that you are authorized to decide if someone is an analyst if, according to you, 'the analyst is authorized only by himself'? Are your criticisms founded on that 'by *him*self'? Those criticisms are, in any case, nothing but rejections: 'she or he is not an analyst,' 'that is not analysis.' What determines this proscription, and this 'foreclosure'? Your own? In accordance with what law? In the name of what name? The name of a father of psychoanalysis to whose unconscious every unconscious must conform? The imperialism of an Unconscious whose subjects everybody, males and females, would have to become? Well then, what you should say is: he or she is not, or is no longer, subject to that Unconscious. And then listen to what the unconscious still has to say. Because, either the unconscious is nothing more than what you have already heard – and so whatever unheard things your female and male patients still might try to say, that is never it, never the id[2] – or the unconscious is desire that tries to speak itself, and as analysts, you have to listen without excluding, however *your own* desire may be implicated in listening to everything, and whatever the risk that *your own* death might ensue . . .

Do you not think that everything that functions in the name of history and in the name of psychoanalysis speaks of the economy of *your* death? Or of *your* economy of death? How can you be an analyst and not deal unendingly with that question? And not wonder, always and everywhere, if analysts might not be protecting themselves from death by imposing it on the other? And if they might not be defending themselves against their own violence or hatred by imputing it or leaving it to the other? And if analysts might become analysts only so that the other can live the relation to death in their stead; while, neutral and benevolent, silent as the tomb, realistic, objective, impartial, and scientific spectators, they are witness to ... tragedies that are not, or are no longer, their own? Should what we call the 'analyst subject' be interpreted as a casting out of death? Or as its effect? As a passage to some beyond? Which would bring forth what? A ghost? Some kind of mechanism? In any case: something in-corporeal? What can the appearance or the persistence of such a status of the subject mean in our history? How can we know without questioning history or retraversing it?

In other words, how do you interpret the effects of a culture on the unconscious: your own and your analysands', both male and female? What if the unconscious were at one and the same time the result of censorship and repression imposed in and by a certain history, *and* a not yet come to pass, a reservoir of the still to come? Then, your rejections, reprimands, and lack of comprehension would just be turning the future into the past. What you would be doing is reducing the still unsubjugated to the level of the already subjugated, the still uspoken or unsaid of language to what *one* language has already paralyzed into mutism, or kept down in silence. Might you be – without your knowledge – the products and defenders of an existing order, its officials of reprimand and repression, making sure that this order is the only one possible, that there is no other imaginable word, desire or language, aside from the ones already in place, that there is no other culture authorized but the monocratism of patriarchal discourse? Are you culturalists without your knowledge? Some of your statements seem to testify to that ... symptomatically.

Now you happen to benefit from prestige, power, love, and transference as a function of the projection onto you of a desire still to come. So, if you are not there to hear it (the id),[3] if that is not your job, if all you care about is invariably reducing every word you hear to what has already been expressed or written, to forcing it into your economy of repetition, your economy of death, then you should say as much, and write it, clearly. Let us know. So that certain men, or women, do not expect from you (and at what price!) what you neither can nor want to give them, so that they do not go on asking questions you neither can nor want to answer.

You could go out and boast about having perfected and put on the market an extraordinarily profitable 'lifetrap' (R. M. Rilke's word), a lifetrap no other economy ever had the notion, or the audacity, to offer its buyer-consumers. Something they have to spend their life-savings on, only to end up with nothing. Something in the name of which they would have the right to ask everything of you, and pay accordingly, only to find, after the demand has exhausted all their resources, that your only answer is *'nothingness,'* or *'dis-being.'* Go ahead and proclaim it openly. The market is such that you will still have clients. But not all men, and certainly not all women. Some men and some women no longer want anything to do with your nothingness. No matter what seductions, simulations, jewels, veils, semblances, or beliefs you employ to dress it up.

So do not keep saying, in some kind of naive pretense, that analysis 'sticks to what is most individual in the desire of the subject – individual as defined by his history and told in his symptoms,' and 'that it is thus out of what is most individual in the symptom that the universal of a science becomes possible'[4] (Eugénie Lemoine-Luccioni, *Partage des femmes*, Paris: Seuil, 1976, p. 11, [pp. 4–5]).[5] Because, aside from the fact that one might ask you what this relationship is between *one science*, yours, and the universal, it very quickly becomes obvious, in reading you, that you establish this relation in a univocally deductive and, above all, normative way. Which is to say that whoever knows *your* universal, the Lacanian code, knows *a priori* how you are going to interpret 'what is most individual in the desire of the subject.' We might even say that a filter is already in place in front of your ears; it closes them off or opens them up as required; or that they have been injured, and fitted with an orthodoxical prosthesis before your analysands begin to speak. Her or his individual only serves as *proof* of the rightness of your universal.

Freud and the first psychoanalysts did not act in quite that manner, at least not right away. For them, each analysis was an opportunity to discover a new facet of practice and theory. Each analysand was heard as if he or she were contributing something new to both. But from the moment psychoanalytic 'science' claimed to have found the universal law of the functioning of the unconscious – each analysis being nothing more than an application or a demonstration of it – this 'science' became nothing more than a dead-end, knowledge from a bygone era, the stuff of university diplomas and theoretical qualifications, enforceable with sanctions.

What if the price to pay for the very existence of psychoanalysis was never submitting to *one* theory and to *one* science? What if the source of its singularity was that it cannot be complete, reduced to an already defined corpus, a knowledge already in place, an already determined law? That it remain 'interminable'? What if each new analysis were as much an elaboration of practice and theory as all those that went before, and if a pre-existing model of analysis indicated only that analysis no longer exists. Would you object that that would be chaos? Well, you would be admitting that you have forgotten that every living body, every unconscious, every psychic economy brings its own order to analysis. You have only to listen. But a pre-existing law prevents that.

And, since you claim that there is only 'individual' desire, how is that you can force analytic material into a lexicon or a syntax, into schemata, and graphs, and mathematical formulas foreign to that individual analysis? What kind of gesture is it that subjugates the language of the analysand to a system of signifiers that is not his or her own? In other words, even if there is a dictionary or a bible of Freudian or Lacanian discourse, there cannot be a dictionary or a grammar of psychoanalysis, under threat of forcing the analysand into adaptation to a language different from the one she or he speaks. Interpretation and listening on the part of the analyst then become nothing more than acts of mastery over the analysand. They are instruments in the service of a master and of *his* truth. The psychoanalyst is already enslaved, and reproduces his or her own enslavement.

In practice, when the language of the analysand is listened to, anticipated, with reference to an already established system – an already articulated, fixed, frozen code – are her or his needs/desires not captured or suspended by that system in a formal and empty ecstasy? Do analysands not end up in some kind of permanent hypnosis or suggestion, whose medium would be a certain type of language-functioning, whose effects would be sustained long-term? Anyone who tried to analyze those effects would automatically be declared outside the ethics of pyschoanalysis ...

So 'patients' – especially if they want to become or to remain analysts themselves – will have to pump life and strength into the system, their own lives and their own strength. The strictly silent benevolent neutrality of the practicing analyst fascinates and inspires the analysand to fill in his or her signifiers–containers–receptacles with the discourse of the other. I mean ... the Other. Not the analysand's other – or the analyst's – her or his unconscious, if you will, but an Other's (with capital O, since you insist), an *a priori* authority, and *a posteriori* as well for that matter, always already and still there, law-trap of an omniscient, omnipotent God the father-mother (the two being merged in the capital letter ...), keeper of the duly veiled Truth of every unconscious. The analysis 'terminates' with the submission of every man and every woman – having thus tautologically become subjects – with no real difference between the sexes – to an order that makes their needs/desires conform to the desire, always invisible, of a Master. Perhaps one might venture to suggest that this Master is of their own making, that it is the Unconscious made School, a sort of micro-culture both primitive in its magical components and decadent in the cult of Truth it imposes, terrorizing precisely in proportion to the amount of ignorance it hides.

Is it not rather surprising that you criticize certain women and men for their philosophical questioning, given that your schoolmaster literally brought you up on philosophy? Not using questions, it is true. But are you not projecting back onto others all that you never digested in his discourse? All that you resent, all that you loathe about him? How does the object of this rejection preferentially end up being a woman's word? In general, is that not a common mechanism in (your) society?

Of course, Lacan delights in not citing his sources or his resources, which does not help in properly assimilating him. He intentionally plays the seduction game of the philosophy professor who 'knows more,' and assures himself of the love of his young pupils. Even so, he did repeat, until you were tired of hearing about it: read *The Symposium* or *De Anima*, for example. He was Hegelian enough to have been credited, during some of his seminars on psychoanalysis at Vincennes, with the discovery of the master–slave dialectic! He admitted, in certain relatively famous instances of acting out, his passion for Heidegger. Etc.

So how is it that you can read the *Ecrits* without having read what the *Ecrits* discuss? How can you understand what 'the Thing' or the 'thing in itself' (that you borrow from him, and label as Freudian) are all about, when you are quite ignorant of how much of the 'Thing' he himself borrowed from Kant? How do you understand the difference he estab-lished between 'to speak' and 'to tell,' without understanding what he understood about it from Heidegger? Two little reminders, among many others ... Since all these 'symbolic' or 'imaginary' components, all this weaving of knowledges and identifications, that constitute your Master's word are little known, or unknown, to you, his word can appear before you only as Truth.

All this must have serious consequences for your listening as analysts 'presumed to know,' since you leave uninterpreted the difference between the knowledge, or knowledges, of your Father–Master, and your own.

What kinds of suggestions, trances, ecstasies, convulsions, and death do you transmit in consequence? Of course, Lacan desires knowledge. That, no doubt, is what commands your admiration, and even a certain kind of beatitude? He loves knowledge more than the unconscious. Or, he loves the unconscious for the knowledge it brings him. Is that what has left you all a bit stupid, like children of a father who knows too much, or a father 'presumed to know everything,' whose limits you cannot even imagine, under pain of confronting your 'lack,' under pain of being forced to question the function of lack within your own desire? You would rather be the sons of God than deprived of your lack? So then, you have Lacan as God of your unconscious, of your School, of your world, of the world? Final avatar of a – psychoanalytic – incarnation of salvation. Do you not know that when science comes to power, God is dead? And your god is a specter that haunts you because you cannot discover his nature. Or interpret, according to your science, his provenance or his cause in relation to desire. Therefore perhaps. . . ? His relation to sex? *Real* sex too.

Your often mixed-up and contradictory statements concerning the status of the phallus in relation to the organ or to real sex – are they not caused by the desire to keep the veil in front of your eyes, and everyone else's, so that you will not see, and we will not see, the sex of your Father in psychoanalysis? To bury in an unsolvable mystery, in a well of invisibility, in a capital letter whose crest rises up to infinity – the relationship your father has with sex: your psychoanalytic primal scene. Does the imaginary and symbolic value of the phallus need a capital letter because, in the real, the sexual relation is not supposed to exist, and some sort of phallo-narcissistic supplement is needed to take its place? Unless we interpret its effects.

It is not a question of underestimating the real. But ask yourselves if the real might not be some very repressed-censored-forgotten 'thing' to do with the body.

Alas! The body, for you, is always already engineered by language, a language. The domination of that language means that 'the sexual relation does not exist,' any more than woman exists, statements whose theoretical impact certainly does not exclude impact on the most banal everyday reality. On the contrary . . . Confining oneself to Truth at the expense of corporeal sex has the most unfortunate consequences . . .

For example: 'Woman is the figure of the scene of the veil that covers over the primal scene: she dances the eternal and often *ridiculous* dance of the veils. She alone knows what nothingness the veil covers, while, fascinated, man watches. Thanks to which the sexual act can take place' (Lemoine-Luccioni, p. 180 [p. 152]). (My emphasis on *ridiculous*: the dance of the veils, dance of a cosmic mystery and reality above and beyond any already constituted subjectivity, is the sexual and religious rite *par excellence* in many traditions. This scene is played out among the mother- or the lover-goddess, the gods, and the universe. Its purpose is not to conceal nothingness, but to break through illusion, and to approach the act of creation or of generation of the world.)

It scares you, doesn't it... ? But why, exactly? If the relation between the sexes can be reduced to man's fascination with the nothingness behind its veils, then there is no recourse against the most profoundly negative effects of nihilism. As for nihilism's constructive goal – the fall of idols – well, about that, you want to hear nothing. Is psychoanalysis today not the practice of a nihilism that unfortunately does not even know it is one? In that case, 'benevolent neutrality,' with respect to 'saying everything,' could also be understood as the ultimate form of a certain kind of indif- ference, where everything would be the equivalent of everything else, with perhaps a few little variously named differences noticeable against a unitary background: it is all the same anyway. How could it really be otherwise if there are not *two* sexes, each with its own imaginary and its own order?

And if 'allegiance to castration'(!) is not the condition for opening up the imaginary and tautological circle of the subject to the perception and desire of some *other,* but rather 'everyone's experience that their desire is the desire of the Other' (Lemoine-Luccioni, p. 180 [p. 152]), and if it subjects the two sexes to the cult of the lack of, or in, the Other, then psychoanalysis is a prorogation of a religion of privation and frustration, in which no incarnation of the divine is possible. Its law is the imposition of nothingness for the sake of Nothingness. It inscribes nothingness onto the deepest unconscious of sexed bodies.

Bodies with no reason even to look at each other any more, since 'there is nothing real to see in either the one or the other' (Lemoine-Luccioni, p. 180 [p. 152]). Hence 'unbearable nudity'? And 'beauty as ornament, that is, as weapon and as cover-up' (Lemoine-Luccioni, p. 181 [p. 153])? But then why, if there is nothing real to see in either one, do we have a 'delib- erate rejection, on the woman's part, of her own body, in favor of beauty' (Lemoine-Luccioni, pp. 181–2 [p. 153])? If for you the scopic drive is constitutive of the subject, and yet there is 'nothing to see,' aside from what has already been ornamented, armed, and covered up, what concep- tion of the subject are we talking about? Woman still has to give up her body in order to perpetuate it. A body so ugly it can be looked at only when covered up ...

Don't you worry about philosophy. Philosophy couldn't care less. All of you, men and women, are stuck in nihilism without knowing it. For example, when you say 'all discourses are equal.' Which is not true, even 'for a subject in analysis or for an analyst' (Lemoine-Luccioni, p. 11 [p. 4]). The subject is determined by certain discourses (by the discourse of mastery – by philosophy) more than by others. After the end of philosophy, philosophy inspires discount discourses among those who are not aware of its end, and the truth, duly exploited by professionals in publishing, comes cheap. The *original* designer label only has to be removed. Actually, there is no reason to put one on in the first place any more. You bring everything down to the same level where it is all equal, and all worth nothing. Your language is nothing more than a knock-off, and you do not even know it. The only thing that still seems to regulate it is a relationship to contradiction, emancipated from all principles, and from all vital imperative. This polemics for the world's end plays with language forms, leaving aside respect for their meanings, order, beauty, and generations.

And so all that is retained from the truth of men is what splits women up, and assigns them their lot, puts them in their place? The effects on women of ambivalence, without the safety catch of a negation that founds truth? The effects on women of the underside of 'male' discourse? In order for them to be one(s), women must take care of the split. Torn between 'yes' and 'no,' women are the site of the irreparable wound (imputed to their sex [organ]); the wound of all the 'I want/I don't want, I love/I hate, I'll take it/I'll leave it' underlying and covered over by the True, the Good and the Beautiful of men. When you affirm that 'man is and he remains, as man – and assuming he exists as a man who would not be a woman at the same time – one' (Lemoine-Luccioni, p. 9 [p. 3]), and that 'knowledge does not divide him' (Lemoine-Luccioni, p. 9 [p. 3]), are you not making woman the bearer of what you call the 'splitting of the subject,' are you not reducing her to the effects of man's relation with the unconscious? Because, if man is not divided in his knowledge, he has no unconscious. Or, at least, he wants to know nothing about it. And his own schiz can be understood only as that which splits women up and puts them in their place. You go on: 'It is understood that woman is not; and yet if she should disappear, man's symptom would also disappear, as Lacan says. Where there is no symptom, there is no language, and therefore, no man either' (Lemoine-Luccioni, p. 10 [p. 4]). So it falls to woman to hold onto her (?) symptoms, to remain within 'her lot and her suffering,' 'the paradise of jouissance' (Lemoine-Luccioni, p. 8 [p. 2]), or else she 'disappears as woman'(Lemoine-Luccioni, p. 10, [p. 4]) . . . !

And 'no sexual revolution will ever move those dividing lines, neither the one between man and woman, nor the one that divides woman' (Lemoine-Luccioni, p. 9, [p. 3]). Let us take note of this statement in a book that claims to be 'an analytic, and not a philosophical or a political, work,' a book that 'is not concerned with the issue of whether women should make a revolution in order to overcome a lack of recognition that has up till now kept them from speaking' (Lemoine-Luccioni, p. 11 [p. 4]).

How is it that such contradictory statements can be made two pages apart? Is the 'neutrality' of the analyst not sticking its neck out a little bit here, handing down dogma about history from the depths of an armchair?

And when you write: 'My thinking always coincides with what my analysands (men or women) are telling me, as well as, through what they are saying, with the analysand that I am; since one hears only what one is capable of saying, but would not say without the other' (Lemoine-Luccioni, p. 11 [p. 5]), 'one' feels like asking you where this 'coinciding' might lead. Might it be leading up to making the other say, or preventing the other from saying, what you aren't capable of hearing? In whose name do you write 'he' or 'she' said such and such a thing, had such and such a phantasm, etc., if you don't reveal where you stand with respect to 'him'or 'her,' to *your* sex, to *your* things and *your* phantasms? How do you decide who is speaking?

It is easy for you to object that being an analyst means listening to what the other says without taking sides or making judgments, but how do you determine which is *you* and which is the *other*? And is this other she or other he not the other of you? How do you know if you do not interpret *your* transference onto that other? Technically speaking, it is true that this is not a simple issue. But hiding behind what analysands tell you in order to affirm: the unconscious is, and is only, what I write in their name, and it is not I who says so, but those men and women, and I take no position whatsoever – ideological, political, philosophical … phallocratic? or sexed? – regarding what I hear, seems at best naive. Nevertheless that naivety leads up to certain judgments and condemnations. Unconscious *oblige*, you protest? Well, whose?

And if you 'impute' to woman an unconscious that is not hers, or if you claim that 'it is only when she is all, that is, as she is seen by man, that the dear woman can have an unconscious' (Jacques Lacan, *Encore*, Paris: Seuil, 1975, p. 90 [pp. 98–9]),[6] or, worse still, if you maintain that woman does not exist except as symptom of man's language (Lemoine-Luccioni, 10 [p. 4]), then certain 'complaints' are less 'untenable' than you would like to think (Lemoine-Luccioni, p. 7 [p. 1]). Women do complain – and sometimes even before the law, in cases of rape, for example – that they have no access to their own desires under your law. But all 'the alleged reasons women give are unconvincing' (Lemoine-Luccioni, p. 7 [p. 1]), and 'although it is true that no one can or should accept slavery, the only question that remains to be asked when it is accepted, and even begged for, is: what is it accepted for, in exchange for what benefit?' (Lemoine-Luccioni, p. 7 [p. 1]). I will let you answer that one . . .

How could you, though, given that your male masters have taught you that 'desire is the same regardless of sex' (Moustapha Safouan, *La sexualité féminine dans la doctine freudienne*, Paris: Seuil, 1976, p. 157),[7] and that it is difficult to sexualize it in the imaginary, and, in a word, that one language – traditionally their language – is the only possible language. Assuming all of that, all you can do with the 'benefits' of slavery reaped by men in their mastery – is attribute them to women. Whether you have begun to say anything in all of this about women's own desire is another question altogether. Because it is not the either devalued or over-valued discovery of their relation to objects that 'leads women astray;' it is rather their exile from whatever might be their space. Ecstasied from their space-time, always moving from place to place in the male phallic imaginary, they seek to incarnate themselves in some 'thing' man can play with, or through which he might be able to rediscover value in his own world of objects (Lemoine-Luccioni, pp. 154–5 [pp. 130–1]). Why not some element in his House? Why not some member of his School? Why not some book-'o' produced in the field of his language-'O'?

For each other, for themselves, women are still not there, anywhere: touching everything, they do not retouch themselves and each other. Lost in space, like ghosts. Dissolved, absent, empty, abandoned, a part of themselves, apart from themselves, apart from each other (Lemoine-Luccioni, p. 154 [pp. 129–30]). Whereas, if they were ever to come into the imaginary of their own desires, they would always be moving and yet always at home, finding their security in mobility, and their jouissance in motion. Nomads with no boundaries other than their own living bodies. But, for that to happen, they cannot stay put where they've been put. They have to be able to leave the property where they have been legally confined, in order to try to find their place(s). And passing a law, in order to protect them from madness by 'allowing them to keep their furniture in case of divorce' could only be the idea of 'an eminent *male* Italian criminal lawyer' (my emphasis; Lemoine-Luccioni, pp. 154–5 [p. 130]). No doubt it is to protect them from going mad that psychoanalysts today keep them on their couches. In any case, once confined there, mad or not, nobody will hear anything more about it/the id . . .[8]

Then you will be able to stay within the circle of your own imaginary. Which is, in your own words, totalitarian. That explains how you are able to force the becoming of the desire of the little girl into the same explanatory schema as the little boy's, without even making the disclaimer that you are really just talking about a child (in the neuter), or about man (in the generic). This power play can be shown for what it is in an example – that is often where parapraxes appear; it is about a 'piece of furniture' (again ...), a piece of furniture 'at odds with the space of language and Truth' (Safouan, p. 23 [p. 133]).[9] Absolutely – if a piece of furniture has some role to play in the schema you apply to the girl's demand – made with 'sealed lips' – you can go right ahead ... It can never contradict your schema. Your appeal to Marx confirms it. The goods speak only the language of their producers–exchangers–consumers. So a 'piece of furniture' will never say anything more than what your desire intends it to say. And if 'none of us gets a dispensation from thinking about ourselves as a piece of furniture' (?) (Safouan, p. 23 [p. 133]), it is a bit different to have to be one without even being able to think about it for lack of a language. Which is what the cult of your hollow divinities requires ... How else are we to take 'seriously' (Safouan, p. 21, [p. 131]) your fetish for capital letters – Other, Thing, Demand, Truth, Phallus – if not, once again, as a nihilistic religion with respect to which all living, corporeal, social reality seems as nothing to you.

Yes, gentlemen psychoanalysts, desire is linked to an epoch (Safouan, p. 19, [p. 130]). That is precisely what allows you today to invest yours in psychoanalysis, but that is also why you find yourselves called into question, whether you like it or not, by women's. And when you reduce what they are trying to tell you to the same old discourse you have always spoken, or when you stick the label of *militant feminism* – now there is a word that does seem to force you out of your neutrality as soon as it comes up – on it, on the unconscious,[10] it signifies your resistance to acknowledging certain limits. Is it because they mark the limits of *your* imaginary?

And you want to keep it absolute. To protect it, you have to deny certain facts by univocally reducing them to phantasms. Some examples, perhaps?

The fact that you attempt, even today, to demonstrate that your analysands' rape anxieties bear no relation to reality will make just about any woman laugh (?). Her/these 'phantasms' (?) must rather come to be understood as memories of traumatic experiences, as images of events submitted to, seen, or heard, or as the effects of a set of restrictions, interdicts, impossibilities, or oppressions, that are everywhere present in the everyday life of all women. But man, who fails to recognize there his own desire to rape –

for not having analyzed it? – can only deny, in the name of woman, the reality of the object of his own phantasms.

When you affirm that, from a very early age, we distinguish between the sexes using all kinds of insignia, especially clothing, that have nothing to do with perceived differences in the body of the other (Safouan, p. 14 [p. 126]), are you not saying that what matters to you is what is hidden, what masks, or ornaments, or makes a relation between two bodies impossible or forbidden, except – occasionally – through breaking and entering? That the cause of your desire is the veil that needs to be lifted – occasionally? The occasional 'semblance' that needs to be deflowered – without knowing it? That it is the seduction of rape that both motivates and disappoints your desire? Because the body already has holes in it? Does it only just have holes? Does your language not have holes? Are your capital letters not just filling in the holes? Does this parade of letters and master-words not trap speech in great holes where the words
ring – and reason – in the void? Hence your fear and anxiety about a certain 'thing'?

When you say that 'the phallic conditioning of the narcissism of the subject, regardless of sex, *is established in, and only in, analytic observation,* a thesis no direct observation could either prove or disprove,' the latter type of observation being 'as useless here as it is with respect to the Oedipus complex' (Safouan, p. 15 [p. 127]; my emphasis), it is really worth it to hold in the laughter long enough to ask you: why do you make statements that so patently contradict reality? What purpose do they serve? Do you really believe in this? If you do ... do you ever leave your consulting rooms? If you do not, then what is your reality?

Reading you, one discovers that, in fact, 'it is not enough simply not to be a feminist to know one's place in the business of sex!' (Safouan, p. 12 [p. 125]). Well, if you were feminists – unlikely hypothesis given the real difference between the sexes, and your existence outside of historical time – perhaps you would know your own place a little better? In that case, you would understand – perhaps – why Freud insists that his patients have vaginal orgasms. It is proof of his own potency. 'That is hardly an injunction to which it would be easy to respond' (Safouan, p. 17 [p. 129]) ... ? On the contrary, actually ... Women do give themselves, give each other, 'vaginal' orgasms with no trouble. All they need do is allow themselves not to satisfy *your* imaginary. You refuse to recognize one fact: women have orgasms very well without you. That does not stop them from wanting to have them with you, even though, generally, it is not quite so 'easy to respond.' However, most of them tell you nothing, 'show' you nothing, about their jouissance, even their jouissance with you. Maybe so that they will not be made frigid, frozen by your gaze, your desire, your discourse, and your theory? That allows you to believe they have no sexual life, or no longer have one. And is it not astonishing that you decree in your erudite way that ' "vaginal" frigidity constitutes a definite symptomatic problem in the sexual life of women' (Safouan, p. 18 [p. 128]), without ever wondering whether it might not really be the effects, on her, of a problem in male sexuality? In your 'verbal parade' (Safouan, p. 16 [p. 128]), you never even question the quality of your male sex life.

You are just as erudite when you state that, 'for us, female homosexuality represents an obstacle on the path toward the assumption of symbolic castration' (Safouan, p. 127), but you are forgetting one fact: your own phantasms are making the law. That symbolic you impose as universal, purified of any empirical or historical contingencies, is *your* imaginary transformed into order, social order too. When you write, on the last page, that 'if we finally come to think of marriage as an exchange between men whose object is woman, we find that she takes on the unconscious significa-tion of all objects of exchange,' and that 'despite the ever increasing liberty that prevails in the choice of a wife, the fact remains that one always marries his father-in-law or his brother-in-law,' but that 'these remarks can easily be transposed into a perspective from which marriage could be considered as an exchange between women whose object is man'(?) (Safouan, p. 127), 'one' might ask you if your own non-assumption of symbolic castration – to put it in your own words – has not led you to 'transpose' just any social organization onto just any other, imagined according to your fantasies and your denial of homosexuality. Has your symbolic ever been anything else but the legal guarantee of strict cultural endogamy among males? Male psychoanalysts, among others.

You remind us that the mother is the first object of desire for the little girl just as she is for the little boy, and then you conclude one more time that 'everything happens for the little girl exactly as for the boy' (Safouan, p. 11), neglecting the fact that desire for a body same as one's own, is not necessarily identical to desire for a body different from one's own. Smelling, tasting, touching, seeing, listening to a body the same as, or different from, one's own has an effect on desire. Is sex not always inscribed, and not in some secondary way, in the qualities of a body? Is sex itself an organ separated/abstracted from its body? Is the imaginary you are listening from, where you situate your male and female analysands, incorporeal? It negates, or denies, from the very beginning, that sex is also constitutive of the body. This might correspond to male phantasms of possible separation between the two, but does not make a lot of sense to a woman, unless she is imprisoned in *your* imaginary. An imaginary that is exclusively dependent on organs? Erogenous zones and their 'objects', sex(es) and language(s).

Is psychoanalysis then a theory and a practice dealing with organs? Like medicine? Generally speaking, psychoanalysis and medicine are both unknowingly caught up in a technocratic process with little concern for sexed matter, or about the site where organs come together in living bodies.

In any case, the system of representations and signifiers accounting for the psychoanalytic experience is unusually poor in representatives of the body: of the blood and circulation, of the air and respiration, of the consumption and metabolism of food, etc. What kinds of vision, of concepts, and of listening, does the psychoanalyst have in relation to the body? Is that body dead? Purely mechanical? A libido-producing machine? What is forgotten or foreclosed about the body, and about sensitive, sexed corporeal matter, when this mechanism is put in place?

You talk a lot about the debt owed to the father, but very little, or never, about the debt owed to the mother. Does that not show that, for you, blood, life, and body are not worth much? Only organs have value, it would seem. One might well ask you if what prevents the relation between the sexes – phantasms, object *o* – could be the symptoms of an unpaid debt to the mother – false bodies, or semblances, pure objects taking the place of a repressed-censured relation to the body that gives life. This unpaid, and at least partly unpayable, debt to the mother, that we would do well to acknowledge, becomes evident in the impossibility of sexual relations, in the obligation to reproduce: children, phantasms, theory, science, etc. But women are the ones who continue to supply the material substrata – the nourishing body, blood and life – while you exercise the power of your organs.

Of course, returning to historically dated anatomical–physiological arguments is out of the question, but we do have to examine the empire of a morpho-logic, the imposition as norms of discourse – and more generally of language – of formations corresponding to the necessities or desires of one sex alone.

The empire of the phallus – of the Phallus – is necessitated by the establishment of a society based on patriarchal power, where the generative power of the natural–maternal is taken over as a – phallic – attribute by god-men, instituting a new order that is supposed to *appear* natural. From then on, "nature" is represented as either good or bad, depending on whether it has been created by men, or engendered by women. The resulting upheavals affecting the organization of the imaginary and the symbolic can still be read in the Greek tragedies and myths from the dawn of our logical era. The values underlying its articulation and deployment have since then been isomorphic with the male imaginary.

And the way that you dismiss as 'anatomical–physiological reasoning' the questioning of phallic domination, bears witness, at the very least, to intentional ignorance, and perhaps even to a refusal to interpret this domination as regulating, through the order of language it commands and which sustains it, all of your systems of representation, as well as to a refusal to examine *your* way of looking at the male–female difference as taking place solely within one discourse that fails to recognize its sexual determinations.

This means that what you claim as universal is sexed according to your own necessities. Since they are *yours*, you cannot see that they are particular. You reject any outside or inside that resists them, and prefer to accuse others of all kinds of stupidity rather than to have to submit to what you call … symbolic castration: that is, the possibility of an order different from your own.

The repression you exercise against women's speech that does not conform to your conception of the symbolic, and to your symbolic world, is therefore absolutely predictable, as are the arguments (?) you invoke, and the tone in which you make your decrees. Since you are implacably programmed by a history you refuse to question, you have not, up to this point, developed or written anything on the subject that is especially astonishing.

Thus when you 'simply tender the remark' that 'the question of what she wants (the girl) is just as much the question of the girl herself as of the Other, whether it is about Freud, or ourselves, or first and foremost about the mother' (Safouan, p. 20 [p. 131]), you do not even bother to wonder about the nature of this 'Other' to whom you relegate the daughter and the mother (graced with a capital letter so she can fit into your system?). You go on: 'There is no 'you' unless coming from the great Other' (Safouan, p. 20 [p. 131]), that is, coming from an ecstatic projection constituted as all-powerful imaginary reality (the 'cornerstone' of your symbolic concatenation?) from where 'I' comes back to me in inverted form.

And what if this schema did not fit the girl's desire? What if this relation to projection, to inversion, to the transcendental, to the imaginary, were dependent on a male sexual economy? On being beside oneself, or outside oneself, as in erection and ejaculation? Man appears to have tried to reappropriate, not without disappropriation, her desire for him, using a phallic morpho-logic constituted through his transcendental imaginary. You want to impose the answer to your own needs as universal law, thereby reducing, in an endlessly repeated gesture, sexual difference to nothing.

Trying to find a possible imaginary, or to find one once more, through the movements of two lips touching each other (cf. *Speculum, de l'autre femme*, particularly 'L'Incontournable volume,' and *Ce Sexe qui n'en est pas un*, particularly the title essay, 'La 'Mécanique' des fluides,' and 'Quand nos lèvres se parlent') is not a regression to anatomy, nor to a concept of 'nature,' any more than it is a call to return to genital norms – women have several pairs of two lips! It is an attempt to open up the autological and tautological circle of systems of representation and their discourses, so that women can speak their sex. The 'at least two' lips no longer correspond to your morpho-logic; they do not conform to Lacan's 'not all,' a model to which the One is necessary. 'There is One,' but something escapes it, resists it, is always lacking; there is One, but with holes, fault-lines, silences that forbid silence, that speak to each other, whisper to each other, etc.: a real in revolt against the law, but already produced under the empire of the law? Woman – unwoman, awoman – is privileged to dwell under the sign of this lack or this fault.

Aristotelian model? Or already Parmenidian? The circle of the same is posited or presupposed. Within the 'at least two' lips, the becoming form – and the becoming form of the circle as well – is not only never complete, or completable, but actually takes place (without ex-sistence) thanks to this incompleteness; the lips and the borders of the body respond to each other, back and forth, and in this movement is born, perpetuated, and developed, a formation of desire, an imaginary of the sexed body whose form(s) are never detached from the matter that engendered them. Form and matter – the very division between the two terms is overcome – engender each other ceaselessly, and no form can be extrapolated from the body-support that gave birth to it.

The constitution of woman's sex does not therefore signify the 'lack of,' or the 'atrophy of,' or 'envy' for, the male sex (except when socio-culturally induced); nor does it signify a univocal call for completion by the male sex in the penile or phallic mode. Sexual difference – when there is any – carries a risk, never foreseeable, of increase or of decrease in jouissance, and even in desire. For woman as for man.

The risk of diminished desire on the woman's part is, on the other hand, completely predictable when, by your definition, sex operates normally. It is easy to understand why, according to you, women are so often frigid, and why you pay so much attention to the extinction of their sexual life, which 'they do not even suspect!' (Safouan, p.16 [p. 128]). Are you ready to question the formations of your own narcissism so that things might change? Have you decided to examine your topo-logic so that sexual difference can be reorganized in order to prevent one side from paying the narcissistic price of jouissance? So that women will not have to renounce, and even forget, their own auto-eroticism in order to become the instruments of yours?

And so, as your master Lacan suggests, we must take another look at the status of the unconscious in women. For, 'if libido is only masculine, then it is only where the dear woman is all, that is, only where she is seen by man, there only, can the dear woman have an unconscious' (Lacan, *Encore*, p. 90 [pp. 98–9]). 'That is why I say that the imputation of an unconscious is an incredible act of charity,' concludes he – as a premise (Lacan, p. 90 [p. 98])? But does this unconscious safeguard women's desire or take it from them? Does it give them libido or take it from them? According to men, it 'imputes' it to them. Well, that does not mean the same thing as structuring their 'drives,' unless sexual difference is once again annulled in a complementarity where the roles are divided up by men?

You say that you hear women speak of their desires – phallic desires among others – the ones you 'impute' to them. Do they have no others? When large numbers of women say that, since their analysis, they feel 'closed in,' 'closed off,' 'withdrawn,' 'that some part of themselves has become inaccessible,' 'that they do not know how to get it back,' etc., what symptoms are they talking about? And the reactions you imagine are very rare: paranoid legal cases brought against you, explosions of hatred, desire for vengeance … More often, it is a question of profound depression or anguish. Caused by the disappearance of their power? By the 'imputation' of a jouissance that is not their own? And the resulting narcissistic effects?

You object: 'Why listen to them? And why are you stuck at the 'manifest' level, and not hearing what is 'latent' in it?' What if it were you who were not hearing yourselves try to close women up in your projections? In the discourse underlying the listening you do? A latent substratum of your economy uninterpreted by you?

At a more manifest level, you have guided women to adapt to your society a little better. Many of them recognize the debt they owe you: you helped them to put up with the various types of conjugal-familial institutions, or to enter the job market, or remain there. They experience fewer crises in relation to your order. But what pain when they confess what it actually costs them! That is, when they are not too ashamed to admit it …

Of course, some of them have, more or less triumphantly, acceded to the phallic 'division,' to their 'lot'; they are past mistresses now in the application of your laws, terrorizing and contemptuous of women who do not submit to it. Like the vestals of a cult they believe in. Not without having sacrificed part of themselves to it. And now they demand that oblation from their peers, the ones you call militants. But the former's militant orthodoxy is invisible to you, so you have as yet not begun to analyze it. It is necessary for keeping order, is it not?

One of its current controversies is the (jubilant) assumption of *bisexu-ality* as the path to salvation. A parry to women's demands to accede to their own desires and their own language? While they are trying to become men, they abandon their 'complaints' and their 'claims'? And then we have peace and quiet once again.

But is bisexuality not both inscribed on the body and a process of identification? And since the anatomical–physiological scares the devil out of you (at least consciously), I imagine that when you claim that Freud is 'more revolutionary' than certain women 'when he posits a fundamental bisexuality and a signifying differentiation' (Lemoine-Luccioni, p. 65 [p. 53]), you are referrring to questions of identity? Therefore – unless you believe in sexual essences? – to the play of identifications. How does it differ in men from in women? Does woman identify herself with the other, or does she identify the other with herself? In the mechanism you describe, and according to your interpretive schemata, she identifies herself with the other. How could it be otherwise when there is *one* language only, structured along principles, particularly principles of identity, deter-mined by one sex alone? As for man, he begins by identifying the other with himself: assimilating, incorporating, introjecting the other, in order to constitute a matrix of identifications.

With respect to sexual representatives and representations, this allotment of identifications ends up being a double polarity within the economy of one sex and one sex alone. For whoever identifies the self with the other abandons the 'identity' of her own sex, and whoever identifies the other with the self reduces the other to his sex. So, where is woman's bisexuality to be found? When she has become the other – masculine or phallic – where are her own desire and jouissance to be found? In whatever these kinds of identification eventually impose upon her?

Making claims for bisexuality does not pose much of a threat really … except the threat of reinforcing the established order. It also has the advan-tage of eluding or masking the question of the relationship to the same body and the same sex. While they are hiding behind – phantasmatic or identificatory – bisexuality, are psychoanalysts not really keeping their own homosexual desires latent? Does that mean they have sublimated them? How?

And are you not ready, even today, to look at and analyze what happens between women, just in order to avoid analyzing *your own* homosexuality? To avoid articulating something about it at last? In that case, might your analytic practice not really be just acting out, whether it is about listening to male or female analysands, or about your organizations and the theories you create there? Why the show? For whom? According to your own expla-nations, as you apply them to relations between women, it would be to signify something to your father, 'something that occurs in the beyond, not the beyond of language, but the beyond of what the subject can articulate in language' (Safouan, p. 39). What is it about your relation to the father – including your father in psychoanalysis – that has 'remained "blocked,"' and requires this detour through acting out so it can be signified?

As for women, might it not be that they are trying to show something to their mother – another woman – instead? The fact that the father sees only a spectacle staged for himself can undoubtedly be interpreted as the prevalence of his own scopic drives, and as the *belief* that a woman's desire can be addressed only to him.

Would that be the reason for the lack, which appears perfectly normal to him, of any possible language between women? For the fact that, in his language, women cannot signify (to themselves/each other) their desires? In order for the mother and the daughter to know that they have same-sexed bodies, they do not need, as you seem to think, to use a mirror. All they need do is touch each other, hear each other, smell each other, see each other ... without unduly privileging the gaze, without donning the masks of beauty, without submitting to a libidinal economy that requires that their bodies be covered with a veil before they can be desirable! However, these two women cannot tell each other their feelings using the existing verbal code, nor can they even imagine them within the governing systems of representations. Love and desire between them, and in them, have no articulable signifiers within language. This results in paralyses, somatizations, and lack of differentiation between them, imposed rejection or hatred, at best 'doing like,' or 'acting like.' The daughter's first pleasures remain wordless, her first narcissisms have neither sentences nor words to speak themselves, even retroactively. When the daughter begins to speak, she already no longer speaks to herself, of herself. She is already incapable of auto-affection, exiled as she is in male speak. From her mother and from other women, she is separated by this male speak, that all women *speak in* to each other, without speaking of themselves.

Is the exclusiveness of this male speak of men among themselves not a guarantee of strict cultural endogamy? Of incest, in indefinitely perpetuated semblance, between father and son, and between brothers? Should it not be our task to try to interpret that incest now? Mother–son incest is supposed to be a threat to the order of culture, but the incest that culture maintains between father and son is a threat to the order of life.

*

Listening too mechanically, you will have no doubt already discovered some palliative interpretation for what I have been trying to tell you. For you, it was all just 'desire for vengeance,' or 'revenge' I am taking, or would like to take, 'against my father' (cf. Safouan), and the need to demonstrate it to him openly; or, more generally, it was the exhibitionistic drive to 'show off,' to 'expose myself' before you men, so that I can exist as a subject – or a female subject (cf. Lemoine-Luccioni). Unless perhaps you can detect 'hatred' resulting from some unresolved – or only too well resolved? – transference, depending on the way you describe the end of analysis. Or perhaps you see here my inability to come through the mourning process? Why?

Do you mind if I have a good laugh? Know you not that you hear only according to your schemata, your code, your imaginary, your phantasms ... and they are really just too partial – in both senses of the word. Women's desire, speech and jouissance elude them for the most part. When it comes to women, you listen to, or you perceive, only what signifies either a mimeticism that is impotent when confronted with the power of your order, or the intention or the need to seduce you by pretending to be what you say they are, out of fear of your various means of retaliation, or a silence filled, through the power of suggestion, by your own statements. Which means: *not all*. And *not all women*.

You distribute certificates of 'femininity' in due form (masculine or feminine?); you assign the rank of 'theoretician of female sexuality' to those males and females who consciously, or unconsciously, march in step with your discourse, support your power, and lend themselves, in accordance with your desires, to the phallo-capitalist-fetishistic market economy. As for any others, you submit what they have to say to your value judgments before listening, or even hearing, without ever giving yourselves time to understand. You exclude them ...

But you use their work, their desire, and their jouissance to fuel the machines producing your writing, seminars, and colloquia. Never citing your sources, except to refute them. Never indicating what's really at stake in your debates; for example, the cause of your interest, all in all rather recent, but oh! so prolific, in female sexuality. This renewed interest goes along with arrogant and derisory verdicts handed down concerning women's struggles to find, or to refind, access to the language of their jouissance.

All of this might or might not be understood as a symptom of rejection, or of contempt for the desire of the other, contempt and rejection related to your own need to remain enslaved to your male masters and their law(s).

Gentlemen psychoanalysts, it is time for you to understand that you are rather pathetic exploiters! Because you have neither the audacity, nor the stamina, nor the joy, nor the pride of your phallocratic convictions and positions. You hide – in shame? – behind scientific honesty (?), benevolent neutrality (?), and conformity to an image – guaranteed by whom? – of the practicing psychoanalyst, nice guy, defender of the one true theory, and of the future of psychoanalysis.

But you know, you have forgotten your age. You are more anachronistic than the oldest man in the west. And in order to understand what our male and female analysands tell us, we would be better off reading Greek myths and tragedies than what you write, which is always already too doctrinaire for any part of what you call the real to speak itself there. With no memory of birth, or of childhood, or of those of *your language*.

So, before you go judging the desire that animates a woman, consider that it is time – in order to re-evaluate the ethics of psychoanalysis – to think about a new ethics of the passions.

Now there's an idea for your future seminars. But better yet: make sure they are even more closed off than ever. Remain among yourselves. Certain women might come and bother you with their 'cries,' 'chatter,' 'naivety,' 'complaints,' or 'claims.' And for those women – so long as you have not interpreted the state of your own passions, and what is going on among yourselves – wanting to come into, or to remain a part of, your circles, can only be fatal.

And, when it comes to law, there is one you forget with a passion: the law of real death.

XVII

The Language of Man

Paradoxically, the issue of the sexualization of discourse has never been broached. As animal endowed with language, as rational animal, man has always represented the only possible subject of discourse, the only possible subject. And *his* language appears to be the universal itself. The mode(s) of predication, the categories of discourse, the forms of judgment, the reign of the concept ... have never been questioned with respect to their determination by a sexed being. The relationship of the speaking subject to nature, to objects both given and fabricated, to God the creator, and to other worldly beings, has been called into question at different periods of history; however, this domain, or this universe, has always been men's. This *a priori* has never appeared, and still does not appear, to call for scrutiny. A perpetually unrecognized law regulates all operations carried out in language(s), all production of discourse, and all constitution of language according to the necessities of *one* perspective, *one* point of view, and *one* economy: that of men, who supposedly represent the human race.

This fact, which is both immediately obvious and inscribed in our traditions, must seemingly remain obscured, and function as the radically blind spot of the entry of the subject into the universe of speech. Opening our eyes to this amounts to an impudence, a heretofore unheard-of madness, and a violence so extreme that all forms of argument – even apparently contradictory ones – must be mobilized in order to maintain the established order.

Such a reaction demonstrates that the question is not an idle one, and that it shakes the very foundations of what is given as universal, as beyond the reach of empirical imperatives, or of subjective or historical particularities. This questioning, therefore, cannot remain local. It is not related to some types of speech only, to certain singularities of expression in one language alone. It cannot be pursued within one existing general code. In sum, it is not idiomatic. The problem of the sexualization of discourse cannot be reduced to an idiolectical problem, unless it is admitted that the language that makes the law is already the idiom of men, the manifestation of man as *idiot*.

Etymology cannot soften the blow of the discovery of this truth: the universal is a particular proper to man. Why not, after all? Has this particular not proved itself effective? Are power or will – doing or saying –

valuable only if they are universally valuable, if they can be imposed as unique and exclusive? Does their unlimited extension not constitute a limitation, and reduce their comprehensiveness? And does there not remain in consciousness, in spirit, in the subject, and in all the figures of discourse, a naivety (in the Hegelian sense of the term) masked by the predication of the absolute: the neglect of the sexualization of discourse, and, more generally, of language. Or in other words: the failure to recognize that male-sexed matter produces *its own* truth, while affirming, and denying, itself in the Truth and the Spirit, in Being and Presence, etc. Or: in Language.

It is true that certain anthropologists studying distant or even local peoples raise the question of the role of the male/female difference in the mechanisms constitutive of a culture and of its language or languages. However, their statements are always subordinate to a 'premier philosophy,' and never examine the foundation of speech in order to interpret it as andrological as opposed to anthropological. A sexed subject imposes his imperatives as universally valid, and as the only ones capable of defining the forms of reason, of thought, of meaning, and of exchange. He still, and always, comes back to the same logic, the only logic: of the One, of the Same. Of the Same as One.

How to reveal what can be revealed only outside this autological circle? What cannot even come to be until after escaping from these types of logic? Difficult question! Not using logic risks maintaining the other's status as *infans*, ceaselessly supplying matter for the functioning of the same discourse; using logic means abolishing difference and resubmitting to the same imperatives. How can the other be spoken without subordinating it to the One? What method will allow this question even to be heard? I will here indicate, modestly, certain applications and implications of the – male – sexualization of discourse, and employ in part its own methods in order to expose its always occulted presuppositions.

(1) An eidetic structure controls the functioning of our truth. No being can speak, no relation to being can be spoken, without reference to a model that determines its manifestation as approximate imitation of its ideal being. The generic dominates the appropriation of meaning. No language is capable of speaking truth without submitting to the common-proper terms that mold it into appropriate, that is, essential, forms.

How then to ask of such a logical economy: what happens to *nature* in this discursive functioning? Always already subordinate to ideas, nature can now be represented only through categories that abstract it from immediate sense perception. Nevertheless, natural causality subsists and fosters the production of ideas.[1] Where and how does it appear in the forms of discourse? What remainder of silence resists such formations? What does truth – or the *logos* – say or do about the immediately sensible?

And, for example, what affects does it permit us to articulate? To translate into language? Can affects ever be ideal and not be diminished as affects? Logic annihilates from the very beginning the specific relation of man *and* of woman to the affect. For each being, and for each apprehension of being, there is nothing more than one idea.

Might this eidetic structure not be interpreted as man's inability to give meaning to his natural beginning, to predicate his relation to a matter-mother who is his origin, but with respect to whom he exists as a man by separating himself from her, by forgetting her, by breaking off any ties of contiguity–continuity, by suspending all sympathy (in the etymological sense of the word) for this primary matter irreducible to his being man? At least in the way that he represents it to himself? The controlling identity principle keeps him safe from any backsliding into a heterogeneity capable of altering the purity of his auto-affection.

Might not woman, women, have something different to say about this relation to the natural? Not merely as complement or supplement to what has already been said, but as a different articulation of the speaking animal with nature, with matter, with the body. Women need not, as men do, distinguish themselves from the mother-nature who produces them; women can remain with her in affection, can even identify with her, without loss of their sexual identity. Which would allow them, were it not for the authority of the male identity principle, to enter differently into the universe of speech, to elaborate differently the structure of language, linking it to primary matter through a type of speech never yet produced.

This would call into question – at least for women? – the obstacle of nothingness and of non-being always at work in our logic, these notions of void, of absence, of hole, of abyss, of nothing ... (the concept of the negative?) to which the history of thought periodically returns. Science continues to assist the latter in progressively naming these notions, and yet, they persist – as attraction of the as-yet-unnamed – for and within man himself. It seems that the closer physics comes to solving the problem of the vacuum, the more often it comes back to haunt man as that which he has projected into and onto nature. Perhaps because there is no answer to the question of how and what it is in himself, and for himself?

The geometric, or more generally mathematical, model he has applied to deciphering the natural world, has allowed man to elaborate and effectively deploy theories; however, the control of this *mathematicizing* over the functioning of discourse has also just as effectively dispossessed him as subject. To what ratio, to what measure, has man, as sexed corporeal matter, submitted? Has the ideal he has imposed as norm not assured his power and his mastery, while simultaneously mortifying-annihilating his relationship to living nature?

While psychoanalysis has been able to interpret certain aspects of this schiz in the man-subject, it also recycles certain philosophical *a priori*. It describes and organizes (male) sexuality according pre-eminence to the death drives over the life drives, to repetition compulsion as privileged spatio-temporal scan, to the triumph of the constancy principle, and to the desire for homeostasis, etc.: love for the same and rejection of difference. It subjugates the unconscious to the fundamental laws of consciousness. Or, more precisely, it uncovers the unconscious as the back, or the reverse side of consciousness, closing off the constitution of the subject within a circle, and leaving it unchanged substantially. It unmasks, at least in part, the underside of a functioning, but does not disturb it. It maintains, even confirms, man in his destiny, his eternal discourse. It does not go so far as to question the sexualization of discourse itself, of theory in general. It is a theory of sexuality that misses its own sexual determination, and it remains naively metaphysical in that way. In submission to the auto-logic of a subject appropriated by and for the needs of the male sex alone, it claims to be indifferent to sex: Truth.

(2) The Reign of the One, of the same as One, in occidental logic, is built on a binarism that has never been radically scrutinized. The localized examination of this regulating model by the sciences (including the logical sciences), and by certain philosophers since the time of Nietzsche, does not so far seem to have required that it be applied to discursive functioning. Yes/no, within/without, good/bad, true/false, being/non-being, along with all the subsequent resulting dichotomies, are still the oppositions ensuring the entry of the subject into language, and they are still subjugated by language to the principle of non-contradiction: yes *or* no, and not yes and no at the same time, at least on the surface. They are henceforth alternatives measured, tempered, temporalized and determined hierarchically: the contradiction being supposedly always capable of resolution in the good term, the right term, according to the right finality.

Founded on this bipolar split, its denial, and the mastery of contradictions, is the substantial consistency of the one (of the subject), capable of surmounting within itself its antagonisms: rational animal . . .

Yes and no to the mother-nature: consumed/rejected, introjected/projected. The identity of the solipsistic subject, indefinitely playing over and over the same game based on the solid ground of his language, is affirmed through the *no* to this denied and unrecognized ambivalence. In him/out of him, the nature-mother is assimilated and rejected, too close, too within and merged with him to be perceived as different; too without not to remain an imperceptible beyond, blind component of the world with its within/without. In self/out of self of the subject, internal/external to discourse, she obscurely nourishes its meaning and remains expelled from the field of all possible references.

This contra-diction, always effective in the order of our reason, must never be revealed as the trace of an original reduction of the other to the same. It is forgotten in a determination of the natural world, in a *physis* that is already man's creation, and whose perceived movements are already subject to the imperatives of his culture, to his own spatio-temporality, which discover in nature only that which his measuring instruments can progressively dominate.

How does the denial of a rhythm specific to the mother-nature, that fundamental *fort-da* always covered over and re-emerging in the multiplicity of the hierarchical oppositions of/in language, *also* come to signify the constitution of the world as a function of the alternations of male sexuality: erection/detumescence? Another question that will be rejected by that which claims to be universal, and refuses the reappearance of the possibility of a contra-diction, where logic was not expecting it and cannot resorb it. A contra-diction in women's speaking that seeks the truth beyond logic's so-called unlimited limits, logic's excess, that which exceeds it, and requires a reorganization of its autarkical economy. Contra-diction showing man that his discourse and his language are the field and techniques of *man*, marked by the particular imperatives of his sex. Intolerable interpretation, which overthrows the order of his pretension to the absolute.

And what if, for women, the dichotomous oppositions did not make sense the way they do for men, unless they radically submit to the phallic male world, leaving themselves mute, or reducing themselves to mimeticism, the only language, or silence, permitted them in this discursive order. What if women were not constituted on the model of the *one* (solid, substantial, lasting, permanent ...) and its base of contradictions, both effective and occulted within a proper hierarchy. What if women were always 'at least two,' without opposition between the two, without reduction of the other to the one, without any possible appropriation by the logic of the one, without autological closure of the circle of the same? Always at least two that can never be reduced to a binary alternative – that logic of distancing from and mastery over the other? What if they always spoke as several at the same time, and if those several were not reducible to a multiple of the one? How would the truth resolve into its economy this enigmatic word, having no principle of identity to the self, nor any known principle of non-contradiction? What would happen to the law-making universal?

(3) And furthermore: what kinds of unforeseen and unforeseeable accidents would happen in the evolution of the essential forms it is the goal of discourse to establish? Would a crisis in truth – or in being – result, if a being, who had always submitted to the laws of predication determined by men alone, actually spoke up? Would a disruption in the premises ensuring their logic ensue? When a being moves out of the ontological status that had been assigned it once and for all, the meaning – of truth, of being – loses its immutability, its impassivity. Discourse comes apart, overflows into the infinite, rediscovers its aporia.

In other words, there results from the privation, for women, of a specificity of language and speech, a domination by logic in a form requiring *both* a God (transcendence marked by the male sex) *and* the interdiction or the impossibility of a regression to primary matter. Under the threat that all substance might fall back into undifferentiation? Into lack of individuation or of identity to the self?

What potency is thus deprived of its own deployment? Remaining as substratum always available for the exercise of man's techniques?

Is discourse then nothing more than the archi-technique used by man in order to evolve in his own being? Does it not constitute, from the beginning, a useful tool for the becoming of man and of man alone? Inaugurated as the space of an exchange, impossible except between man and himself.

But if form could no longer be extrapolated from matter, and if matter and form each engendered the other, without the end prescribed by the domination of the one – the One – over the other, might other types of exchange not be opened up in this perspective? Exchanges in which the one and the other – man and woman, for example – would give each other matter and form, potentiality and action, in a never teleologically determined becoming, having no stable transcendence or immanence.

Would the opposition, as well as the complementarity, of the matter/form couple – woman/man – come undone, thus confounding both the power of binarism and the origin-substance it sustains and maintains? Reference points of a single agent-subject, affected by his own activity, producer and consumer of the energy he has always already appropriated in a circular movement out of and back into himself: translocation having in no other either its beginning or its end? Woman appears, or is signified, at best as nothing more than non-man, with no specificity other than negative, with no difference other than aporetic – the pole of lack – and she must try to elevate herself to the level of the only valid human, or divine, model. Within this logic, 'man' and 'woman' form strictly *one* notion, still hierarchically dichotomized.

What if that other speaking nature acceded to (her own) language?

What if that *subjectum* heretofore non-subjectifiable unveiled herself as the source of another logic? In what ways would the status of the subject and of discourse be disrupted?

(4) Discourse, the *logos*, bear witness to the necessity and the mode of the separation of man from the mother-nature. This separation, constitutive of man as man, requires that he erect himself as solid entity out of an undifferentiated *subjectum*.

In the pre-Socratics, we observe the casting out – or at least the framing – of fluids by solids: the world-*cosmos* surrounded by a shell in Empedocles, the world-thought closed off in a circle by Parmenides. Occidental logic appeals to and is based on the mechanics of solids. Fluids always overflow reason, the ratio, exceed the measure, plunge back into undifferentiation: they are the universe of myths and magic, of darkness resistant to the light of the philosophers who approach it only to enclose it within the confines of their thought. Forgetting that, without fluid, there would be no unity, since fluid always remains *between* solid substances in order to join them together, to reunite them. Without fluid intervention, no discourse could hold together. However, the operation of fluids is not expressed as condition of the truth or of the coherence of the *logos*. That would unveil its unstable edifice, its shifting foundations.

Have the sciences, in their own way, not interpreted the end of philosophy as the end of the predominance of the logic of solids? Have they not discovered or rediscovered the properties of a dynamics of flux to which discourse remains resistant, constraining us in obedience to a world of outdated reason, even though we are actually living in a universe where the power of fluids is increasingly dominant?

The economy of flux requires a re-evaluation of that which has been determined as subject. It exists only as scoria from an ancient world, as debris submerged by the force of energies it can no longer master. Man's discourse perpetuates itself as language overwhelmed by the technical power of scientific formalizations, engendered according to their own necessities, destroying and creating universes of which man is not even aware. Man accompanies, witnesses, participates in or annihilates such processes almost at random. These random connections or interferences escape him, and their relation to a dynamics of flux, deploying itself beyond the control of reason, still remains to be thought.

The so-called human sciences, methods of description and of normalization of the *psychè*, are seemingly trapped in a conception of subjectivity whose relationship to metaphysics has been insufficiently questioned. Thus, when psychoanalysis bases its theory of the mechanisms of the unconscious on thermodynamics, it reconstrains libidinal dynamics within a closed circuit, imprisoning the flux of the drives within a reservoir of solids. The importance of the constancy principle must be correlated with the pre-eminence of the death drives. Psychoanalysis re-encloses desire within the framework(s) of classical rationality, a circumscription against which desire struggles, but from which it has not yet escaped. This economy repeats itself indefinitely with no radical modification, as if the subject were forced to remain immutable with respect to all becoming, physical or historical. The subject's permanence is law for all nature and all history; it can never be determined by them. Interpretive model for the already past, psychoanalysis refuses to listen to what, in that past, was not yet able to speak. It recycles the censorship and the repression of the dominant order.

Thus, in the theorization of women's desire, psychoanalysis, with no fundamental reservations, continues to manifest and practice an allegiance to male-sexed logic. And yet ... The formalistic discontinuity–continuity marking the rhythm of this logic is very different from what women's speaking would be: continuity–discontinuity whose movement would no longer be subordinate to some assignable goal – neither 'ex-sistence' nor ecstasy, neither temporary nor definitive – but engendered gradually with quantitative and qualitative heterogeneities, physical modifications or alterations, a dynamic unforeseeable from within the laws of the displacement of bodies, a dynamic originating in an actual vacuum between two infinitely close bodies. Speaking where infinity would really be actualized physically, within the dynamics of flux where it would no longer represent an aporia to be enclosed in some ideal reality, but a power whose energy can never be closed up/closed off in *one* act, the potential and the actual engendering each other without end.

However, this woman's/women's language(s) is today still censored, repressed, unrecognized, a language held up and held back in latency, in suffering, deciphered only in so-called hysteric symptomology, even though the science of the dynamics of fluids could already provide a partial explanation. The science of the subject is resistant to carrying out its own 'Copernican revolution.' It refuses to question, in its mono-sexual causality, the truth it has established as normative. Whatever the other sex contributes is unacceptable, except as stylistic figures *added on* to a logical functioning that remains unshakable. The reality of the dynamics of fluids is dissolved into a few flowers of rhetoric, within a fundamentally unchanged dis-course, regulating principle that does not recognize that the *logos* represents a rhetoric of solids. . . .

Thus, psychoanalysts object that it is only a question of metaphors when their definitions of the mechanism of the unconscious are questioned from the vantage point of an economy of *real* flux. They have not understood that the constancy principle, homeostasis, and the whole Freudian theory of the libido come down to a system of metaphors. They listen, interpret, and normalize the psyche according to a thermodynamic metaphorizing whose effectiveness is not nil, but limited.

*

The artificialist perspective, from which the issue of natural evolution is approached, is taken seriously as universal and eternal truth, even though it has never been anything more than a hypothesis valid in certain places at certain times. The subject and its discourse are correlates or counter-weights, both indispensable and complementary, to the measuring forced upon the natural-material universe at every moment in history. The subject is then nothing more than an effect, or a residue, a reservoir, constituted as a function of the partial techniques man uses to construct himself a world, a kind of meta-stable reality, pre- and post-discursive, more than ever overwhelmed by techniques being developed without its knowledge.

How many subjects today still believe that their discourse is true, unique, and definitive? In the name of which God do they still order their Truth? For psychoanalysts, the answer is relatively obvious: the Phallus.

Let us imagine the death of this 'God' also. Does that mean that the void he leaves behind will result in the disintegration of all language, its grinding into dust, its splitting into atoms, as well as in the reduction of the world into ever tinier and more innumerable units, and in the decomposition, into infinity, of the entire universe? Or will this death leave a place for that for which the Phallus has always stood: an excess in the economy of solids which would no longer think of itself as a transcendent entity, shielded from all evolution, but rather as extrapolated from the infinite of a dynamics of real fluids.

XVIII

The Limits of Transference

The cathartic operation is analytic work's major difficulty; when accomplished without amputation or sacrifice, it is a task on the frontier of the realm of the possible.

A pathway has yet to be invented, or created, in analysis of women, between women. Women have always been the hidden stakes of the sacrificial, already deprived of themselves, already outside themselves at the moment when the subject–object separation is posited in discourse. Our grammar, within which female jouissance loses its auto-affection, and the possibility of speaking itself, remains foreign to its evolution.

Unable to create words for themselves, women remain and move about within an immediacy having no transitional or transactional object. They take–give without mediation, commune unknowingly with, and within, a flesh they do not recognize: maternal flesh, not reducible to a reproducing body, amorous matter more or less unformed, with respect to which there is supposedly no debt and no possible return.

Oedipal law forbids the daughter's return to the mother, except insofar as she *does as* the mother does in maternity. It cuts her off from her beginnings, from her conception, from her genesis, from her birth, from her childhood.

According to the norm, only half of herself is left her to make her journey: the half that is not herself, but is all (all that) (the id that)[1] remains for her to love.

Split in two by Oedipal law, (situated henceforth between two men, the father and the lover?), she is exiled into the male, paternal world. An errant beggar in relation to values she will never be able to appropriate.

In this respect, she is the only one desiring; desiring, however, from within a lack or a dereliction that dispossesses the father himself of his potential plenitude, since the accomplishment of desire can take place only in an attraction that maintains the course of evolution of both.

According to Freud, the becoming of woman is never finished (which does not rule out woman's being arrested at some point in her development). From this perspective, it is effectively interminable, impossible. The beginning and the end, the roots and the efflorescence, the memory of the moment of embodiment, and the anticipation of the blossoming – all are lacking. Women are thus dispossessed of access to life and death as affirmative responsibilities, depositing in the other their identity as living and free subject.

Imagined and thought of as sheath or envelope for the sex of the man, the woman's sex puts her in a position of double closure. What is lacking is a porousness that exceeds enclosure, fluidity that is not loss but rather source-resource of new energy. Might the depth of immersion be proportional to as yet undiscovered depths?

That does not mean regression to the intra-uterine, but rather access to the as yet, or the never yet, formed, delimited, identified, or spoken. Not yet born? Overflow of a flux that disconcerts entropy, reopens the world and regenerates the organism in a difference that is neither complementarity nor inversion: the latter two figures always linked with the quantitative, to calculations, and to the maintenance of what has already been economized, assimilated, and disassimilated, rather than with access to the qualitative, or to the source.

Two qualitative differences remain to be discovered and related to each other – the difference in sexual difference and the difference that can be lived in sympathy between women. There is no doubt that one is not without the other, but they do not correspond to the same affection. Folding them into each other, or effacing the one into the other, risks reducing both to the quantitative; the effect of forgetting, or of not recognizing, that there can be, that there are, two great others, two Others – a female and a male? Each sex must measure itself against an ideal, its corresponding transcendent. If each does not tend toward the accomplishment of its potential, the alliance or the encounter between the energies of both remains impossible. One always encroaches upon the other, without ever accomplishing its own destiny, without rejoining the flowering of its becoming and its fecundation by the other.

Deprived of an autonomous ideal, does the woman-mother not risk being reduced to fiction? Simple gestures of an imposed everyday routine, unique or plural image, mechanism or dream, shadow, phantom even, she is never unified in her insistence, or in her existence,[2] for lack of words that envelop her, cover her, situate her in an identity, help her to move from inside to outside herself, cloak her in herself, like a shelter that accompanies and protects her without adherence or allegiance to the world of the other. In that way could she open herself to that world while remaining separate, without being continually split within herself. Discord between the sexes takes place within a forgotten, repressed, denied, confounded maternal: universe same and other that creates neither difference, nor encounter, nor alliance.

Without a setting for sublimation through and between women, does the analytic scene not become impossible?

Since women have no soul, how can female analytic partners mark off the limits of their bodies, of their desire? Not to mention the fact that, for them, there is no transitional or transactional object unless they create it, and are able to exchange it or share it between them.

Traditionally, creation and sharing took place around food. The lot of women was to provide food. Since that scene is forbidden in the so-called analytic scene, and since that creation has no words to speak itself within its own act, a practice must be invented that alienates neither analysand nor analyst in unavoidable devouring, a scene must be invented that moves beyond orality and the subsequent stages, but that carefully – and not in the same way as the child psychoanalyst would – establishes a space for the intra-uterine, and access to respiration, and to the gaze opening up onto what is not yet an object: sensitive, sensual touching, a still contemplative opening of the eyes, prior to any capture, or precise objectival definition.

The limit of transference would be this proximity without distance between women – between mother and daughter? – without distance because no symbolic process is able to account for it. Rather than recognize this deficiency and try to overcome it, those who should articulate this difference, both in the particular and in analytic practice in general, often play at being mother, play the card of archaism and of psychoticizing regression – doubles or understudies for the maternal who cannot fulfill the same relationship to the placenta, to milk, to skin, or to the mucous, and therefore aspire in empty transparency or in nothingness.

Playing the mother, the man-analyst renounces his own sex and deprives the analysand of hers, reducing to nothing, or to oneiric charm, the carnal mother-to-daughter, woman-to-woman relation. The man-to-woman relation as well, except as aspiration to lost flesh, to lack, to nostalgia.

Although it is relatively common to speak of fusional relationships, what is played out in those relations must be interpreted diversely. The placental habitation and the adherence of the placenta to the mother's womb represent another economy and a different liberation.

There exists, however, another mode of confusion between subjects or rather between psyches: the consumption (?) of the sex and body of another woman, turning her inside out, and closing the threshold of her partial opening. Woman therein is not in the place of, does not take the place of, the mother. She is taken as woman, worn out well before the reproduction, or before the imitation, of her appearance. What is most intimate in her, the jouissance of her retouching, is used so that the other may become, without becoming, what she is by her birth and her history. This becoming therefore lacks roots and growth. It envelops itself in the jouissance of another woman, or uses it as grounding for a flight that neglects to secure its foundations, its landing, something of its identity, of its identity to itself, of its fidelity to itself in the unfolding of a trajectory. The lack of any imaginary and symbolic ground accorded, or recognized, 'on the part of women,' means that all of this happens in what could be a death-dealing immediacy, prior to any master–slave dialectic.

A chiasmus ensues directly, without a mirror. Left and right are inverted in a face-to-face leaving no place for the image of the other, appropriated and traversed on the way to some traditionally paternal infinity. What are taken as movements of the woman-mother are forgotten there.

It remains for women to come back to some tactile unfinished in-finite. Foundation of all the senses, touch operates prior to clear-cut positioning of subject and object. Its action is always almost immediate, the space of a jouissance that cannot be posited as such, but that calls out for boundaries, for covering over, for filling in . . .

Without subject or object, what 'do women want'? Absolute wanting. Without identity, what 'does she want'? The wanting of the Other. Not the want of the God-Father, but wanting *more*. Women want the mystery of the infinity of enumeration, the infinitely great, for lack of tactile perception of the infinitely small, or the infinitely close. Women want something that overflows the numeric within numbers, that insists within the form of the accounting. Women want what has not yet taken place, what appears, becomes, takes shape before their eyes, or even what they perceive prior to any gaze. Women want the movement of generation because they lack a language that would grant them their participation in engendering. Women want to appropriate unto themselves all that grows, all that is coming into being, emerging from the chaos where they seek the place where they are lost. They want what is not yet fixed-frozen into finite architecture, what has yet to be born.

Women do? But as something borrowed from the desire of the other, or the Other, who is still in night. Barely unveiled? That is already saying too much. Becoming is more important to them than the secret of any fetish. Always unsatisfied? If that means women want the very movement of engendering, because they are arrested in their generation. Women want, without end or model, the presumed wanting of anyone who follows the path of wanting – model without a model, example whose paradigm they efface. Women want to seize hold of what already exists in order to bring it back to an invisible source (theirs?), a space out of which they would create and create themselves *ex nihilo*? Has history not imposed the following impossibility on them: they are to continue to live cut off from their beginning and their end?

Woman must ceaselessly measure herself against her beginning and her sexual determination, re-engender the maternal in herself, give birth in herself to mother and daughter in a never-accomplished progression. Mother is she who in shadow is in possession of the subterranean resource; daughter is she who moves about on the surface of the earth, in light. She becomes woman who can in herself unite in her body-womb the most secret, the deepest energies, to life in the light of day. Then no longer is the alliance attraction in an abyss, but encounter in the flowering of a new generation.

Something happens on the order of the psychic and on the order of the cosmic. An encounter that would never have taken place between the two? A whole history to sort out and spread out, between morning and evening, between evening and a new dawn, a history related to time and to our ways of marking it, that could have an impact on the numeric itself? Another economy of the whole requiring a new language.

The lips? Open, in-finite, unfinished – not the indefinite retreat from what cannot be lived – but partially open here and now all the time. Retouching? The most subtle return that progresses without going back, without closing off in a circle or knot, feeling without feeling resentment.

How to make retouching perceptible to those who are nourished by this touch in order to envelop and enclose themselves in it, to those who turn this gift of space-time into skin folded over on the refusal to respond or correspond in openness. How – in particular, women among themselves – can they not take from this gift what they need to save themselves from dereliction in a quasi-immediate and paradoxical mimetic identification? The latter operation turns any giver inside out before any gift object is given, and does not leave the path open for whoever takes, a gesture in which a kind of capitalization of the mucous is played out, ejecting to the outside what is most intimate. The daughter-woman tries to re-envelop herself in the desiring flesh of the other, covers herself in it more and more, spurning her own birth and her own retouching. She turns herself into protected gestures, without knowing from where she obtains what shelters her, helps her.

Then, feeling secure, she can try to turn back toward the woman who is the origin of her journey and of that other birth that covers her – that other is no more. Or at least she is no longer apparent to her, clothed as she is now in what, of the other, could appear. The Other-woman? Never perceived as such, except insofar as she might be inexhaustible?

In the absence of an identity for the woman-mother, the word of the 'daughters' is either spoken as gestural mimeticism, or flows into the mysterious desire of that female Other. Verbal exchange thus becomes impossible or useless. Everything is played out before the word intervenes.

What is most terrifying is mimetic appropriation by women, because it takes place without ideals or female models. Because they lack an ideal female maternal figure, when woman imitates woman, one gets under the skin of the other, in the reduction of the skin and of the very mucous itself into figures into which they flow in order to exist, often completely unconsciously. They take over the appearance of the other prior to any image, eventually leaving her the one they no longer want – their own – for lack of a representation of themselves to venerate, contemplate, admire, and even adore.

This abduction takes place before any positioning in love or hate. In the absence of a valid representation of themselves in the other – or the Other – they destroy the face and appearance of the other-woman in order to nourish and clothe themselves in it. They are deprived of an artistic, iconic, religious (?) mediation that would permit them to look at and admire themselves through some ideal supporting the perspective of their face-to-face, some work of beauty that is neither the one nor the other, that facilitates the passage from the in-finite, the unfinished, that they are morphologically, to their quest for the infinite. Lacking this connection, they either close off the infinite in a never-ending game, or they collapse it into the unformed, as archaic primitive chaos.

The constitution of temporality, of habitable space-time no longer takes place, or else is accomplished in blindness, in a night where the other has no face. The other woman is exhausted from within, not recognized in the contours of a carnal existence. And the word, unless it becomes the word of the flesh, gift and message of flesh, is a skin that wears out, peels, falls and grows back over and over again, without giving up its secret.

Two lips? Retouching, unclosed enclosure of the body. The envelope of the skin is neither sutured nor open onto a 'canal' that takes in or rejects, but partially open onto the touch of two mucouses, or of four, at least: the lips above and the lips below.

If the skin is removed or turned back, there is no more retouching. The mucous of one becomes that which surrounds the other. The skin inside out? The absence of possible caresses and the capture of the intimacy of the body, consumption of the flesh becoming the placental envelope of the other. Woman tacitly becoming daughter? Inside this inhabiting, all regressions can be imagined, or lived, prior to imaginable phantasms. Unconscious exploitation of a primitive shelter and of what is given there – what is necessary for life.

In this nourishing shelter, oral, anal, and phallic scenarios are played over again. The one this excess is borrowed from pays dearly for this fiction, in usage and usury of a first home without debt, without payment, without acknowledgment. Without consciousness or memory therefore, except the anguish of abandonment?

So this primitive cavern or womb is imagined as a dangerous fault-line, as chaos, as 'empty vase'? This container does not correspond, on interpretation, to a procreative matrix: maternal-feminine space capable of engendering beyond conception in the strict sense of the term, intimacy of a receptacle as potential for engendering, out of the retouching of the lips, female desire.

Without this, without this reversal or positioning of female jouissance within its relation to the maternal, how do we articulate limits between women? The partial openness of their bodies, of their flesh, of their sex, makes the question of boundaries difficult. Qualitative difference is required. Of course, no woman has the morphology of another. Does this alone allow us to move beyond competition within the quantitative? *More, Better* – two sames each trying to outdo the other – persist for lack of discovery and valorization of a – female – sensible transcendental, against which every woman could measure herself, rather than developing only through taking the place of the mother, of the other woman, or of man. Is that the task assigned her? With no sign of the subjective operation in play there.

Most often, the step of *like* (the other) is skipped, effaced. Through lack of identity? If *like* is explicit, it becomes the minimal object: 'like you.' And I owe you the remainder of the leap between past and future? Priceless. Like you – and I owe you my development and the scale of my development.

What is lacking is a double scale, double stakes, a double game, and qualitative difference. Can sexual difference potentially be a function of a relation to the divine? In reserve there? If God is always imagined as a Father, how can women find a model of identity in him, an accomplished image or representation of themselves allowing them to escape from trying to outdo each other quantitatively?

For women, how can the greatest be joined to the least at every instant? And especially how can they move from one qualitative to another? Difficult question of energy, notably when the object or measure between the two poles is lacking. They must become creations. *Objets d'art*? Two subjects can thus come to be, one for the other, and an alliance between the two is made possible.

It is less a problem of mastery than of a creative goal, open to participation in the enjoyment of the object and its co-creation: a useful work since it marks without destruction the limits of energy, of the flesh and the body, of desire and its possibilities. The creation or elaboration of the object becomes an architectonics of the body, of a life and a death that do not kill the other.

This creation could be the only thing that would permit the resolution of transference. Used to privation, women do not deal well with frustration, with the intervention of a discontinuity different from the one they know, with a fragmentation of space-time that cannot be assimilated to the amputation of one part of the world. Of themselves as part of the world? They tolerate not existing, or not insisting,[3] more easily than feeling they are measured off in time and space; they tolerate remaining pure reservoir more easily than perceiving their limits, which do not constitute the limits of a body or of an envelope, but the living boundaries of partially open flesh.

Keeping the lips closed? Feeling, without feeling resentment, the touch that doubles before doubling in consumption: fetal, oral, mimetic ... That is what is said in silence, and exchanged only with difficulty ... The amorous female gesture that can be affirmed and preserved without deprivation or closure remains to be found or created.

In transference, a certain limit, a certain threshold, are never crossed and are ceaselessly transgressed – the porosity of the mucous membranes. Many events may take place, even meetings of hands, of eyes, of ears, of odors, but the mucous never retouches itself carnally in transference.

Already constructed theoretical language does not speak of the mucous. The mucous remains a remainder, producer of delirium, of dereliction, of wounds, sometimes of exhaustion. The mucous that is deployed during the course of an analysis risks death if it is not relocated in its own space. In that case, all thought becomes skin torn from the other, speculation lacking roots and branches, feet and head, and it consummates–consumes the intimacy–interiority of the body that ensures the passage from lowest to highest.

It so happens that the projection of 'good' can turn into 'no good,' anchored in an orality that has forgotten that it is already secondary. If the source is invisible, the other can believe she is the source; the site where she received herself is seen in reverse, as she situates herself above the place from whence flows that which gives birth to her, quenches her thirst, nourishes her.

How can women – in particular? – be prevented from taking from this gift that which would save them from dereliction in a quasi-immediate mimetic gesture, turning the one who gives (herself) inside out, and closing the path to the one who would like to be nourished? What economy(?) can be taught women so that they, understanding the full import of the question, become without becoming closed, so that they exchange in openness something that is not nothing, that cannot be reduced to nothingness.

At times naively vitalist, do women not become murderers through indifference to the meaning of death? Our traditions have not taught them to take responsibility for and keep their own deaths.

However, transference is not merely projection or reprojection of a history; it is also appropriation of the other – here and now, nourishment the analysand feeds on in order to carry out his or her analytic task and life. The analyst also functions as raw material for the cure. The fact that the analyst is the security for, or the guarantor of, knowledge does not spare her or him from having to make the two extremes meet: remaining a reservoir of dynamism, of breath, of all that the analysand comes to seek in order to sustain himself or herself, and remaining the analysand's anchoring in knowlege. The analyst must hold as the guarantor of these two spaces, of the two bridges (that can always be renovated), between the other and herself or himself, without complacency for consumption and without closing in or closing off in theory the needs or desires of the one who has confidence in him or her.

Transference comes down to who best perceives the other, who returns the other, or in the other, the closest to his or her source, a gesture that is almost never perceived as bilateral. The third term in transference becomes the limit not only of the skin but of the mucous as well, not only of walls but of the most extraordinary experience of intimacy: communication or communion respecting the life of the other while tasting of the strangeness of his or her desire. Impossible to touch bottom? At the very boundaries of interpretation, beyond which the risk of conflict is most implacable.

That is also where the perception of the possibility or the necessity of calm is discovered. Interval between two, temporary lull in quantitative measuring, opening for an encounter of a different, peaceful quality. Another ground, and yet the same as the most highly intense? This access is required for there to be otherness.

Peaceful does not mean death, either violent or contained within neutrality. It is rather a state of tranquillity permitting two to be, without life-and-death struggles, and without lethal fusion. What is peaceful can be engendered as harmony with the self, both prior to and beyond the closure of language, harmony that lets the other be, a kind of reserve outside transference, allowing the analyst to ensure his or her own solitude, and to guide the other in or toward his or her own.

Within sexual difference, this peace and this harmony would signify acceptance and accomplishment of one's own sex, without will to outdo the strange or the stranger who insists in the other. This dimension of sexual difference constitutes a horizon for the potential deployment of analysis as opening or enigma, rather than as peremptory imposition of the authority of a word, a language, or a text. It organizes a space or a site for liberty between two bodies, two types of flesh, that protects the two partners by refixing their boundaries.

For this to be a possible alternative, the analyst must always keep in mind the dimension of his or her own transference, must always remain close to and yet distant from the one to whom he or she listens, in a transferential relationship, reversible and open, linking up all possible positions in time and space. Remembering the configuration of bodies and of their synchronic and diachronic relations, the analyst perceives herself or himself as she or he is, was, and will be, in order to hear the other without confusion. This listening marks the limit of what is possible for her or him, what passes for horizon between analysand and analyst: horizon of life and death, matrix-like envelope to be ceaselessly reconstituted as it nourishes and protects, remaining partially open for its own becoming and for reception of and by the other.

This matrix, both anterior and posterior to that of all constituted discourse, matrix of the singular history of a subject, is required in the transferential relationship between women; it is an absolute necessity. This does not imply that it is not a necessity in any analysis. However, in its absence, one woman listening to another becomes the destruction of the one, or of the other, or the assimilation of both to a word or a discourse they have not produced, and of which they make themselves the object.

Analysts must ceaselessly reinterpret their own transference, and not simply their own counter-transference, but the ground from which they listen and give space-time, from which they give themselves as space-time where they listen. This space-time they give remains non-perceptible for most, who never return to the analyst his or her own skin or intimacy: space-time that gives itself, crossing from the inside to the outside, like a body already become flesh, offering itself or proposing itself as space in which the analytic scene is held.

But who understands that analysts are giving space at the same time as listening? That they are giving the horizon, listening in a setting made possible thanks to their relation to space-time. No analysand can success-fully constitute an irreducible horizon for himself or herself. Such, however, is the goal of analysis – access for the one and the other to their respective horizons, no longer constituted by rejection, hatred or mastery, but fluid and remaining partially open to the other. Permanent construc-tion without closure, of amorous and musical rhythm and scansion.

The goal of analysis could be expressed thus: 'Let us invent together that which will allow us to live in and to continue to build the world, and first of all, the world that is each of us.'

XIX

In Science, Is the Subject Sexed?

How does one speak with scientists?[1] What is more, with scientists of different disciplines, each discipline a separate domain, and each system within each domain claiming, at one time or another, to be global? Since, at every moment, every one of these domains is totalized, closed off, how can the various fields be reopened in order to encounter and speak to each other? In what language? Using what type of discourse?

The problem has no evident solution. Each scientific field seems to have its own vision of the world, its own goals, its own experimental protocols, its own techniques, its own syntax. Each appears isolated, cut off from all the others. Can one take a bird's-eye view of all these different horizons in order to locate common ground, viable intersections, possible passages from one to the other? Does one have the right to take an outside point of view? How does one claim this right? Historically, there was God, transcendent to any *episteme*. But if, as Nietzsche said, 'when science is in power, God is dead,' then how can these different worlds be brought together? My hypothesis is that the place for collective questioning is *inside* and not *outside*, subjacent and not simply transcendent, 'underground' as well as 'in the sky,' deeply buried and not relegated to some absolute, unquestionable guarantee.

How can we discover this space for inquiry and make it perceptible? How can we speak of it? In the language of science, there is no *I*, no *you*, no *we*. The subjective is prohibited, except in the more or less secondary sciences, the human sciences, and we cannot seem to decide whether they are indeed sciences, or substitutes for science, or literature, or poetry?... Or even whether are they true or false, able to be proved or disproved, formalizable or always ambiguous because expressed in natural languages, too empirical or too metaphysical, dependent on the axiomatization of the so-called exact sciences or resistant to such formalization, etc.? Old debates and old quarrels, potentially involving reversals of power, rises and falls of imperialism, that are still current.

These cycles can repeat themselves indefinitely. However, one could perhaps wonder if, in some subterranean underground, there might not be one common producer making science. But who? Is anyone there?? Can

we see them? How do we question them? Not for a long while have I
experienced so much difficulty with the idea of speaking in public. Most
of the time, I can anticipate to whom I will speak, how to speak, how to
argue, make myself understood, plead my cause, even please or displease
my audience. This time, I know nothing, because I do not know whom I
have before me. Is this the reverse side of scientific imperialism: not
knowing to whom one speaks, or how to speak? Anxiety in the face of an
absolute power that hovers in the air, in the face of judgment by an imperceptible but ever present authority, in the face of a tribunal without judge,
lawyer or defendant! The judicial system is in place nonetheless. There is a
truth to which one must submit without appeal, against which one can
unintentionally and unknowingly transgress. This high court is in session
against your own will. No one is responsible for this terror, or this
terrorism. Nevertheless, they are in operation. In this very classroom or
conference hall. For me, in any case. If I met individually with each one of
you, male or female, it seems to me that I would be able to find a way to
say *you*, *I*, *we*. But here? In the name of science?

My first question would be: what schiz does science impose on those
who practice or convey it in one way or another? What desire is in play
when men and women are making science, and what other desire when
they are making love or creating love, individually or socially?
   What schiz or what rupture: pure science on one side and politics on
another, nature and art on a third or as conditions of possibilities, love on
a fourth? Are not this schiz and this rupture, which you claim are above
scientific imperialism, already *programmed by it* in the separation of the
subject from itself and from its desires, as well as in its dispersion into
multiple sectors, including those of science, among which encounters
become impossible, verifications of responsibility impracticable. What
remains is an imperialistic *there is/there are,* or a *one,* that the power-
holders, the politicians, take advantage of as opportunities arise. By the
time the scientists react, the game is already over: in the name of science?
Imperialism without a subject.

*

- So, looking at things a little bit differently, and playing the game of
  those questionnaires that flourish in women's magazines (replacing the
  crossword puzzles found in gender-neutral daily newspapers, which
  actually are all too often exclusively male?) let us make an effort:
  If I tell you that two ova can engender a new life, does this discovery
  seem to you possible? Probable? True? Purely genetic? Or related also to
  the social, economic, cultural, political order? To be within the domain of
  the exact sciences? Check the appropriate box or boxes. Is this type of

discovery going to be encouraged, and funded? Will it be discussed in the media? Yes? No? Why or why not?

Your answer? How do we interpret the answer? Through the importance of sperm in partriarchy, and its link to property and the symbolic? Through the importance of reproduction and its ambiguous correlation to pleasure and desire in sexual difference?

And, while we are dealing with reproduction and its hormonal components:

- Is male contraception hormonally possible? Yes? No? Why or why not? If it is, is this information disseminated, is the practice encouraged?

- Is the left hemisphere of the brain less developed in women than in men? Yes? No? Would this discovery be used to justify the social, cultural, and political inferiority of women? Yes? No? Would this affirmation concern innate or acquired characteristics? Give your own interpretation and your own hypothesis. Explain how you establish a parallel with the inhabitants of certain oriental countries who, as science tells us, share the same anatomical destiny as women. Do the types of mental and physical practices found in these Asian countries signify an unconscious (?) desire on the part of men to become women? Or a resistance to the liberation of women and an appropriation of all values, accompanied by lack of recognition of a symbolic sexed morphology?

- The girl-child, according to a certain number of observations, develops more precociously than the boy-child: she speaks earlier on and her social skills are precocious. Yes? No? Can it be proved? Disproved? Does she employ these early accomplishments to make herself into a desirable object for others? Resulting in regression? True? False? Justify your response.

- What percentage of the world's population is men and what percentage is women? What are the percentages of men and women in positions of political, social, and cultural leadership? Does that seem a foregone conclusion to you, does it correspond to a male or a female *nature*, and to men's and women's desire? Is it innate or acquired?

- Are women *naturally* more limited, more ignorant, more animalistic, or better at language than men are? Are they inept at political, economic, social, or cultural leadership? Innate? Acquired? Verifiable? Unverifiable?

- Is a woman scientist really just a man? A genetic aberration? A monster? A bisexed individual? A submissive or a non-submissive woman? Or . . .?

- Is there or is there not a dominant discourse that claims to be universal and neuter with respect to sexual difference? Do you agree that it should be perpetuated? For a year? Two years? One hundred years? Or forever?

- Who, according to our epistemological tradition, is the keystone of the order of discourse?

- Why has God always been, and why is He still, at least in the west, God the *father*? That is, the strictly masculine pole of sexual difference? Is that the way we designate the sex that is hidden within and beyond all discourse? Or ... ?

*

In fact, what claims to be universal is actually the equivalent of a male idiolect, of a male imaginary, of a sexed world – and not neuter. There is nothing surprising in this, unless one is a passionate defender of idealism. Men have always been the ones to speak and especially to write: in the sciences, in philosophy, in religion, in politics.

However, nothing is said about scientific *intuition*. It is supposedly produced *ex nihilo*. Certain aspects or qualities of this intuition can nevertheless be distinguished. It is always a question of:

- positing *one* world that one confronts, constituting a world before oneself, as separate from oneself;

- imposing a model on the universe in order to appropriate it, an invisible, imperceptible model, projected over it like some piece of clothing. Is that not the same thing as clothing it blindly in one's own identity?

- claiming that one is rigorously exterior to the model, in order to prove that the model is purely and simply *objective*;

- demonstrating that the model is not dependent on the senses, even though it is always prescribed at least through privileging the visual, and through the absence and distancing of a subject who is nonetheless surreptitiously present;

- ensuring independence from the senses through the mediation of instruments, through the intervention of techniques that separate the subject from the object of investigation, and through processes that distance and delegate power to that which intervenes between the observed universe and the observing subject;

- constructing an ideational or ideal model, independent from the physical or psychical existence of the producer, according to ideally elaborated rules of induction and deduction;

- proving the universality of the model, at least for x amount of time, and its absolute power to constitute (independently of its producer) a unique and totalized world;

- backing up this universality with experimental protocols about which at least two (identical?) subjects agree;

- proving that the discovery is efficacious, productive, profitable, exploitable (exploitative? of a more or less inanimate nature?), all of which means that it is progress.

The above characteristics exhibit isomorphism with the male sexual imaginary, a fact that is supposed to remain rigorously concealed. 'Our subjective experiences and our feelings or convictions can never justify any statement,' affirms the epistemologist of the sciences.

It should be added that discoveries must be expressed in a formal language, a language that makes sense. And that means:

- expressing oneself in symbols or letters, substitutions for *proper names*, that refer only to intra-theoretical objects, and therefore never to any real persons or real objects. The scientist enters into a world of fiction incomprehensible to all who do not participate in it.

    The signs forming terms and predicates are:
    + : or the definition of a new term
    = : which marks a property through equivalence and substitution (belonging to a set or a domain)
    ∈: signifying belonging to a certain type of objects.

    The quantifiers (not qualifiers) are:
    > <
    the universal quantifier
    the existential quantifier, subordinated, as its name indicates, to the quantitative.

In the semantics of incomplete entities (Frege), the functional symbols are variables taken from the limit cases of the forms of syntax, and the preponderant role is accorded the symbol of universality or the universal quantifier.

The *connectors* are:
- negation: P or not P
- conjunction: P or Q
- disjunction: P or Q
- implication: P results in Q
- equivalence: P equals Q.

There is therefore no sign:
- for *difference* other than quantitative difference;
- for *reciprocity* (other than within the same property or the same set);
- for *exchange*;
- for *permeability*;
- for *fluidity*.

Syntax is dominated by:
- *identity to*, expressed by properties and quantities;
- *non-contradiction,* or reduction of ambiguity, of ambivalence, or multivalency;
- *binary oppositions*: nature/reason, subject/object, matter/energy, inertia/movement.

Undoubtedly, formal language is not simply a set of game rules. It serves to define the game so that all the participants play the same way, and so that a decision can be made in case of disagreement over a move. But who are the participants? Is it possible to intuit something outside the language utilized? How could such an intuition be translated for the participants?

*

The non-neutrality of the subject in science is expressed in many ways. It can be extrapolated from what is, or is not, being discovered at any given moment in history, and from what science sets, or does not set, as goals for its research. For example, in relative disorder and disrespect for the hierarchy of the sciences:

- Psychoanalysis is based on the two main principles of thermodynamics underlying the Freudian model of the libido. These two principles appear to be more isomorphic with male sexuality than with female sexuality. The latter is less subject to alternations of tension and discharge, to conservation of required energy, to the maintenance of states of equilibrium, to functioning as a circuit that is closed and then reopened by saturation, to the reversibility of time, etc. Female sexuality may harmonize better, if we must evoke a scientific model, with what Prigogine calls 'dissipative' structures, which function through exchange with the outside world, which proceed in energy stages, and whose ordering is based not on seeking equilibrium, but on crossing thresholds corresponding to leaving disorder or entropy behind, without discharge.

- Economics (and the social sciences as well?) has emphasized scarcity and survival phenomena rather than those associated with life and abundance.

- Linguistics remains attached to models of the utterance, to synchronic structures of speech, to models of language that every normally constituted subject can intuit. It has not considered the question of the sexualization of discourse, and sometimes even refuses to do so. It accepts – out of necessity – that certain terms of the lexicon have been added to the accepted stock, that new figures of style eventually impose themselves, but is unable to imagine that syntax and syntactic–semantic organization could be sexually determined, and neither neuter nor universal nor atemporal.

- Biology is beginning to approach certain issues rather late: for example, the constitution of placental tissue, or the permeability of membranes. Are these questions more directly correlated with the female and maternal sexual imaginary?

- Mathematics is interested in set theory, in closed and open spaces, in the infinitely large and the infinitely small. It shows little interest in the question of the partially open, of fluid sets, of analysis of the problem of boundaries, of passages between, of fluctuations taking place between thresholds of defined sets. Even these questions are raised by topology, it emphasizes that which closes back up, rather than that which remains outside circularity.

- Logic is more interested in bivalent theories than in trivalent or multivalent theories that still appear marginal.

- Physics conceives its object of study according to a nature it measures in ever more formalized, ever more abstract, ever more modeled, ways. Its techniques, expressed through increasingly sophisticated axioms, deal with matter that does still exist, of course, but that is not perceptible to subjects conducting experiments, at least for the most part. Nature, the target of physics, risks being exploited and disintegrated by the physicist, even without his or her knowledge. The Newtonian revolution ushered scientific practice into a universe where sense perception is almost non-existent, and where the matter (however it is predicated) of the universe and of the bodies that constitute it – the stakes and the object of physics itself – may be annihilated. Inside physics itself there are cleavages: quantum theory/field theory, mechanics of solids/dynamics of fluids, for example. In any case, the imperceptibility of the matter that is studied often leads to a paradoxical privileging of solidity in discoveries, and to a lag in, even an abandonment of, analysis of the unfinished in-finite of force fields. Could this be interpreted as a result of the refusal to take into account the dynamics of the researcher-subject?

*

In the face of these observations and questions, are we faced with an alternative: *either* be a scientist *or* be a 'militant'? Or even: continue to be a scientist *and* divide oneself up into different functions, into several different people or characters? Should the truth of science and the truth of life remain separate, at least for the majority of researchers? What kind of science and what kind of life are we dealing with then? The question is all the more pertinent since life in our times is largely dominated by science and its techniques.

What is the origin of this schiz that is both imposed by and inflicted upon scientists? Is it a non-analyzed model of the subject? A 'subjective' revolution that never took place: the splitting of the subject having been programmed by the *episteme* and the power structures put in place by it? Is it that the Copernican revolution has occurred, and that the epistemological subject has so far neither acted upon nor moved beyond it? Has it modified this subject's discourse about the world in such a way that it is even more disappropriating than the language that preceded it? Scientists now claim to be standing *before the world*: naming it, establishing its laws, axiomaticizing it. They manipulate nature, use it, exploit it, but forget that they are also *in* it, that they are still physical, and not simply confronting phenomena whose physical nature they sometimes fail to recognize. Progressing according to an objective method that shelters them from all instability, all moods, all feelings and affective fluctuations, all intuitions not already programmed in the name of science, all interference from their desires, notably sexual ones, that could affect discoveries, they settle down into the systematic – into what can be assimilated to the already dead? Fearing, sterilizing the destabilizations that are, nonetheless, necessary for the coming of a new horizon of discovery.

Inquiry into the subject of science, and its psychic and sexual implication in discourse, and in discoveries and their development, is one of the sites most capable of provoking a re-evaluation of the scientific horizon.

In order to ask oneself if the so-called universal language(s) and discourse(s) (including those of the sciences) are neuter with respect to the sex that produces them, we must pursue research in view of accomplishing two goals: the interpretation of the law-making discourse as subject to an unrecognized sexual dimension of the speaking subject, and the attempt to define the characteristics of what a differently sexed language would be.

In other words: is there, within the logical and syntactico–semantic mechanisms of accepted discourse, an openness or a degree of liberty that would permit the expression of sexual difference? We must analyze, in order to interpret their position within a sexed logic, the laws (including those that are not explicit) that determine the acceptability of language and of discourse. This work can be pursued from different angles:

- The causal mode that currently dominates discourse considered normal, as well as the conditional, unreal, and restrictive modes, etc., that fix its 'practicable' framework, limiting the liberty of a subject of enunciation who does not necessarily obey certain criteria of normality, may be studied. While these causal and restrictive modes (the two are linked) permit the accumulation of information and a certain type of already coded communication, do they not inhibit intra-discursivity and prevent all possibility of any qualitatively different enunciation?

- The means or conjunctions of co-ordination also participate in the economy of the principle of causality dominating so-called asexual discourse: juxtaposition, including the summation of clauses and subjects (and ... and); alternative (either ... or); exclusion, including the eventual elimination of the subject of enunciation (neither ... nor); co-ordination proceeding in the direction of the syllogistics regulating discourse (for, therefore, but).

What modes of subordination or co-ordination would authorize the discursive relationship between two sexually different subjects?

- The symmetry (notably right–left) in intersubjective relations and its impact on the production of language may be analyzed. Can the issues of symmetry and asymmetry result in criteria that would be able to determine a qualitative difference between the sexes? Is the 'blind spot in the old dream of symmetry' (cf. *Speculum*) situated in the same place in a relationship between individuals of the same sex, as it is in a relationship between individuals of different sexes? The dream itself, however, dream that may underlie the economy of the speaking subject, seems to be invalidated by cosmic laws in the face of which no observer of nature and language can remain indifferent, any more than a speaker or interlocutor from the outside.

• When women are held back in a potential language, they constitute a reservoir of energy that could be eliminated, or could explode for lack of possible forms of expression. When they represent only the underside or the reverse side (in specular symmetry?) of discourse, they close it off on itself. Forced into a mimetic defense or offense, women risk absorbing the meaning of discourse, by collapsing it through lack of any possible response. They may be intercepting the goal or the intentionality of discourse, and thus accelerating the destructuring process – which could be acceptable if a new language were to ensue. The question that must be asked is whether women's language would fulfill an as yet unrealized potential for meaning, while remaining within the same general discursive economy, or whether what women think and may be able to say would require a mutation of the horizon of language. That would explain the resistance to their entry into the networks of communication, and the even greater resistance to their entry into the spaces – theoretical and scientific – that determine the values and laws of exchange.

*

Certain questions should be asked regarding the access of women to language and discourse.

(1) Why is their potential energy for language always on the vanishing point, never able to get back to the subject of enunciation? Recent research in discourse theory, as well as in physics, may shed light on the site, in darkness until now, of women's lack of access to discursivity. We must come back to a study of temporalization and its relationship to the place from which the subject is either able, or unable, to position itself as producer of language. If the discourse of the hypothetical interlocutor intercepts the word, cutting it off from memory of the past and from anticipation of the future, all that is left for the subject are attempts to get back to that place from which she or he can be heard. We should emphasize in this context the importance of locality in the constructions of women's language. The circumstances of place largely determine the programming of 'discourse.'

(2) Do we not find, in this insistence on the question of place, an attempt to give form to a subject of enunciation, for lack of temporalization in a dynamics of communication? The utterance's potential for reversibility, or lack thereof, notably between speaker and interlocutor, should be approached from this perspective, as well as its eventual repetition or reproduction. These conditions are absolutely essential for admissible discourse, since the other is placed in the position of a mirror

that both inverts the received discourse, and responds to it after this retro-action.

(3) The problem of the possible, or impossible, mirror in the other, dominates the enigma of the language and silence of women. Whatever the case may be, 'they' do not say nothing, and the fascination felt, by certain practitioners in particular, for what they do say certainly indicates that some kind of deciphering of the production of language is expressed through them.

These issues could also be approached from the following angle:

(1) Does what we call the *mother tongue* establish a space for a specific production of language by the mother, and for exchange between mother and children? Is socially admissible language not always paternal? Does a fault-line open up at the entry into discourse? A fault-line that ceaselessly threatens discourse with total collapse, with madness, with sclerotic normalization.

(2) The creation of language – in all forms – by the maternal has been barred since the origin of our culture. The maternal has been allocated to the procreation of children, and has never been a site for the functioning of a productive matrix. From this perspective, it is useful to reinvestigate and reinterpret the Freudian texts – notably *Totem and Taboo* – that define the foundation of the primitive horde as the murder of the father, and the sharing of his body by the sons. Deeper than the murder of the father, at the origin of our culture, can we not decipher (in Greek tragedy, mythology, and even philosophy) an even more archaic matricide? This murder of the mother in her cultural dimension as fecund lover, continues to govern the establishment of the symbolic and social order that is our own. What consequences does this matricide have for the production of language and the programming of discourses, including scientific discourses?

(3) Since psychoanalytic 'science' is supposed to be the theory of the subject, Freud's hypothesis concerning the constitution of the relation of the subject to discourse calls for reconsideration and reinterpretation. Freud puts forth, as the scene of the introduction of the subject into language, the 'spool game.' The child – a boy, as it happens – tries to master the absence of his mother by using an instrument he throws away and then pulls back, first banishing it, and then bringing it in close to his space, into his space, alternating vowel sounds along with his gestures: o-o-o (far), a-a-a (near).

This 'game,' the so-called *fort-da* game, complete with its alternating vowels, supposedly marks the entry of the child into the realm of symbolic distancing. The boy-child (Freud does not provide any hypothesis as to how all of this might happen for a girl) is able to make this transition – while producing sounds, a kind of musical scale – by assimilating his mother to an object attached to a string that allows him to control, or even eliminate, the distance between her and himself. Does the *fort-da* scene still have a significant function in the constitution of the meaning of language? How are the vowels articulated with the consonants?

This scenario, as it is described by Freud, requires the absence of the mother as interlocutor, and the presence of the grandfather as observer and regulator of 'normal' language. What gestures, what other kinds of language, between child and mother, mother and child, are left out of acceptable discourse? Do the systematicity and the madness of so-called admissible discourse not result from this 'outside' of the spoken and the speakable, since a scenario for *exchange between* mother and son, mother and man-subject, has not been put into place in language? We had better make sure that this means of distancing does not become deadly.

(4) Freud says nothing about the entry of the little girl into language, except that it takes place earlier than for the little boy. He does not describe her first scene of gestural and verbal symbolization, in particular in relation to her mother. On the other hand, he does affirm that the girl will have to leave her mother, turn away from her, in order to enter into the desire and the order of the father, of man. A whole economy of gestural and verbal relations between mother and daughter, between women, is thus eliminated, abolished, forgotten in so-called normal language, which is neither asexual nor neuter. Does discourse then consist only of partially theoretical exchanges between generations of men, concerning the mastery of the mother and of nature? What is lacking is the fecundity of the sexed word, and of a creation, beyond procreation, that is sexual.

Notes

II LINGUISTIC AND SPECULAR COMMUNICATION

1 *Translator's note.* Although I have everywhere tried to use gender-fair language in this translation, in the case of 'Linguistic and Specular Communication' I have decided to maintain the generic masculine in which it was originally written. The topic itself is ambiguous in this respect, in that it deals with the moment of the emergence of subjectivity, when gender identities are only just coming into being. It would be questionable in this context to interpret the third person singular pronoun 'he/it' (the French *il*) as identifying a particular gender. '*Il*' is in this case neither a 'he' nor a 'she,' and the use of the generic masculine 'he' is, at least debatably, appropriate in this context. It would have been theoretically possible to use 'she,' the equivalent third person singular. However, given the cultural and linguistic resonances of 'she,' I believe that that choice of translation would have risked skewing the meaning of the text in the direction of gender identification, and would have misrepresented its principal theme, which is the emergence of subjectivity.

2 *Translator's note.* I have used the numeral to distinguish between the French *un* (the numeral 'one') and *on* (the pronoun 'one').

3 *Author's note.* Brackets indicate that the concept has been laid down without being actualized in discourse. Parentheses indicate the partners of enunciation. Quotation marks: for example, 'I,' are used to designate the subjects and objects of the utterance.

4 *Author's note.* Today I would not write this statement. The father and the mother are not permutable unless they are sexually undifferentiated. We are dealing with a more complex operation: a sexually marked triangulation which engenders a sexed subject in its relation to language. I leave the text as it is, as the trace of theoretical distance covered, and of a question about the constitution of the subject of discourse.

5 *Author's note.* G. Frege, *Les fondements de l'arithmétique*, Paris: Seuil, 1969.

6 *Author's note.* K. Togeby, *Structure immanente de la langue française*, Paris: Larousse, 1965, p. 157, quoting S. Mill, Brondal, L. Hjelmslev.

7 *Translator's note.* The French 'one' Irigaray refers to here is more appropriately translated into English as 'we.'

8 *Author's note.* R. Jakobson, 'Les Embrayeurs,' *Essais de linguistique générale,* Paris: Minuit, 1963, p. 177, and Togeby, p. 157, referring to Hjelmslev.

9 *Author's note.* At the specular level, the terms of the schema of communication can never be understood as realizations of actual discourse. Hence, the

constant usage of brackets in the paragraphs devoted to specular 'communication.'

10 *Author's note.* J. Lacan, 'Le stade du miroir comme formateur de la fonction du Je,' in his *Ecrits*, Paris: Seuil, 1966.

11 *Author's note.* I leave in abeyance here the question of the creation of writing that is not duplication of the word.

12 *Author's note.* The transformations carried out here on the theoretical model previously defined make no claim to explaining all of the disorders of linguistic and specular communication. They serve as examples and block out a program for future research.

13 *Author's note.* J. de Ajuriaguerra *et al.*, 'A propos de quelques conduites devant le miroir de sujets atteints de syndromes démentiels du grand âge,' *Neuropsychologia*, 7:1, June 1963, 59–73. Cf. also my book: *Le Langage des déments*, in *Approaches to Semiotics*, Paris: Mouton, 1973.

14 *Author's note.* At the level of the theoretical model, the subject can be found in the 'zero' that founds it, and in the structure that singularizes it.

III NEGATION AND NEGATIVE TRANSFORMATIONS IN THE LANGUAGE OF SCHIZOPHRENICS

1 *Translator's note.* The ambiguities referred to here are not always easily translated into English. In some cases they can be made clearly 'ambiguous' in English, and in others will remain so only in the French, especially where these ambiguities are phonetic. For example, *to be born (naître* in French*)* cannot be distinguished phonetically from *not to be (n'être* in French).

2 *Translator's note.* Obviously 'to be reborn,' 'not to be,' and 'to disappear' do not rhyme in English. The French terms *renaître, ne pas être, disparaître*, most definitely rhyme.

3 *Translator's note.* Since most adjectives in English are not marked by gender, it is impossible to show the distinction being made here. Even the previous distinction between *handsome* and *beautiful* is only partially valid in English, since the two adjectives are not invariably, but only sometimes, gender-specific.

4 *Author's note.* We find here perhaps one of the divergences noted in the performances of schizophrenics depending on whether we are dealing with adjectives or verbs. In the case of adjectives, the cue word can be understood as an acceptance or a rejection of certain aspects of the word, whereas for the verbs, especially if they imply an animate subject, it would necessarily be received as a request to transform a statement after having assumed responsibility for it as one's own.

IV TOWARDS A GRAMMAR OF ENUNCIATION FOR HYSTERICS AND OBSESSIVES

1 *Translator's note.* The French *hystérique* is the same for both masculine and feminine, and I have translated it as 'he or she', 'him or her', and so on, because in Irigaray's work it is almost always female but not exclusively so. The French text uses the masculine form *obsessionnel*, which I have translated as 'he', 'him', and so on because in Irigaray's work the obsessive is almost always male.

2 *Translator's note.* The following abbreviations will be used in the text: NP1 = noun phrase 1 = the subject of the sentence; V = the verb; NP2 = noun phrase 2 = direct or indirect object of the verb; NP3 = noun phrase 3 = adverbial phrase, complement of a preposition of time or place.

3 *Author's note.* These are the terms of traditional clinical and phenomenological nosology. Why use them in this work? It is impossible to move, without transition, from one code to another, from one dictionary to another. Using the already existing terms is one way, among others, of finding the means to subvert them. As for the risk of tautology between the provisional naming of the speaking subject and the analysis of the discourse, it is nil: *the first time.* It is no longer nil when the relation has been established through work on the corpus. Only that which remains at the level of metalanguage goes into its own feedback loop, rediscovering only its own hypotheses.

V ON PHANTASM AND THE VERB

1 *Translator's note.* Although the theological reference is obvious in this sub-heading, it is useful to point out explicitly here that the French *verbe* means *word*, in the sense of the *logos* – 'In the beginning was the Word . . . ' – as well as *verb*. I have chosen to use *verb* in the English translation, since the article deals with verbs, in the linguistic sense.

2 *Author's note.* That is to say that what will be designated as subject and object does not belong to the register of the utterance. Nor will it be a question of a specific subject or object, but rather of the subject function – f(s) – and of the object function – f(o) – determined by the structuring in question. In cases where the term subject designates the whole of the structuring, or even of the structure, it is written <subject> and designates another functional level.

3 *Author's note.* *Phantasm* is to be understood here as the primordial formation of the subject resulting from the reciprocal integration of its body and an individual discourse. It must therefore be distinguished from the *drive* – a limit concept, the effect of the union of the body and of language – and from the projection of phantasms specified in the form of animated scenes, the stage where representation appears, and which is, as spectacle often passively undergone, to be opposed to the more active structuring which presupposes *the image*.

4 *Author's note.* However, a passive form anterior to an active form, and not the result of a passive transformation: to live – to absorb – to be absorbed.

5 *Author's note.* The term 'partner of enunciation' – sometimes written as (you) – indicates the space of the possible functioning of an other <subject>.
6 *Author's note.* I continue to use the term *analysand* in the text. Strictly speaking, the 'analyst' and the 'analysand' are both *analyzing* and *analyzed*.

VI LINGUISTIC STRUCTURES OF KINSHIP AND THEIR PERTURBATIONS IN SCHIZOPHRENIA

1 *Translator's note.* The example given in this context does not make sense in English. The French word *'parent'* does indeed mean both 'relative' in the general sense and, more specifically, 'parent.'
2 *Translator's note.* The words *'ormeaux'* (elm striplings), and *'jumeaux'* (twins) rhyme in French; their English translations do not.
3 *Translator's note.* In French, the plural generic masculine *'neveux'* can include both nephews and nieces.

VII SENTENCE PRODUCTION AMONG SCHIZOPHRENICS AND SENILE DEMENTIA PATIENTS

1 Translator's note. Sea (*mer*), mother (*mère*), and mayor (*maire*) are homophones in French. The point is that the respondents with dementia do not notice this ambiguity.
2 Translator's note. See note 1, above.
3 Translator's note. The word for 'window-shutter' in French is *volet*, which sounds exactly like the verb *voler*, 'to fly.' The word for 'sheet of paper' in French is *feuille*, which also means 'leaf.'
4 Translator's note. See note 1, above.

VIII THE UTTERANCE IN ANALYSIS

1 *Author's note.* For the meaning of the term 'phantasm,' see Chapter V, 'On Phantasm and the Verb.'
2 *Author's note.* See Chapter I, 'Linguistic and Specular Communication.'
3 *Translator's note.* Savoir ['to know'], *s'avoir* ['what he/she has'], *ça voir* ['to see that'] are homophones in French. The context here indicated a literal translation, but the rhyming word-play should be noted.
4 *Translator's note.* Irigaray frequently uses the term *'insister'* in contrast to the verb *'exister.'* I have chosen to maintain this usage in English. 'Insist' here indicates *being within*; 'exist' would indicate *without*, or *being outside*.
5 *Translator's note.* The 'puns' do not literally translate Irigaray's examples, but are meant to illustrate the psychoanalytic operation on language she is discussing.

IX CLASS LANGUAGE, UNCONSCIOUS LANGUAGE

1 *Translator's note.* My translation of Saussure. The page reference is to Luce Irigaray's citation of the French text.
2 *Translator's note.* The 'I' in parentheses, here in brackets, is the subject of enunciation.
3 *Translator's note.* See Chapter IV, note 1.
4 *Author's note.* See Chapter 4, 'Towards a Grammar of Enunciation for Hysterics and Obsessives.'

X THE RAPE OF THE LETTER

1 *Author's note.* For example, those of J. Derrida: *De la Grammatologie*, Paris: Minuit, 1967; *L'Ecriture et la différence*, Paris: Seuil, 1967; 'La Différance,' in his *Marges de la philosophie*, Paris: Minuit, 1972; or 'La double Séance,' in *La Dissémination*, Paris: Seuil, 1972.
2 *Author's note.* Derrida's text also includes the ambiguity that its scribe is marked as simultaneously included and excluded in the closure he or she designates and denounces.
3 *Author's note.* For the meaning of the term 'phantasm' see Chapter V, 'On Phantasm and the Verb.'
4 *Translator's note.* Irigaray here notes that Derrida translates *Aufhebung* into French as *relève.*
5 *Translator's note.* Irigaray uses the term '*différance*,' and notes in a footnote, 'This term is Jacques Derrida's. Cf. "La Différance," in *Marges de la philosophie*. It means the temporalization of difference as J. Derrida tries to think it in our *epoch* after Nietzsche, Heidegger and Freud.' Some writers use the term 'differance' in English, while others do not. I have used 'deferral' to translate '*différance*.'
6 *Author's note.* This is not to say that the constitution of *my* image as *other* does not require movement. A certain number of reiterations or displacements with respect to the environment are necessary for the articulation of the play of same and other. (Cf. Lacan, 'Le Stade du miroir,' in his *Ecrits*.)
7 *Author's note.* It is, on several accounts, deceptive to say 'the' phoneme, or 'it,' etc.
8 *Author's note.* Phonological analysis, in what it takes or defines as the field of articulation, founds for the *act* of articulation a structural method that is not without suspensions or reservations.
9 *Author's note.* The fact that phonological features are accounted for in binary terms is obviously another issue. Still 'open at present.' In addition, 'only phonological features are strictly binary.... . Phonetic features can have many values' (Sanford A. Schane, Introduction to *Langages*, 8, on 'La Phonologie générative')
10 *Author's note.* Historically linked to the consignment of language to writing? The *logos*, logic, are determined only by the coming of *literal,* as opposed to figurative, graphism.

11 *Translator's note.* 'Between' (*entre*) and 'cavern/antrum' (*antre*) are homophones in French.

12 *Author's note.* Not necessarily the split involved in 'archi-writing,' or even in 'writing' (cf. Derrida's text). The letter and the grapheme cannot be confused.

13 *Author's note.* Thus one interpretation, among others, of Freud's discourse could be as an encyclopedic 'after the fact,' after-effect of a double submission to the alphabetic order.

14 *Translator's note.* See note 11, above.

15 *Author's note.* And not only phonetic articulation, which has been wrongfully privileged.

16 *Translator's note.* See note 11, above.

17 *Author's note.* Is the history of silence surrounding writing the result of the silence imposed by its non-figurative *alphabetic* apparatus? The absence of writing from history could be interpreted as the reaction to the rejection, the answer to the foreclosure, acted out in literal writing.

XI SEX AS SIGN

1 *Translator's note.* *Entrer*, 'to enter,' and *entre*, 'between,' present a homophony in French that Irigaray is both playing with and emphasizing. See Chapter X, note 11.

2 *Translator's note.* The word '*ça*' means 'this/that/it,' as well as the 'id' in French.

3 *Author's note.* Cf. what Lacan articulated about the way they function, in the *Ecrits* and particularly in *Subversion du sujet et dialectique du désir*.

4 *Author's note.* For the problematic of *writing*, refer to Derrida, in particular to 'La Dissémination,' in *La Dissémination*, Paris: Seuil, 1972.

5 *Author's note.* The question of the hymen, of its structure and its functioning, was taken up by J. Derrida in 'La double Séance,' in *La Dissémination*.

6 *Translator's note.* See Chapter X, note 11.

7 *Author's note.* In this context, one should consider the *androgynous* structure of the enunciating machinery.

8 *Author's note.* And especially not: *I, here, now*, the traces, by now so obvious that they are not even read as such, of the metaphoric process taking place.

XII IDIOLECT OR OTHER LOGIC

1 *Translator's note.* These terms translate the French, but do not illustrate the 'rhyming' phenomenon discussed here. Appropriate expressions in English might be: *to be reborn, to deform, to be torn.*

2 *Translator's note.* See Chapter VI, note 2.

3 *Translator's note.* See Chapter VI, note 3.

4 *Translator's note.* The first of these is really a 'proverb' in English; the others are translated French. In any case, the results from the exercise on 'Like father, like son' are the only ones discussed at length in the analysis.

5 *Translator's note.* The terms translate the French, but do not illustrate the phenomenon in question. An appropriate choice might be 'master → remaster.'

6 *Translator's note.* The terms are literal translations from the French, and while they do present certain ambiguities, these are not necessarily the same ones as in French.

7 *Translator's note.* The terms given do not attempt to illustrate the concept discussed, but are literal translations from the French. 'Body – booty' would illustrate the phenomenon more appropriately.

8 *Translator's note.* Se note 7, above. 'Tile – toll' would illustrate the example more appropriately.

9 *Translator's note.* See Chapter IV, note 1, for an explanation of abbreviations.

XIII DOES SCHIZOPHRENIC DISCOURSE EXIST?

1 *Translator's note.* Irigaray here gives an example to illustrate the point she is making. The respondent answered: 'I *kill* everyone.' 'I *kill* ['je *tue*'] in French is a homophone of the second person singular pronoun *tu* [you].

XIV SCHIZOPHRENICS, OR THE REFUSAL OF SCHIZ

1 *Translator's note.* This and all subsequent translations from Saussure are my own. Page references are Luce Irigaray's references to the French text.

2 *Translator's note.* This and all subsequent translations from the Ruwet text are my own. Page references are Luce Irigaray's references to the French text.

XV THE SETTING IN PSYCHOANALYSIS

1 *Author's note.* This text was first presented, in March of 1975, at the University of Strasbourg, in a seminar entitled 'The science of texts,' directed by P. Lacoue-Labarthe and J. L. Nancy. It could also be called: 'Philosophy Viewed from behind,' or: 'What is the Psyche of a Vegetarian?'; 'What Kind of Philosophy Is Written while Dancing?'; 'Why Does Nietzsche, the Mobile One, Spend the End of his Life Lying down, and Not Writing?'; or finally: 'Who Is this Freud, Never from Both Sides?'

2 Translator's note. I have used 'backside' for the noun Derrière, 'back side' / 'behind' / 'in back' for the preposition, but the French text puns on the single word.

3 *Translator's note.* See Chapter XI, note 2.

4 *Translator's note.* See note 3, above.

XVI THE POVERTY OF PSYCHOANALYSIS

1 *Translator's note*. '*Misère de la psychanalyse*' would theoretically require a very long and unwieldy title, since no one word in English can account for the multiple meanings of the French '*misère*.' After much consideration, I have selected 'poverty,' a translation already used by David Macey and Margaret Whitford, in the English-language collection edited by Margaret Whitford, *The Irigaray Reader*, London and Cambridge, MA: Basil Blackwell, 1991, pp. 79-104). I would now like to express my appreciation and respect for the entire Macey–Whitford translation, a text I have long known, and knew for many years before undertaking this translation. I have tried, in the opening paragraphs of the article, to render some of the other resonances of '*misère*,' which are not represented in the title.

2 *Translator's note*. See Chapter XI, note 2.

3 *Translator's note*. See note 2, above.

4 *Author's note*. The journal *Critique*, in which '*Misère de la Psychanalyse*' was published in 1977, required that examples be cited; the 'you' to whom the text is addressed should nevertheless be understood as plural. My decision to write this text is linked to the suicide of a woman friend, a psychoanalyst. The psychoanalytic world is reponsible for her suicide, among others – particularly in its rejection of the ethical and theoretical questions asked about psychoanalysis by women and men who then have no other choice but to kill themselves.

5 *Translator's note*. This, and all subsequent translations, from *Partage des femmes* are my own. The first references given following the citations are Luce Irigaray's, and refer to the French edition of *Partage des femmes*. For an alternative translation of *Partage des femmes*, the reader should consult Eugénie Lemoine-Luccioni, *The Dividing of Women, or Women's Lot*, trans. Marie-Anne Davenport and Marie-Christine Réguis, London: Free Association Books, 1987. The second page numbers, given in brackets, refer to this translation.

6 *Translator's note*. This and all subsequent translations from Jacques Lacan's *Encore* are my own. The first reference given following each citation is Luce Irigaray's reference to the French edition of *Encore*. For alternative translations of the *Encore* citations, the reader should consult Jacques Lacan, *Encore: 1972–1973*, an English-language edition of which is *On Feminine Sexuality: the Limits of Love and Knowledge. Jacques Lacan*, trans. Bruce Fink, in the series Seminar of Jacques Lacan, Book XX, New York: Norton, 1998. The second page reference, given in brackets, is to this translation.

7 *Translator's note*. All translations from the Safouan text are my own. See note 9, below.

8 *Translator's note*. See note 2, above.

9 *Translator's note*. A translation of Chapter 1 of Safouan's *La Sexualité féminine dans la doctrine freudienne* has been done in the collection *Jacques Lacan and the Ecole Freudienne: Feminine Sexuality*, ed. Jacqueline Rose and Juliet Mitchell, London: Macmillan, 1982, under the title 'Feminine sexuality in psychoanalytic doctrine,' trans. Jacqueline Rose. As mentioned in note 6,

above, all translations of the Safouan text are my own. The first page reference included for all citations is Luce Irigaray's reference to the French text. When the citation is from Chapter 1, I have indicated the reference to the alternative translation in brackets.

10 *Translator's note.* See note 2, above.

XVII THE LANGUAGE OF MAN

1 *Author's note.* Cf. the analysis of the myth of the cavern in *Speculum of the other woman.* [An English-language edition, trans. Gillian C. Gill, was published in New York by Cornell University Press, 1985.]

XVIII THE LIMITS OF TRANSFERENCE

1 *Translator's note.* See Chapter XI, note 2.
2 *Translator's note.* See Chapter VIII, note 4.
3 *Translator's note.* See note 2, above.

XIX IN SCIENCE, IS THE SUBJECT SEXED?

1 *Author's note.* The following questions were presented, in part, at the 'Seminar of the history and sociology of scientific facts and ideas,' at the University of Provence, in Marseilles.

Index